Teaching and Learning Online

Teaching and Learning Online, Volume 2, provides practical advice from academics, researchers, practitioners and designers who are currently engaged in defining, creating and delivering the increasingly important world of online learning. This powerful guide avoids trends in technology, instead focusing on the articulation and development of the learning theories that underpin the use of technology.

Topics covered include:

- Theory that informs practice – emerging models and understanding from academia;
- Research – new understandings of learning, collaborative sense-making and learning preferences;
- The practitioner view – real examples from around the world of groundbreaking developments in online learning that are transforming education, adult learning and corporate training;
- Guidance for designers and producers – pedagogical advice and skills for a range of people who may have had little exposure to the body of knowledge surrounding learning design;
- Looking to the future – what to expect in the next five to ten years and how to prepare to take full advantage of the opportunities an increasingly connected society will provide for learner-managed learning.

The second volume of this bestselling guide addresses key gaps in the available literature including the inequality of access to technologically enabled learning and cutting-edge design issues and pedagogies that will take us into the next decade of e-learning and future Web 3.0+ approaches.

Brian Sutton is the founder and director of Learning4Leaders, an educational consulting group in the UK. Brian@Learning4Leaders.com

Anthony "Skip" Basiel is an e-learning thought leader and freelance consultant as an Adobe Education Leader (alumnus), London, UK. abasiel@gmail.com, http://abasiel.wordpress.com

Teaching and Learning Online

New Models of Learning for a Connected World

Volume 2

Edited by Brian Sutton and Anthony "Skip" Basiel

NEW YORK AND LONDON

First published 2014
by Routledge
711 Third Avenue, New York, NY 10017

Simultaneously published in the UK
by Routledge
2 Park Square, Milton Park, Abingdon, Oxon OX14 4RN

Routledge is an imprint of the Taylor & Francis Group, an informa business

© 2014 Taylor & Francis

The right of the editor to be identified as the author of the editorial material, and of the authors for their individual chapters, has been asserted in accordance with sections 77 and 78 of the Copyright, Designs and Patents Act 1988.

All rights reserved. No part of this book may be reprinted or reproduced or utilized in any form or by any electronic, mechanical, or other means, now known or hereafter invented, including photocopying and recording, or in any information storage or retrieval system, without permission in writing from the publishers.

Trademark Notice: Product or corporate names may be trademarks or registered trademarks, and are used only for identification and explanation without intent to infringe.

Volume 1 published 2001 by Routledge

Library of Congress Cataloging-in-Publication Data

Teaching and learning online : new models of learning for a connected world / edited by
  Brian Sutton and Anthony 'Skip' Basiel. — Second volume.
    pages cm
  Includes bibliographical references and index.
  1. Web-based instruction.   2. Distance education—Computer-assisted instruction.
  3. Teaching—Computer network resources.   4. Education—Computer network resources.
  5. Educational technology.   I. Sutton, Brian.
  LB1044.87.T425 2014
  371.33'44678—dc23
  2013006026

ISBN: 978-0-415-52856-6 (hbk)
ISBN: 978-0-415-52857-3 (pbk)
ISBN: 978-0-203-11101-7 (ebk)

Typeset in Minion
by Apex CoVantage, LLC

Contents

Foreword   ix
CURTIS J. BONK

Introduction   xvii

Part 1
Contextual Positioning

1 Merging the Best of Both Worlds: Introducing the CoI-TLP Model   3
MELISSA LAYNE AND PHIL ICE

2 Online Learning: Models and Impact in the 21st Century   20
LEN CAIRNS AND KHALID ALSHAHRANI

Part 2
Theory that Informs Practice

3 Strategies for Supporting Students' Metacognitive Processes in Ill-Structured Problem Solving in Online Environments   35
YUN-JO AN

4 Coping Together: Collective Self-Regulation in a Web-Based Course   53
JACKIE HEE-YOUNG KIM

Part 3
Researchers

5 Learner Use of Online Content   75
PAUL BACSICH AND GILES PEPLER

6 Open Educational Resources: Understanding Barriers to Adoption and Use   96
GABRIEL REEDY

7 Designing Dynamic Online Learning Environments
That Support Knowledge Construction   111
MARK WEYERS

Part 4
Practitioners

8 Explorations in Self-Managed Online Learning   131
IAN CUNNINGHAM

9 People's Open Access Education Initiative: Peoples-uni   148
RICHARD F. HELLER

10 A Case Study of the Tensions and Triumphs in Building an
Online Learning Community   161
TAREK ZOUBIR AND IAN TERRELL

11 Metaphor and Neuroscience: Implications for Online
Learning   176
MIKE HOWARTH

Part 5
Transition

12 Virtual and Virtuous: Creating New Pedagogies for
a New South Africa   193
NAREND BAIJNATH AND PAMELA RYAN

13 Online Learning in Virtual Academia   207
PAMELA McLEAN

Part 6
Designers and Producers

14 Gaming Learning   227
CLARK QUINN

15 Lights, Camera, Action: Experiential Learning with Digital
Media Simulations   243
DAVID JAMES CLARKE IV AND DOUGLAS BECKWITH

16 Towards a Method of Improving Participation in Online Collaborative Learning: Curatr BEN BETTS	260
Endpiece Putting the Learner in Charge – A Pedagogy for Online Learning Comes of Age BRIAN SUTTON AND ANTHONY "SKIP" BASIEL	275
Notes on Contributors	281
Index	285

Foreword

Online Learning Yesterday and Today

This story begins at the turn of the century. It was also the dawn of a new millennium for the learners of this planet. Those of us studying online learning in the previous one realise that 1999 was a bellwether year for online learning; it was then that educators began to take stock of the skyrocketing enrolments in online classes in college and university settings across the globe. Look at any line graph or bar chart of online learning credit hours or course enrolments since the emergence of the Web in 1991 and that year – 1999 – will typically leap from the page. It was often the first data point of the staggering growth we all felt. Indeed, administrators enamored with massive open online courses (MOOCs) and distinctive blended forms of learning today continue to marvel at that one year even though course enrolments then pale significantly in comparison to daily figures found in the news today.

Those of us in the online teaching and learning trenches or employed by research institutes studying different forms of distance learning at that time began to worry that expanded enrolments without corresponding enhancements to online instruction might be a dagger to this movement and doom it to failure. We witnessed firsthand the immense dropout rates of most online learning initiatives during those initial years. In reaction, many of us wanted to understand more about how to create active and engaging learning environments. At that time, my research team and I conducted a series of national studies in both higher education and corporate training settings in North America. Dropout rates of over 50% in the corporate world and 30% in higher education were not uncommon. We later expanded this work to national studies in other countries (e.g., the UK, Korea, China and Taiwan) and found similar trends and concerns.

Enter John Stephenson, the editor of the first volume of this book, *Teaching and Learning Online: Pedagogies for New Technologies*. He was deeply concerned about the issue of online pedagogy in this explosive new e-learning world. Consequently, in August of 2000, he organised a powwow of e-learning experts to take place at the International Centre for Learner Managed Learning (ICLML) at Middlesex University where he was housed. It was a meeting of the minds, and John and his colleagues at Middlesex were to be the spiritual leaders.

Unfortunately, with a heavy speaking commitment in Australia for two weeks prior to the event, I had just arrived home and had to participate from a distance. Like everyone else, my colleagues and I submitted a paper for the seminar. This paper, written with Drs. Jamie Kirkley, Noriko Hara and Vanessa Paz Dennen, discussed the four roles, or hats, of the online instructor – managerial, technological, social and pedagogical. It was the latter role in which this event was the most focused – namely, pedagogy. Given that synchronous Web conferencing technology was still evolving at the time and was primarily used in corporate settings rather than higher education, my live online presentation that August was filled with trepidation on both sides of the Atlantic. Sitting at my desk at Indiana University (IU) that afternoon, we used an experimental technology I had never heard of. I really was not sure it was going to work. To make matters worse, I could not see my fellow participants seated at the other end in London, but I could hear them and hoped they could hear me as well as view my slides clearly enough. Fortunately, it went well.

Other participants included a number of well-known online learning gurus such as Shirley Alexander, David Boud and Ron Oliver from Australia; Robin Mason from the Open University in the UK; and Marion Coomey from Canada. Additional participants came from Belgium, Finland, Italy and the United States. Some were academics. A few of the participants were program managers. Still others were instructional materials designers and commercial producers of online content. Papers were shared before the expert seminar and then discussed at the summit in London. These papers were later revised and reformed into the 17 chapters comprising the first volume of this book. That bright orange book came out a year later with Kogan Page in the UK and Stylus Publishing in the United States.

As documented by Brian Sutton and Skip Basiel in the introduction as well as their endpiece to this second volume, much has transpired during the past 12 years related to online pedagogy. As Sutton and Basiel accurately point out, emerging technologies for learning seem to steal all the headlines. Yet it is really the unique pedagogical uses of such technology that I (and perhaps many of you) encounter on a daily basis with notes from colleagues, friends and others around the world that reveal a teaching and learning world much different from the one in London in the summer of 2000.

Online learning that was once quite suffocating, redundant and dreary and best described as shovelware or electronic page turning at the end of the last century is now highly collaborative, social and individually driven. Times have changed. Learners have markedly different roles when online. For instance, they do not just discuss, debate, or add comments to learning content made available for a class; instead, they often generate new content in the form of podcast shows, blog posts, videos, wiki-based glossaries and mobile applications others might use now or in the future. A culture of producers has arisen to augment – or, at times, entirely replace – the browsing or consumption-based online learning common in the mid to late 1990s and early 2000s.

Many of us writing for the first volume were concerned with what effective instructors could do to facilitate and enhance the online environment so as to overcome inferior course management systems, stale prepackaged content and nervous online learners and instructors. The focus for our various recommendations and guidelines was highly centered on asynchronous aspects of learning online. At the time, it was quite common for universities to equate online learning with asynchronous technology since that was all that they could afford. Those in corporate settings back in the late 1990s and early 2000s thought of asynchronous learning as self-paced. If an instructor was in the loop, it occurred during a synchronous Web conference using highly expensive systems at the time like WebEx, Centra and PlaceWare (now Live Meeting). In contrast, those of us in higher education were often working on shoestring budgets and had to rely on free synchronous tools such as CU-SeeMe as well as various forms of videoconferencing.

Today, the systems for synchronous interaction have truly proliferated as seen by those of us using Adobe Connect Pro, Google Hangouts, Google On Air, Blackboard Collaborate (formerly Elluminate) and trusty old Skype. With the evolution of such synchronous conferencing systems, online learners have come to expect increased social presence on the part of the instructor. Also common are online presentations or chats with world-renowned guest experts on any topic at any time as well as cross-cultural collaboration with peers in distant lands. The entire world of 2013 seems to be at one's very fingertips. Seek and you shall find.

Despite this optimism, we all know the Internet was filled with a plethora of online text and dead links back in 2000. In fact, such online text has proliferated to trillions upon trillions of pages of content that online learners too often feel they must trudge through without much guidance. Fortunately for those who have limited bandwidth, this same text-centered form of learning in the format of open access journal articles and reports has fostered new forms of free online courses and programs. Much is now transmitted to those at the other end of the digital divide to improve health care, business practices and education.

However, it is video that has exploded upon the online learning scene during the past decade. When you ponder online video, many of you may think of YouTube, TED talks, National Geographic specials and CNN as well as BBC News and Video. Video-based learning is not just coming from YouTube and major news and media outlets but from a slew of new online learning start-ups and unique resource initiatives such as Academic Earth, Big Think, LinkTV, HowCast, Book TV, LearnZillion and TED-Ed, among hundreds of other shared online video portals. Not convinced? A few years ago, I decided to create a portal of dozens of such shared online video sites to help educators grasp the learning possibilities (see Web resources available from my homepage). At about the same time, I also wrote a few papers on how to use such content from a learner-centered as well as instructor-centered perspective; they are also freely available from my homepage.

The pervasive nature of online video enables greater use of multimedia in online learning, thereby fostering the dual coding of content (i.e., both text and video retrieval cues). In short snippets, such video can be used to anchor instruction and provide a base for later readings, presentations and discussions. As shown by the Khan Academy, online instructors are increasingly cognizant that the forms of blended learning expand when they can record a video lecture and make it available for future students. Classes can be flipped with students watching such videos or listening to podcasts prior to coming to class. And when medical emergencies (e.g., SARS, H1N1, serious strands of the flu, etc.) or natural catastrophes (e.g., hurricanes, ice storms, tornados, tsunamis, earthquakes, etc.) arise to affect a region of the world, learning no longer skips a beat; learners – at least those who still have an Internet connection – can find their content and course activities online.

There are myriad other educational technology trends that have arisen since the start of the century to affect learning in significant ways. Among them are the increased use of e-books and other digitized resources. Back in 2000, a digital book was a rare find that most publishers did not know how to market or price. Today students can find free textbooks at sites like Beyond Textbooks and OpenCollegeTextbooks. At the same time, as my colleague Mimi Lee at the University of Houston and I showed in a series of research projects, students can jointly write Wikibooks across sections of a class or across institutions around the planet and make them freely available to use, change, or share. Such learners might also upload a final course project as a mobile book in BookRix or exchange ideas about a book in Subtext, a free iPad application. Speaking of mobile applications, there are billions of downloads of mobile applications each year. Back in 2001, there were none.

Tools and resources for social networking are also in the limelight today. Back in 2001, many contributors to the first book talked about the pedagogical possibilities of networked learning even though there was no Facebook, Ning, or Twitter. Their glimpses of the future of networked learning were quite provocative. Nevertheless, as the authors and editors to this second volume highlight, there was no mention of OpenCourseWare (OCW) or open educational resources (OERs) at that time. Today, individuals wishing to learn from such content can form online study groups in Open Study. They might also meet at local cafes and bookstores to talk with other learners struggling to get through such free and open content. The cyber world now often blends seamlessly with the physical one.

Just as the two volumes of this book mark the shift from asynchronous to synchronous learning, OCW and OER are no longer the only means in which to learn for free online. Today, there is much discussion and debate as well as a diverse array of initiatives related to massive open online courses. A MOOC expands online learning in directions few people back in the summer of 2000 thought was possible. Those making futuristic predictions at that time likely did not envision the sudden emergence millions of individuals learning for free from top-tier universities like MIT, Harvard, Stanford, Rice University, the University of Melbourne and the University of Edinburgh.

MOOCs stretch the limits of online pedagogy. They are a test bed for nearly any idea, activity, or form of collaboration one can dream up. While we hear about companies and organisations such as Uadicity, edX, Coursera, Udemy and Future Learn emerging during the past year or two to coordinate MOOCs as well as their business plans, procedures, partnerships and success stories, there should be equal press devoted to unique and engaging pedagogical activities in a MOOC. For instance, there are highly innovative tools for cross-cultural collaboration from the Stanford Venture Lab, crowdsourced office hours that hundreds of thousands of learners now use for free with Piazza and interesting ways that MOOC participants interact using Twitter and Facebook. Volume 3 of *Teaching and Learning Online* will undoubtedly have plenty of text space devoted to MOOCs and the various MOOC offspring that will materialize during coming decade.

Upon review, we see that static online content is now dynamic, passive online learning consumers are now high-end producers, Wikipedia learning has morphed into "Videopedia," and solitary learning has been replaced by highly social and connected e-learning. Of course, e-learning, which was quite rare and unusual in primary and secondary schools back in 2001, is often mandated as a learning option and serving tens of millions of learners in 2013. Small class pilot tests of different types of e-learning have given way to tens of thousands of learners in a single MOOC. And prepackaged online content with limited learner choice or control is often replaced by "free-range learners" who have ample opportunities to self-select their learning content. Those are but some of the trends of the past decade.

The big shift is toward learners embedded in an endless sea of content and using myriad Web 2.0 tools to add to it. With that, the pool of learning resources is expanding. Of course, the free-range learners we all have become need advice, mentoring and peer ratings from which to select the content that works best for them. As my good friend Paul Bacsich and his colleague Giles Pepler note in chapter 5 of this book, the pervasive concerns about the quality, credentialing and usability of open educational contents have shifted to questions of why, how and when learners use such content. At the same time, in the next chapter, Gabriel Reedy points out that instructors, especially those early in their careers, need help selecting from and using the wealth of OER now found online. These were not the questions my colleagues and I were dealing with in the first volume. Clearly, times have changed in the online world.

I am delighted to see that some of my friends and colleagues from the United States like Yun-Jo An, Jackie Hee-Young Kim, Clark Quinn and Phil Ice contributed chapters to this volume. Both chapter 3 from An and chapter 4 from Kim better inform us about the issues, challenges and opportunities facing self-directed online learners. Their advice about the principles and strategies to support self-directed learners should prove valuable for those involved in designing as well as assessing the impact of various forms of OER and MOOCs.

In chapter 12, Baijnath and Ryan expand these ideas by discussing the potential impact of this shift from traditional forms of learning to self-directed online learning on an entire nation – in their case, South Africa. In the following chapter, McLean puts a face on such self-directed learners while offering practical suggestions to all potential free-range learners. In effect, the scantily clad ideas related to self-directed and learner-centered networked learning offered by just a few authors in the first volume are now more pervasive and fully dressed up here in the second one. As a result, I am excited by the myriad learning possibilities discussed throughout this splendid book.

It is also fantastic to see associates of John Stephenson like Len Cairns from Monash University in Australia and Skip Basiel and Brian Sutton from the UK make major contributions to this volume. Chapter 2 from Cairns and Alshahrani takes the reader on a journey from the paradigms and learning models offered in the first volume to those of a more participatory learning environment today while also offering several glimpses of the exciting online learning world of tomorrow. Whereas that chapter may be the heartbeat that connects the two volumes together, it is Sutton and Basiel who are the eyes, ears, fingers, feet and brains of this book project. Their introductory and ending pieces will make you reflect on the learning choices available today as well as the pedagogical possibilities for elevating online learning to new heights. In their recap of the book chapters of volume 2, they also remind us of the limitations, obstacles, constraints and realities we must now confront before online teaching and learning can advance further.

As with the first volume, the contributions of this one span the globe. In this second volume, the authors come from Australia, Canada, Saudi Arabia, South Africa, Scotland, England and the United States. These contributors are professors, lecturers, directors of nonprofit organisations, corporate and higher education consultants, learning technologists, company executives, learning explorers, research directors, deans and pro vice chancellors. Given the breadth of backgrounds and experiences, there is much you can learn from each one.

I think you will find as many online learning nuggets in this second volume of *Teaching and Learning Online* as were made available in the first. There are hundreds of millions and perhaps even billions of free-range learners who at the time of the first volume had no access to education. Their learning world was closed. Today it is wide open. In the coming decade, the tools and resources for free-range learners to mine the Internet for online learning gems will dramatically expand, as will the possibilities for certificates and other forms of credentialing of that learning. As the chapters in this book make apparent, there will be greater opportunities for experiential learning, game-based learning, inquiry-based learning, learner-learner connectivity and still other novel learning formats.

Nevertheless, we still need to make vast inroads into this open learning world. As John Stephenson hoped, such journeys will likely occur in the land of novel and impactful online learning pedagogy. Learners at all corners of the globe are banking on it. I cannot wait to read the updates in the third and fourth volumes of this book series to understand when and how those dreams were fulfilled. One thing is certain, the worlds of 2025 and 2037 will be vastly different than the one we are experiencing today as well as that back in 2001. In fact, by the fourth volume of this book, I suspect that most people will be referring to this as "The Learning Century." Stay fit, my friends; I want you to experience it. And I hope to be around to make a comment about our wondrous world of online teaching and learning at that time. Till then.

Curtis J. Bonk
Indiana University
February 20, 2013

Introduction

Scope

For the purposes of this book, "teaching and learning online" refers to electronic means of distributing and engaging with learning. Throughout the book we refer to online learning as shorthand for the full process of teaching and learning online on the assumption that all teaching activity is aimed at producing learning. It is not assumed by any of the authors that online learning will exist entirely without interaction between teachers and learners or between learners and learners. Indeed, what we are seeing is that the medium tends to produce richer and wider-ranging collaborations between learners, and in some cases the distinction between teacher and learner is starting to blur as the roles merge and alternate. Neither is it assumed that online learning will replace existing schooling or campus-based education, although here again we are seeing the transformative power of the technology to produce what might be termed "fluid walled" classrooms and institutions. It is assumed that online learning may meet the needs of the many stakeholders for whom a conventional educational experience is either inappropriate or not available.

Why the Need for a Second Volume?

The first volume of this book was published in 2001, coincidentally the same year as the Massachusetts Institute of Technology (MIT) announced it would put its complete programme catalogue online. This was a seismic shift and gave birth to the open educational resource (OER) movement, examined in greater detail in part 3.

Whilst this book is not solely about technology, it cannot be denied that technology, and the social mores it creates, fundamentally shapes our approach to what is possible and/or desirable in terms of an online learning experience. At the writing of the first volume, online was largely thought of as a medium to deliver content to distant learners or a means of facilitating asynchronous discussion within a prescribed network of contributors. It is worth reminding ourselves of some of the technologies that have risen to dominate our every waking hour since we published our last collection of articles in 2001. That year also saw the official launch of iTunes and the emergence of Wikipedia. The first 3G mobile telephony networks started to emerge in the following year. In 2003, we saw the launch of Web video conferencing in the guise of Skype, and the same year also brought us Facebook and LinkedIn, and so we entered an era of user-generated content, online resumes and online portfolios of work and personal recommendations.

xviii • Introduction

In 2004, open source networked learning – Elgg – was founded, the same year that YouTube brought us the ability to instantly share movies, often shot using a mobile phone, and with that came a major disruption in the way breaking news from around the world could be reported, accessed and shared, and the age of the "citizen publisher" was born. After that, 2006 ushered in Twitter and the seemingly previously untapped need to instantly share all your most mundane everyday activities and thoughts with the rest of the world. Not to be outdone by this, the BBC launched iPlayer the following year and thus moved television from a broadcast-once medium to an anytime, anyplace tool that could be accessed on any phone, tablet, or appropriate mobile device.

We mention these technological developments not because they are interesting in and of themselves but because together they have quite unexpectedly, and quite fundamentally, changed the way young people expect to engage with the world and each other. Whilst educators and learning professional are pondering how best to take advantage of these capabilities within their offerings their potential customers are reinventing everything about how they access, reshape, share and exploit what is available on the Net.

The Trend Towards Sharing Everything Online

In the introduction to the first volume the editor opined the following:

> The trend to "online everything" is powerful and difficult to resist. Education is part of that trend. But does it really amount to anything other than doing what was previously done but doing it faster, on a greater scale and for more people? Economies of scale are, of course, desirable in themselves, but does the medium add value to the learning experience? Is there anything about the medium that suggests that a new educational pedagogy is emerging – one that has something positive to offer teachers and learners alike?

He went on to suggest the following:

> Many commentators have observed that much online learning appears to have been developed because it was possible, technically, to do so and without explicit reference to any pedagogical principles.

Have we moved on? We think the answer is an unequivocal yes. But not perhaps in an orderly fashion, nor does the movement appear to be driven by the educational establishment; rather it appears that society and its relationship, one might even say love affair, with technology is reshaping the value proposition of post-school-age engagement with learning. Nowadays learners appear to have an insatiable appetite for engaging content, regardless of its provenance, and a compulsive need to tell their personal stories as they share and build collective experience.

Do we need a new pedagogy? Perhaps; the jury is still out on this one. But what is clear is that teachers need to concern themselves less with serving up content and more with creating engaging and socially relevant experiences, and we need to provide much better guidance for our online learners to support their cognitive processes so they can collectively gain maximum value from the experiences we create.

Is it possible that professional social networked learning provides the start of a new online pedagogy? This bottom-up approach sees the learner as the content generator, and Web 2.0 tools provide the opportunity to collaborate in ways that were not possible at the time of our first volume.

The Book Structure

The chapters have been arranged into six parts according to their general themes and mirroring the structure of the first edition. Each group of chapters explores the phenomena of online learning from a different perspective. In part 1 we revisit the online paradigm grid, proposed by Coomey and Stephenson, that provided the theoretical anchor for the 17 chapters that made up the first volume in 2001. Part 2 is made up of two chapters that draw upon a solid research base and sound practical discovery to show how online learners can be supported in their cognitive processes and can help each other to become more "strategic" learners. Part 3 is given over to the researchers and draws together insight from across Europe and the United States to examine how the ubiquitous accessibility of education content has implications for both institutions and teachers alike. There are also big questions about the role of the instructional designer when learners are increasingly shaping and directing their own learning destiny. Part 4 turns to the practitioner view. Here we look at a range of cases drawn from all educational levels and involving learners in different cultures and professional communities. Part 5 looks at the potentially disruptive effect of online learning as it examines an organisation in transition and also gives a glimpse of the "free-range" learner – these tend to be lifelong learners whose motivation stems from a deeply felt personal need to make a difference in their community. For these people learning is not about collecting accreditations but all about socially constructing, and immediately applying, new insight to resolve pressing issues. Part 6 is an opportunity for commercial providers to show how they are working with industry and educational providers to field rich learning experiences. These chapters are authored by some of the industry's thought leaders and represent not just a view of the current state of the art but also an intriguing glimpse of what may be just around the corner. The book concludes with an endpiece composed by the editors after reviewing all the contributions looking for pointers on the pedagogical way forward.

Part 1
Contextual Positioning

It is now over a decade since the first volume of this book, and it is timely to start with a reminder of the thinking that provided the initial impetus. In the first chapter, Layne and Ice look in detail at two theoretical frameworks that underpin much of the thinking in this book, namely the Teaching Learning Paradigm (TLP), which was proposed by Coomey and Stephenson in the first volume, and the Community of Inquiry (CoI) framework. They provide a comparison of the two frameworks and a review of current thinking and in so doing develop a unified representational model that incorporates the best of both frameworks. Cairns and Alshahrani also provide a reminder of the "paradigm grid for online learning" in the second chapter and then move on to discuss how pedagogy may be affected by any of a wide range of technological developments being embraced by the education sector. The ideas explored in these two chapters set up the discussion that will be picked up and expanded in many of the ensuing chapters.

1
Merging the Best of Both Worlds: Introducing the CoI-TLP Model

MELISSA LAYNE AND PHIL ICE

American Public University System, USA

Editors' Introduction

The authors provide a detailed review of the elements, categories and indicators associated with two of the dominant frameworks for online learning, namely the Teaching Learning Paradigm (TLP) and the Community of Inquiry (CoI) framework. They contend that whilst on the surface the models appear dissimilar, significant insight can be gained by combining the two models to provide a more holistic model, specifically with regard to the intersections of teaching, social and cognitive presences and the appropriate balance of these presences as we progress from instructor-led to learner-managed learning.

Introduction

Acquiring information has always been a prefacing factor towards acquiring knowledge. However, supporting the transformation of information to knowledge are teaching and learning frameworks guiding educators that enable them to lead students towards academic success. Depending upon the physical or virtual space used to accommodate teaching and learning, consideration of the attributes and affordances these spaces offer narrows the framework options from which to build and execute learning processes. In online learning spaces, there exist few, but very robust, models that aid in the implementation of online learning, yet many of these models contain duplicity in terms of constructs or variants.

Albeit far from a wicked problem requiring immediate attention in the field of online learning, the authors of this chapter aim to provide efficiency through the use of a holistic online learning model by (a) aligning the constructs from two widely used online learning frameworks, the Teaching Learning Paradigm and the Community of Inquiry framework, and (b) merging the constructs from both frameworks to form an integrated process model. The rationale for this focus is to eliminate redundancy and extraneous information, extract information from the best of both worlds, and combine the information into a unified process model.

Both frameworks boast increasing numbers of citations and have gained respect among learning theorists and practitioners alike. To begin the chapter, we will introduce the first of the two frameworks, the CoI. The CoI is a collaborative, constructivist, process model that explains the interactions within online learning environments through three distinct but interrelated presences: teaching, social and cognitive presence. Teaching presence is defined as the design, facilitation and direction of cognitive and social processes for the realisation of personally meaningful, and educationally worthwhile, learning outcomes.

Social presence refers to the ability of learners to project themselves socially and emotionally, "as real people," in an online environment, as well as the degree to which they feel socially and emotionally connected with others in that environment. Cognitive presence is described as the extent to which learners are able to construct and confirm meaning through sustained reflection and discourse.

The second framework, the TLP, comprises four major characteristics of online learning considered to be essential to good practice. These characteristics include dialogue, involvement, support and control (DISC). The TLP places a focus on the importance of structuring the learning activity and designing the materials in order to promote dialogue, secure active involvement of the learner, provide personal or other support and feedback, and enable the learner to exercise the degree of control expected.

This chapter explores how both models can be utilized in a cohesive, holistic fashion, allowing for the integration of and transition between the main elements of the CoI and TLP – CoI presences and the teaching learning quadrants. The chapter is outlined as follows:

- Presenting seminal and current research for both frameworks and their associated elements supporting the propositions put forward in this chapter
- Explaining the process used to merge the frameworks' elements, categories and indicators
- Introducing and describing the unified representational model
- Concluding the chapter with suggestions for further exploration and application

Community of Inquiry Framework

Garrison, Anderson, and Archer (2000) initially developed the CoI framework to explain how features of written language used in computer conferencing activities could promote critical/higher-order thinking. The authors contend that higher-order learning experiences are best conducted as a community of inquiry composed of teachers and learners requiring both the demonstration of critical thinking and the engagement of "real" persons to be successful. The framework assumes that effective online learning is a function of the interaction of three elements: teaching presence, social presence and cognitive presence (see Figure 1). In this section, we describe each of these three elements and their associated categories and indicators with supporting seminal and recent literature.

One misconception we, as educators, often make in online learning is that social interactions among teachers and students serve as a catalyst for the development of a learning experience. Often overlooked, however, are the vital roles and responsibilities of the instructor to create a learning space that supports and sustains the students' ability to explore and integrate learning experiences leading to reflection and resolution. According to Kanuka and Anderson (1998), this misconception has been shown in online discourses among educators, whereby much of the exchanges result in lower-level critical thinking. Similarly, this diminishing opportunity for higher-level thinking is represented in the literature in academic settings as well, whereby an emphasis is placed upon the *number* of online interactions over the *quality* of interactions (Garrison, Anderson, & Archer 2001; Meyer 2003; Pawan, Paulus, Yalcin, & Chang, 2003). The CoI framework is predicated upon the assumption that the sequential integration of quality teaching, social and cognitive elements builds upon one another to spark higher-level thinking (Garrison & Anderson 2003; Rovai, 2002).

Teaching Presence

Teaching presence is described by Garrison and colleagues (2000) as the design, facilitation and direction of cognitive social processes as precursors to attaining rich, meaningful learning. Specifically, the authors assert that teaching presence is comprised of three categories: (a) instructional design and organisation; (b) direct instruction; and (c) facilitating discourse.

Instructional design and organisation Anderson, Rourke, Garrison, & Archer (2001) describe the design and organisation aspect of teaching presence as the planning and design of the structure, process, interaction and evaluation aspects of the online course. Further research on teaching presence has evidenced the instructor's role as manifesting in various ways. For example, in their study on teaching presence, Garrison and Cleveland-Innes (2005) validated the importance of the instructional design and organisation of the course as significant contributors to teaching presence. Conversely, in their study examining the instructional design of a graduate-level course in literature, Anagnostopoulos, Basmadjian, and McCrory (2005) determined that the students found the navigational characteristics to be so well-designed and straightforward that the need for the instructor's presence decreased over the duration of the course.

Direct instruction Anderson and colleagues (2001) contextualized direct instruction as the instructor provision of intellectual and scholarly leadership in part through the sharing of their subject matter knowledge with the students. They also contend that a subject matter expert and not merely a facilitator must play this role because of the need for diagnosing comments for accurate understanding, injecting sources of information and directing discussions in useful directions, scaffolding learner knowledge to raise it to a new level.

In addition to the sharing of knowledge by a content expert, direct instruction is concerned with indicators that assess the discourse and the efficacy of the educational process. Instructor responsibilities are to facilitate reflection and discourse by presenting content, using various means of assessment and feedback (Swan et al., 2008). Explanatory feedback is also crucial; this type of communication must be perceived to have a high level of social presence/instructor immediacy to be effective (Arbaugh, 2001; Richardson & Swan, 2003).

Facilitating discourse The CoI conceptualizes facilitating discourse as the means by which students are engaged in interacting about and building upon the information provided in the course instructional materials. This role includes sharing meaning, identifying areas of agreement and disagreement, and seeking to reach consensus and understanding. Therefore, facilitating discourse requires the instructor to review and comment upon student comments; raise questions and make observations to move discussions in a desired direction, keeping discussion moving efficiently; draw out inactive students; and limit the activity of dominating posters when they become detrimental to the learning of the group (Anderson et al., 2001; Coppola, Hiltz, & Rotter, 2002; Swan et al., 2008).

The importance of teaching presence as an essential element in the learning process has been realised in research focusing on the construct's dimensions and the reliance on the instructor maintaining a constant presence within the online environment (Arbaugh & Hwang, 2006; Shea, Fredericksen, Pickett, & Pelz, 2003).

Social Presence

Garrison (2009) describes social presence as an opportunity for students to engage and interact with other students in an online community, meaningfully communicate with each other towards a goal or purpose, and foster relationships through sharing their individual personalities and personal experiences related to the discussion topic. To date, social presence within the CoI framework is the most frequently researched of the three presences (Gunawardena & Zittle, 1997; Richardson & Swan, 2003; Rourke, Anderson, Garrison, & Archer, 2001; Walther, 1992). A possible explanation for this delves into constructivist views as the pedagogical theory for rich discourse. In this light, constructivists maintain that knowledge is transferred from one person to another through meaningful and coherent discussion of newly acquired information as it is situated within a person's prior knowledge.

Presently there is an emerging debate on whether social presence has a causal or co-relational relationship with online course outcomes. Recent research on social presence in online learning has also focused on its role in facilitating cognitive development and critical thinking. To date, this research suggests that while social presence alone will not ensure the development of critical discourse in online learning, it is extremely difficult for such discourse to develop without a foundation of social presence (Garrison & Cleveland-Innes, 2005). Crucial to the development of social presence is (a) open communication; (b) group cohesion; and (c) emotional expression.

Open communication Open communication refers to risk-free discourse among students within an online learning environment. The ability to communicate electronically with others, without the fear of rejection or being subsequently degraded, is key to developing the sense of openness that catalyzes online communities (Arbaugh et al., 2008). Notably, this may be more of a given among younger learners who have been online and participating in social communities from an early age (Garton et al., 2013).

Group cohesion Group cohesion, a category within social presence, indicates the encouragement of students to collaborate with one another. Whether this encouragement comes from the instructor or among the students themselves, group cohesion provides a catalyst to explanations, elaboration and defending one's position to others (as well as to oneself) and further prompts learners to integrate and elaborate knowledge in ways that facilitate higher-order learning (Oliver & Naidu, 1996).

Emotional expression Emotional expression, as described by the authors of the CoI model, is an inherent characteristic within social presence whereby learners use emoticons or textual symbols to represent a particular emotion. However, in their study examining educational presence within the CoI, Cleveland-Innes and Campbell (2010) explore emotional expression as its own CoI presence construct apart from social presence that influences learning and learning outcomes.

Cognitive Presence
Cognitive presence is the extent to which learners are able to construct and confirm meaning through sustained reflection and discourse (Garrison et al., 2001). The field of higher education has distinguished cognitive presence as a necessary element for students at this level. This collective perspective originates from Dewey's (1933) work on practical inquiry leading to critical thinking and will most assuredly continue to frame teaching and learning for years to come.

Garrison and colleagues (2001) assert that four categories help develop online cognitive presence: (a) *triggering event*, where some issue or problem is identified for further inquiry; (b) *exploration*, where students explore the issue both individually and corporately through critical reflection and discourse;

(c) *integration*, where learners construct meaning from the ideas developed during exploration; and (d) *resolution*, where learners apply the newly gained knowledge to educational contexts or workplace settings.

Of the three types of presence in the CoI framework, cognitive presence continues to be the most challenging presence to develop within online courses (Celani & Collins, 2005; Garrison & Cleveland-Innes, 2005; Moore & Marra, 2005).

Emerging research suggests a complementary relationship between teaching presence and cognitive presence. While social presence lays the groundwork for higher-level discourse, the structure, organisation and leadership associated with teaching presence creates the environment where cognitive presence can be developed. Garrison and Cleveland-Innes (2005) found that course design, structure and leadership significantly affect the extent to which learners engage course content in a deep and meaningful manner. These findings suggest that the role of instructors in cultivating cognitive presence is significant, both in terms of how they structure the course content and participant interactions. Delineated in *Table 1.1* are the CoI elements, categories and indicators previously described.

Teaching Learning Paradigm

The Teaching Learning Paradigm, developed by Coomey and Stephenson (2001), is an online learning framework that represents the learning process as transitioning from teacher managed to learner managed. The process embeds characteristics facilitating this transition to the point where learners are able to decide and control their own direction and learning process. Some of these embedded characteristics of this process include the following:

- Learner ownership and responsibility
- Negotiated, flexible provisioning
- Instruction tailored to individual student needs
- Students manage their own work and learning priorities
- Learning enhanced when applied to work/life/personal experiences
- Elements of personal development
- Opportunities for personal reward and/or recognition for effort and progress

These characteristics were extracted from research studies whereby students rated the extent to which they perceived learning to manifest. For example, students highly rated everyday work activities, mentors and hands-on activities as enriching their learning experiences (Stephenson & Basiel, 2001; Stephenson, Williams, Cairns, & Critten, 1999). These findings add further credence to previous studies focusing on online learning frameworks that apply learner-centeredness and learner-management (Boud & Solomon, 2001; Cairns & Stephenson, 2001).

Table 1.1 The Community of Inquiry Coding Template (Garrison, Anderson, & Archer, 2000)

Elements	Categories	Indicators
Teaching presence	Instructional design and organisation	Defining and initiating discussion topics
	Facilitating discourse	Sharing personal meaning
	Direct instruction	Focusing discussion
Social presence	Emotional expression	Emoticons
	Open communication	Risk-free expression
	Group cohesion	Encouraging collaboration
Cognitive presence	Triggering event	Sense of puzzlement
	Exploration	Information exchange
	Integration	Connecting ideas
	Resolution	Applying new ideas

The Teaching Learning Paradigm Model (*Figure 1.1*) illustrates a straightforward approach of classifying online learning instructional design in terms of teacher control versus student control over content and the learning process. Much like the CoI, the Teaching Learning Paradigm is rooted in constructivism; however, the instructional design supporting this pedagogical framework is situated along two axes: the locus of control of learning (teacher controlled versus learner managed) and the task specification (specified tasks versus open-ended, strategic learning). Coomey and Stephenson further identified and divided four major dimensions (more commonly known as "quadrants") that reside above and beneath the axis. The quadrants include these:

- North West quadrant (teacher-controlled, specified learning activities)
- North East quadrant (learner-managed, specified learning activities)
- South West quadrant (teacher-controlled, open-ended, or strategic learning)
- South East quadrant (learner-managed, open-ended, or strategic learning)

The majority of existing online learning research has largely focused on the NW quadrant, leaving the SE quadrant yet to be thoroughly explored. Coomey and Stephenson contend that this lack of exploration is caused by the lack of communication and understanding between teacher and student and the lack of awareness of existing research in online learning. Additionally, they suggest that much of the research is directed to other researchers and not to practitioners. The Teaching Learning Paradigm grid attempts to serve as a guide for practitioners to use for the design, organisation and management of online learning so they can customize their own practice according to their students' learning styles and needs. Therefore, within each of these quadrants exist common indicators that distinguish the extent to which learning tasks are tightly controlled or open-ended and strategic. These indicators include: (a) dialogue; (b) involvement; (c) support; and (d) control (see *Figure 1.1*).

Dialogue

Dialogue can occur with the use of several online tools including discussion forums, e-mail and chat rooms (asynchronous and synchronous). Online learning literature supports the concept that for online discourse to be meaningful and rich, it should be designed in such a way that facilitates student learning. Instructors should not make the assumption that students will be able to navigate and use these tools simply because they are instructed to do so (Angeli, Bonk, & Hara, 1998; Funaro, 1999; Mason, 1998). Gregor and Cuskelly (1994) stress that if interaction is not clearly defined according to the parameters set forth by the instructor, students may not interact with each other (or the

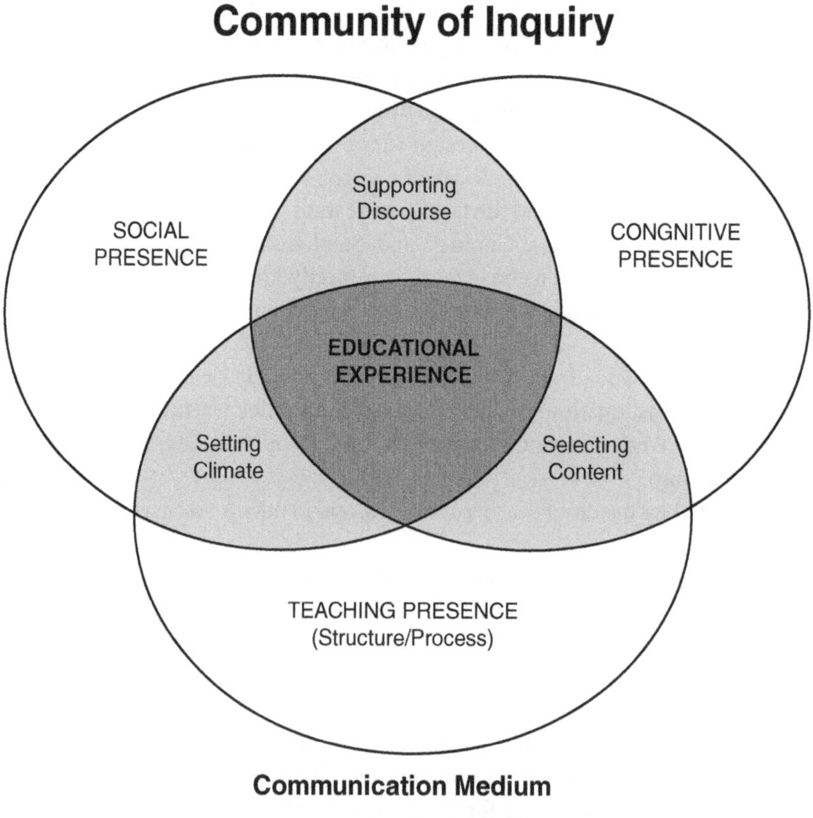

Community of Inquiry

Figure 1.1 The Community of Inquiry Model (Garrison, Anderson, and Archer 2000)

instructor). Beaudin (1999) and Bonk (1999) suggest that instructional design should include the instructor as a moderator and facilitator and that predefined questions help guide students and encourage them to keep on topic. Doherty (1998) and colleagues assert that the instructor should view asynchronous discussion as a means for students to actively participate and engage in reflection and higher-order thinking.

Involvement

Involvement includes instructor-designed tasks whereby students can interact, collaborate and guide their own learning. Dee-Lucas (1999) contends that when these tasks are clearly defined and integrated into the course, it is easier (and faster) for students to locate the answers and respond to these tasks. Chan and Repman (1999) maintain that if students are immersed in online activities, they are more likely to attain optimal experience, better known as "flow." Flow, as described by Csikszentmihalyi (1990), is associated with challenge, clear feedback, learner control and concentration. In their research on structured course design, Wilson and Whitelock (1998) found that students who took online courses that lacked the facilitation of student involvement became less involved and engaged and eventually considered online discussions as an extra task with no relevance or purpose to their learning.

Support

The need for support is the most frequently mentioned feature of online learning. Support may come in the form of instructor feedback, moderation of online discussions, support from peers, student services, outside expert advice, or even face-to-face meetings with the instructor. The importance of student support in online courses is further developed by Alexander (1999), Ewing (1999), Funaro (1999), Mason (1998), Oliver (1995), Thompson and McGrath (1999), and Warren and Rada (1998). The majority of this research maintains that students believe that the more support they receive, the more success they achieve. Students who are new to online learning typically expect the same traditional support they receive in face-to-face classes. Lewis and Vizcarro (1998) contend that by the very nature of online learning, there should be protocols in place that accommodate the same level of support students are used to receiving from a traditional face-to-face course. In an online course students must be encouraged and guided by the instructor to develop and support a comfortable and congenial learning atmosphere in order to feel as though they are a part of a learning community (Rimmershaw, 1999).

Control

Control, in this context, does not refer to the control of the instructor, but rather, the control a student has over his or her own learning. For a student to reach the point of confidence in his or her ability to take control, there must be gradual scaffolding by the instructor to insure a student does not feel "thrown into" this learning environment (McConnell, 1995; Oliver, 1998).

Condensed (in *Tables 1.1 through 1.5*) are the specific indicators for each quadrant and category as outlined by Coomey and Stephenson (2001). These indicators provide various degrees of teacher management and student management in an online course and are meant to serve as a guide for practitioners to gauge the level of dialogue, involvement, support and control that would, ideally, lead students to establish their own goals and outcomes, relate learning to their own needs, take control of their own learning, and monitor and reflect on their own progress.

The Mapping Process

Given the elements, categories and indicators provided from both frameworks, it is necessary to identify similarities common to both in terms of these components. By identifying these similarities, alignment becomes easily recognisable and further validates our rationale for merging both frameworks. We began the mapping and alignment process by examining the main elements first, the categories second and the indicators third.

Elements: Quadrants (TLP) Versus Presences (CoI)

Both the CoI model and the TLP grid evidence the importance of (a) *an instructor* and (b) *communication/discourse* (instructor-to-student and student-to-student) as precursors to the development of a student's (c) *higher-level thinking processes*. Although the TLP implies more of a gradual "process" with distinct quadrants towards this development, the CoI emphasizes the same core components required to achieve these higher-order thinking levels (presences). One slight advantage that the TLP grid modestly demonstrates to researchers and practitioners is its sequential direction and incremental immersion of instructor and communication leading to a student's cognitive processes.

Categories Each category underlying both frameworks represents the direction and extent to which the *instructor, communication* and *higher-level processes* unfold. Only minor distinctions exist between each framework's categories. For example, while the TLP outlines the extent to which each category manifests within each quadrant, the CoI provides specific areas within each presence that are necessary for this manifestation to occur.

Indicators At this level, the identification and translation of keywords and phrases provide the highest level of alignment between both frameworks. For example, under the shared category *communication*, keywords and/or phrases such as "[students] communicate with each other toward a goal or purpose (CoI)" aligns with "[students] collaboratively exchange online dialogue to formulate ideas and

Table 1.2 The North West Quadrant (Teacher-determined, task-specific)

Dialogue	Teacher defines/controls online dialogue and interaction Student responds to teacher questions and mini tasks
	Dialogue with peers specified as part of task
	Focus of dialogue is usually task-oriented problem solving and that problem is set by the instructor
Involvement	Little or no scope for learner to influence content
	Activity is strictly defined and related to preset task
	Site is structured to lead learner directly to specific information
	Students can access information from a Web site before or during lectures to illustrate points and after lectures to seek support from the instructor
Support	Assumed to come only from the teacher via e-mail or phone calls or "traditional" face-to-face meetings
	Time-tabled face-to-face support by teacher or through e-mail
	Online tools to help understanding of content
	Could involve assignments being posted online and read, with feedback by other students but main feedback from instructor
Control	Learner control confined to responses to tasks
	Some control over sequencing and level of engagement
	Teacher controls reading materials, content to be learned, deadlines and time required to work on tasks
Teacher role	Instructor

Table 1.3 The North East Quadrant (Learner-determined, task-specific)

Dialogue	Teacher sets out the general responsibilities and procedures, but not the participation, content, or usage
	Scope is confined to the task, but the systems and protocols support student-managed dialogue with other students, peers and experts
	Much use of asynchronous dialogue and frequently asked questions
Involvement	Task-focused self-managed groups
	Groups can be self-selected and/or self-moderated, deciding own agenda and program
	Learner able to relate or adapt tasks to own circumstances and aspirations
Support	Online support tools, learning support framework
	Tutor provides advice on nature of the task, learning goals, etc.
	Tutor feedback available on progress towards task
	Mainly e-mail contact, or tutor-moderated discussion groups
	Students provide feedback to members of their own groups and others
Control	Conduct of task up to learner
	Emphasis on navigable links to wide variety of sources
	Use of resources outside the program
	Wide discretion over activities, content, learning outcomes
	Relates learning to own personal goals
Teacher role	Coach

Table 1.4 The South West Quadrant (Teacher-determined open-ended strategic learning activities)

Dialogue	A combination of dialogue styles found in NW, during the instructor-led segment of the course, and SE during the learner-managed segment of the course.
	Could be managed by teacher, focused on the overall direction and purpose of the study
	Use of asynchronous dialogue but with instructor setting out roles for students, making students participate as leaders or respondents in discussions or asking students to categorize their response
Involvement	Could start out as solo activity with student learning rules/concepts/theories from online texts and possibly traditional lectures
	Text may be online but there are also locations for students to write and place their "discoveries," the links that they find, the data and content they discover, once students have mastered "the basics," they create something new of their own
	Group activity mainly confined to course group
	Discovery, problem-solving activities
Support	Tutor support could be online or occasionally face to face
	Range of support from traditional instructor feedback to assignments in the first phase of the course (NW quadrant), to the instructor reacting as a facilitator, offering suggestions but not answers to student posts during the "discovery" phase of the course (SE quadrant)
Control	Learner has control of specific learning goals within the generalized goals
	Manages own unstructured discovery activities within given parameters
	Free to set own personal goals within the generalized activity
Teacher role	Guide

exchange materials" (TLP). Another example falling under the shared *instructor* category, the instructor's role in the CoI framework includes "defining and initiating discussion topics, sharing personal meaning, and focusing discussion." These roles map directly to the TLP paradigm whereby the instructor "controls content," "defines online dialogue" and "moderates discussion groups."

Combining the CoI Framework and Teaching-Learning Paradigm to Form a Unified Representational Model

Once the elements, categories and indicators were thoroughly aligned, the CoI-TLP Graph (see *Figure 1.2*) was developed to illustrate where, and to what extent, each CoI presence should reside within the TLP quadrants. During this development of both the graph and the model, we ensured that all components of both frameworks were equally represented. One immediately notices the vast difference between the amount of teaching presence between the NW quadrant and the SE quadrant. Similarly, the NE quadrant emphasizes the increasing importance of social presence integration.

Merging the Best of Both Worlds: Introducing the CoI-TLP Model • 15

Table 1.5 The South East Quadrant (Learner-determined open-ended strategic learning activities)

Dialogue	Self or collaboratively (peer-group) directed
	Wide discretion over choice of discussion groups, from peers to "public" specialist interest groups
	Asynchronous dialogue with other specialists
	External source of specialist assistance, formulation of ideas and exchange of materials
Involvement	Total involvement in the learning activity
	Could be working alone or in a team
	Learner relates the learning to own needs – personal, vocational, academic
	Reflection on progress and meaning
Support	Access to instructor and experts and peers for advice and support
	Contacts with supervisor initiated and monitored by the learner, facilitated by the system
	Teacher in background, offering advice on procedures and resources
	Feedback sought from variety of sources and experts
	The structure and design of the online learning facilities provide a framework of support within which the learner has considerable discretion
Control	Learner controls the direction and the task
	Learner determines the goals and outcomes
	Learner monitors progress
Teacher role	Facilitator

Interestingly, cognitive presence represents a gradual increase from the NE quadrant to the SE quadrant as teaching presence gradually decreases.

Following the development of the CoI TLP graph, we further simplified our dual framework merger into a unified CoI-TLP model (see *Figure 1.3*). Although it is expected that online instructors will provide various degrees of the three CoI presences within each TLP quadrant, this model is meant to serve as an all-encompassing guide representing both frameworks. As the graph illustrates, and the model reiterates, there exists a "tipping point" or apex in between the NE quadrant and the SW quadrant which signifies where the interconnections of teaching, social and cognitive presences trigger the progression from instructor-led to learner-managed learning.

Conclusion and Future Directions

The CoI framework posits that each of the three presences, while independent, interact to create an optimal learning experience. As previous research has demonstrated, varying degrees of emphasis can be placed on each presence to adjust for constructivist or objectivist outcomes. From this perspective, the process orientation of the CoI is highly complementary to the paradigmatic underpinnings

16 • Melissa Layne and Phil Ice

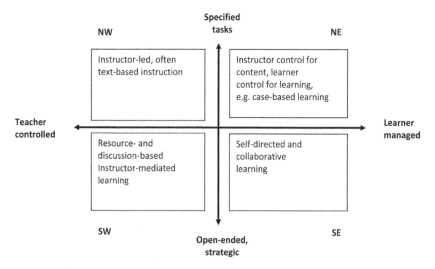

Figure 1.2 The Teaching Learning Paradigm Model (Coomey and Stephenson, 2001)

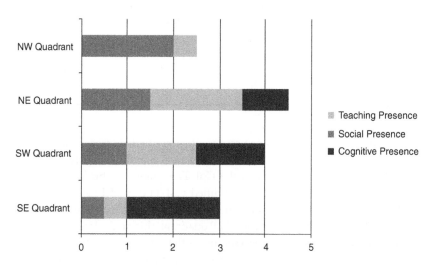

Figure 1.3 The CoI-TLP Graph (Burgess and Ice, 2012)

of the TLP model. Specifically, we suggest that by making one or more of the presences a foci and deemphasizing the remaining presences proportionally, one can achieve directionality vis-à-vis a desired quadrant of the TLP.

While still theoretical we believe that optimization of the presences could easily target a given TLP quadrant. To understand the feasibility of such techniques it is suggested that mixed methods analysis be employed. From a quantitative perspective three-dimensional mapping of factor analysis should reveal discrete and unique separation of the factors when weighting emphasis for one of the

Merging the Best of Both Worlds: Introducing the CoI-TLP Model • 17

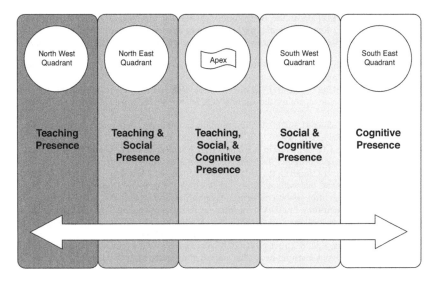

Figure 1.4 CoI-TLP Model (Burgess and Ice, 2012)

TLP quadrants. Additionally, decision tree analysis would be highly revealing in understanding the relationship between each of the CoI elements given a different, quadrant-based, targeted outcome. Ideally, rich qualitative work using an iterative, interpretive approach and data nesting could be applied to student and instructor interviews, with cross case and within case analysis of the two groups. These data could then be used as an explanatory tool with respect to the quantitative data.

Given our interest in and support for both the models discussed herein, it is our hope that this chapter will serve as a basis of inquiry in both communities. Given adequate research we further hope that combining the process orientation of the CoI with the philosophical directionality of the TLP will provide guidance for practitioners in various online learning scenarios.

References

Alexander, S. (1999). Selection dissemination and evaluation of the Top Class WWW based course support tool. *International Journal of Educational Communication, 5*(4), 283.

Anagnostopoulos, D., Basmadjian, K. G., & McCrory, R. S. (2005). The decentered teacher and the construction of social space in the virtual classroom. *Teachers College Record, 107*, 1699–1729.

Anderson, T., Rourke, L., Garrison, D. R., & Archer, W. (2001). Assessing teaching presence in a computer conferencing environment. *Journal of Asynchronous Learning Networks, 5*(2), 5.

Angeli, C., Bonk, C. J., & Hara, N. (1998). Content analysis of online discussion in an applied educational psychology course. *CRLT Technical Report*, No. 2-98.

Arbaugh, J. B. (2001). How instructor immediacy behaviors affect student satisfaction and learning in web-based courses. *Business Communication Quarterly, 64*(4), 42–54.

Arbaugh, J. B., Cleveland-Innes, M., Diaz, S. R., Garrison, D. R., Ice, P., Richardson, J. C., & Swan, K. P. (2008). Developing a community of inquiry instrument: testing a measure of the Community Inquiry framework using a multi-institutional sample. *Internet and Higher Education, 11*, 133-136.

Arbaugh, J. B., & Hwang, A. (2006). Does "teaching presence" exist in online MBA courses? *Internet and Higher Education, 9*(1), 9–21.

Beaudin, B. (1999). Keeping online asynchronous discussions on topic. *Journal of Asynchronous Learning*, 3(2). Retrieved from http://www.aln.org/alnweb/journal/jaln-vol3issue2.htm

Bonk, C. J. (1999). Breakout from learner issues. *International Journal of Educational Telecommunication*, 5(4), 387–410.

Boud, D., & Solomon, N. (2001). *Work-based learning: a new higher education.* Buckingham: Open University Press/SRHE.

Cairns, L.G., & Stephenson, J. (2001). Peripheral social learning in the workplace and the development of corporate capability: the role of NVQs. *Journal of Vocational Education and Training*, 53, 443–466.

Celani, M.A.A., & Collins, H. (2005). Critical thinking in reflective sessions and in online interactions. *AILA Review*, 18, 41–57.

Chan, T., & Repman, J. (1999). Flow in web based activity: an exploratory research project. *International Journal of Educational Telecommunications*, 5(4), 225.

Cleveland-Innes, M., & Campbell, P. (2010). Emotional presence, learning, and the online learning environment. *International Review of Research in Open and Distance Learning*, 13(4). Retrieved from http://www.irrodl.org/index.php/irrodl/article/view/1234/2333

Coomey, M., & Stephenson, J. (2001). Online learning: it is all about dialogue, involvement, support and control – according to the research. In J. Stephenson (ed.), *Teaching and learning online: pedagogies for new technologies* (37–52). London: Kogan Page.

Coppola, N. W., Hiltz, S. R., & Rotter, N. G. (2002). Becoming a virtual professor: pedagogical roles and asynchronous learning networks. *Journal of Management Information Systems*, 18(4), 169–189.

Csikszentmihalyi, M. (1990). *Flow: the psychology of optimal experience.* New York: Harper and Row.

Dee-Lucas, D. (1999). Hypertext segmentation and goal compatibility: effects on study strategies and learning. *Journal of Educational Media and Hypermedia*, 8(3), 279–314.

Dewey, J. (1933). *How we think.* Boston: Heath.

Doherty, P. (1998). Learner control in asynchronous learning environments. *ALN Magazine*, 2(2). Retrieved from http://www.aln.org/alnweb/magazine/alnpaga.htm

Ewing, J. M. (1999). *Enhancement of student learning online and offline.* Retrieved from http://www.norcol.ac.uk/departments/educas/JimEwing/webversion/studentlearning/htm

Funaro, G. M. (1999). Pedagogical roles and implementation guidelines for online communication tools. *ALN Magazine*, 3(2).

Garrison, D. R. (2009). Communities of inquiry in online learning: social, teaching and cognitive presence. In C. Howard et al. (eds.), *Encyclopedia of distance and online learning* (2nd ed., 352–355). Hershey, PA: IGI Global.

Garrison, D. R., & Anderson, T. (2003). *E-learning in the 21st century: a framework for research and practice.* London: Routledge/Falmer.

Garrison, D. R., Anderson, T., & Archer, W. (2000). Critical inquiry in a text-based environment: computer conferencing in higher education. *Internet and Higher Education*, 2(2–3), 87–105.

———. (2001). Critical thinking, cognitive presence, and computer conferencing in distance education. *American Journal of Distance Education*, 15(1), 7–23.

Garrison, D. R., & Cleveland-Innes, M. (2005). Facilitating cognitive presence in online learning: interaction is not enough. *American Journal of Distance Education* 19(3), 133–148.

Garton, S., Garrison, R., Heinz, S., Ice, P., van Tets, I., & Williams, M. (2013, January). *The community of inquiry framework as a theoretical base for research efforts to improve online learning.* Honolulu, HI: 11th Annual Hawaii International Conference on Education.

Gregor, S. D., & Cuskelly, E. F. (1994). Computer mediated communication in distance education. *Journal of Computer Assisted Learning*, 10, 168–181.

Gunawardena, C., & Zittle, F. (1997). Social presence as a predictor of satisfaction within a computer mediated conferencing environment. *American Journal of Distance Education*, 11(3), 8–26.

Kanuka, H., & Anderson, T. (1998). Online social interchange, discord, and knowledge construction. *Journal of Distance Education*, 13(1), Spring, 57–74.

Lewis, R., & Vizcarro, C. (1998). Collaboration between universities and enterprises in the knowledge age, in *The virtual campus: trends for higher education and training.* F. Verdejo and G. Davies (eds.). New York: Chapman & Hall.

Mason, R. (1998). Models of online courses. *ALN Magazine*, 2(2). Retrieved from http://www.aln.org/alnweb/magazine/alnpaga.htm

McConnell, D. (1995). *Learning in groups: some experiences of online work.* Berlin: Springer-Verlag.

Meyer, K. (2003). The Web's impact on student learning. *T.H.E. Journal*. Retrieved from http://thejournal.com/articles/16350

Moore, J. L., & Marra, R. M. (2005). A comparative analysis of online discussion participation protocols. *Journal of Research on Technology in Education, 38*, 191–212.

Oliver, R. (1995). Measuring users' performance with interactive information systems. *Journal of Computer Assisted Learning, 12*(3), 89–102.

———. (1998). Training teachers for distance education programs using authentic and meaningful contexts. *International Journal of Educational Telecommunications, 4*(2/3), 147.

Oliver, M., & Naidu, S. (1996). *Building a computer supported co-operative learning environment in medical-surgical practice for undergraduate RNs from rural and remote areas: working together to enhance health care*. Lawrence, KS: University of Kansas.

Pawan, F., Paulus, T. M., Yalcin, S., & Chang, C-F. (2003). Online learning: patterns of engagement and interaction among in-service teachers. *Language Learning and Technology, 7*(3), 119–140.

Richardson, J. C., & Swan, K. (2003). Examining social presence in online courses in relation to students' perceived learning and satisfaction. *Journal of Asynchronous Learning Networks 7*(1). Retrieved from http://www.sloan-c.org/publications/jaln/v7n1/v7n1_richardson.asp

Rimmershaw, R. (1999). Using conferencing to support a culture of collaborative study. *Journal of Computer Assisted Learning, 5*(3), 189–200.

Rourke, L., Anderson, T., Garrison, D. R., & Archer, W. (2001). Methodological issues in the content analysis of computer conference transcripts. *International Journal of Artificial Intelligence in Education, 12*(1), 8–22.

Rovai, A. P. (2002). Development of an instrument to measure classroom community. *Internet and Higher Education, 5*(3), 197–211.

Shea, P. J., Fredericksen, E. E., Pickett, A. M., & Pelz, W. (2003). A preliminary investigation of "teaching presence" in the SUNY learning network. In J. Bourne and Janet C. Moore (eds.), *Elements of quality online education: into the mainstream: Vol. 4* (279–312). Needham, MA: Sloan-C.

Stephenson, J, (2001). Learner Managed Learning: a holistic approach to work-based learning, in D. Boud and N. Solomon (eds.). *Work-Based Learning: A New Higher Education?* OU Press, Milton Keynes.

Stephenson, J., Williams, R., Cairns, L., & Critten, P. (1999). *The contribution of national vocational qualifications (NVQs) to the learning milieu of the work-place*. Commissioned by OCR (Oxford and Cambridge RSA Examinations Board), published by Middlesex University Press. Retrieved from http://www.johnstephenson.net/ocrrep.pdf

Swan, K. P., Richardson, J. C., Ice, P., Garrison, D. R., Cleveland-Innes, M., & Arbaugh, J. B. (2008). Validating a measurement tool of presence in online communities of inquiry. *e-mentor, 2*(24).

Thompson, M., & McGrath, W. (1999). Using ALNs to support a complete educational experience. *Journal of Asynchronous Learning Networks, 3*(2). Retrieved from http://www.aln.org/alnweb/journal/jaln-vol3issue2.htm

Walther, J. (1992). Interpersonal effects in computer mediated interaction: a relational perspective. *Communication Research, 19*(1), 52–90.

Warren, K. J., & Rada, R. (1998). Sustaining computer-mediated communication in university courses. *Journal of Computer Assisted Learning, 14*, 71–80.

Wilson, T., & Whitelock, D. (1998). Monitoring the online behaviour of distance learning students. *Journal of Computer Assisted Learning, 14*, 91–99.

2
Online Learning: Models and Impact in the 21st Century

LEN CAIRNS AND KHALID ALSHAHRANI

Monash University, Australia

Editors' Introduction

The authors review the state of practice in online learning and provide a reminder of the "paradigm grid for online learning" that was proposed by Coomey and Stephenson in the first volume. They look at the implications of the grid for the key features of dialogue, involvement, support and control and contrast the classification with the model of teaching conceptions, proposed by Kember. The authors then move on to discuss how the potential for cocreation that emerged from the deployment of Web 2.0 may have transformed our approach to making content accessible whilst doing little for the advancement of underlying pedagogy. The chapter closes by looking at the promise of Web 3.0 and poses big questions about the future directions of pedagogy and educational practice.

Introduction

This chapter presents a consideration of online learning and the implications for teaching, learning and workplaces that have emerged over the first two decades of the 21st century. The field has emerged from the rapid and challenging development of technological advances to sound theory, research and practice in this area of study.

Much has been written about this field, particularly in the last years of the 20th century and in the first decade of the 21st century. Much of this work has either offered predictions about the potential of the technology advances and their application or has suggested that a new era of pedagogy has arrived and the educational endeavour, at all levels, and in a range of sites, has been changed and challenged like never before (Driscoll, 1998; Palloff & Pratt, 1999; Wallace, 2004; Beetham & Sharp, 2007; Bonk, 2009).

On other hand, some academics (See Crook, 2012; Selwyn, 2012) called for bursting out of the "ed-tech bubble" and blamed academics in the field of educational technology for being "inward looking" and not interacting with academics and practitioners in different levels of education. The need is stressed for educational technology academics to engage in public debate about the challenges and hot topics of e-learning. Indeed, critical and probably disruptive debate is needed more now than ever with the spread of new initiatives such as massive open online courses (MOOCs), Khan Academy and the potential of using social media in learning.

What is significant in the consideration now, however, is that online teaching and learning has moved beyond a fascination with technology and possible applications to a more mature consideration of its impact and the consideration of pedagogical successes (and failures) of some of the fanciful dreams that were bound up in the excitement of the rapid technological advances from the 1990s to 2010 (Garrison, 2011; Rudestam & Schoenholtz-Read, 2010).

It is proposed, in this chapter, that online teaching and learning has reached a point in time and development of theory, research and practice integration where there is a robustness and understanding of the impact the range of experiences more and more people across the planet have within their life space.

Whilst there has been a rapid and pervasive expansion of contact, impact and influence of the online world, there are still many people across the world who are yet to join the online community; this is an issue for humanity akin to the impact of the written word over past centuries. Initially, issues of access, equity and a new form of poverty in relation to involvement in the online community (now amongst the largest populated "nations" in the world) raised concerns about the haves and have-nots. Whilst this aspect has not been resolved on a global scale, the spread and coverage of online potential has started to become more universal at a greater rate in one century than the spread of literacy did over many centuries. The historical parallels with the advent of the printed word and the spread of literacy to the point of an almost assumed basic human right should not be lost in this electronic era.

There are many areas of learning that have been and will be affected by the general conceptualisation of what has become encapsulated in the term "online" learning; schools and higher education institutions are one area of obvious expansion and application. Less known but still significant has been the impact and activity in vocational and workplace learning, though online technology and related applications have long been a staple of the business world, especially in the information technology (IT) areas, some of which support developments in online learning, others in software and hardware development for application elsewhere (Wallace, 2004).

A further related application has been in the area of training (Driscoll, 1998) where aspects of online and Web-related planning design and delivery of adult training programmes have flourished over the past 15 to 20 years. The impact on this area has led to many organisations that specialise in corporate training and support systems online where employees can take personality profiles, tests about their learning styles and more sophisticated psychometric analyses.

Along with these developments has been an enormous uptake of uses and ideas across the online world where social media and applications have even led to an entirely new set of terms and "e" vocabulary where F2F (face-to-face) communication is, in many cases, the least used communication genre for many of our youth and other groups. Blogs, wikis and many other approaches to social communication have blossomed with amazing frequency and growth.

There have been a number of well-constructed and thought-throrough models that have tried to assist in the understanding of online learning, the range of possible elements and approaches, and how to better theorise, discuss and analyse them. This is particularly so in relation to the teaching and learning in educational settings or where there is an educational "intent."

One such model, which underpinned a good deal of the thinking of the first volume, *Teaching and Learning Online: Pedagogies for New Technologies*, was that developed and explicated by Coomey and Stephenson (2001).

The Coomey and Stephenson Paradigm

In the first volume of *Teaching and Learning Online*, in 2001, Coomey and Stephenson, in their chapter entitled "Online Learning: It Is All About Dialogue, Support and Control – According to the Research," presented what they described and detailed as a "paradigm grid" to establish a rubric to enable the aspects of teaching emphases and learner roles across the spectrum of possible uses in online learning to be analysed and discussed. It is presented in this chapter as still a significant and relevant model to enhance the understanding of the central issue inherent in considering pedagogical impact and approaches in this field – who should and who does "control" or direct the learning that takes place. As the online learning "world" has shifted from what has been labelled Web 1.0 to Web 2.0, the emphasis on student control and interaction is more and more relevant to the discussion.

The Coomey and Stephenson "paradigm grid" sets out four quadrants on a two-dimensional "grid" to represent four different paradigms for consideration. As stated by Coomey and Stephenson, "much of the current experience of online learning falls within four paradigms (see Figure 2.1):

- Teacher-controlled, specified learning activities;
- Teacher-controlled, open-ended or strategic learning;
- Learner-managed specified-learning activities;
- Learner-managed, open-ended or strategic learning" (2001, p. 41)

The Coomey and Stephenson "online learning grid" amounts to a model that emphasises two dimensions: *learning activity* set against a dimension of *locus of control* (teacher versus learner locus).

Online Learning: Models and Impact in the 21st Century • 23

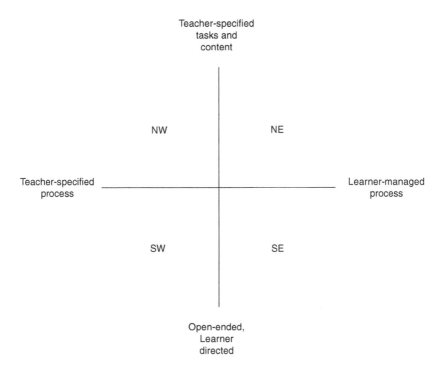

Figure 2.1 Online Paradigm Grid (Coomey & Stephenson, 2001)

The four quadrants generated by this model clearly show the four different paradigms, and Coomey and Stephenson go on, in their explanation of each quadrant, to elaborate on the characteristics of each variant and the implications of each for the roles of teaching and learning expected and exposed by the consideration of the two dimensions.

Central to the Coomey and Stephenson model was what they referred to as "four major features of online learning," which were identified as "dialogue, involvement, support and control (DISC)" (p. 38). Drawing on around 100 research studies, the authors elaborated on the four quadrants of their model as applied to the reports of these studies, which led them to conclude that to a large extent, "the range of teaching and learning paradigms described in this study is comparable to that found in learning contexts not based in Information-and Communications Technology (p. 49). Further, they suggested, along with others in the field at that time, "that teachers using online learning merely re-create their normal pedagogical stance" (p. 49).

Coomey and Stephenson do not leave the matter there, however, and offer a caveat of sorts. "However, it would be misleading to conclude from this evidence that educationally nothing is changing." (p. 49). They suggest that from 2000–2001 when this chapter had been written, there was a gradual shifting from traditional didactic modes of teaching and learning to more learner-managed modes.

What is fascinating to anyone who has been following the emergence of the "computer age" in educational terms is that as early as 1980, Seymour Papert in his landmark work, *Mindstorms: Children, Computers and Powerful Ideas*, suggested the following:

> In most contemporary educational situations where children come into contact with computers the computer is used to put children through their paces, to provide exercises of an appropriate level of difficulty, to provide feedback and to dispense information. The computer programming the child. In the LOGO environment the relationship is reversed: The child, even at preschool ages is in control: the child programmes the computer. (1980, p. 19)

While Papert's work received widespread adoption and support at the time and through the early 1980s, to a large extent the idea that children needed to learn to program (no matter how simply) appears to have passed most by. The key impact of this work, however, is that the locus of control shifting to the learner in the IT world has become more and more of a reality.

Another model, with similarities to Coomey and Stephenson's later one, is that offered by Kember (1997) (see Figure 2.2), where the emphasis on the role of teaching conceptions is on shaping teaching and learning practices.

Studies that examined teaching conceptions categorized it into two main categories: student-centred/learning-oriented and teacher-centred/content-oriented orientations (Devlin, 2006; Entwistle, Skinner, Entwistle, & Orr, 2000; Kember, 1997). This categorization is in line with Coomey and Stephenson's online paradigm grid in terms of the locus of control. However, Kember (1997)

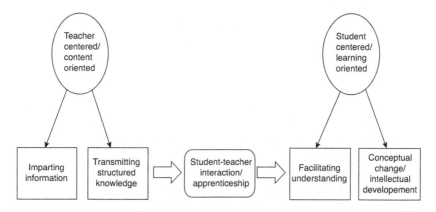

Figure 2.2 Conceptions of Teaching (Kember, 1997, p. 264)

Online Learning: Models and Impact in the 21st Century • 25

further suggested that each of these two categories has subcategories. That is, teacher-centred/content-oriented can be divided to (a) teaching as imparting information and (b) teaching as transmitting structured knowledge. On the other hand, student-centred/learning-oriented can be divided into (a) teaching as facilitating understanding and (b) teaching as promoting intellectual development/conceptual change. An intermediate/transitional conception was situated between the two categories: teaching as student-teacher interaction (Kember, 1997). While Commey and Stephenson explained the nature of how online learning tasks are carried out, Kember described teachers' conceptions about teaching underpinning some of the learning and teaching behaviours. Therefore, understanding teachers' conceptions of online learning can help us further understand the way learning tasks are carried out.

Whatever the models or paradigms emphasising learning and teaching and the roles of educators in using different forms of the latter to enhance learning, the second decade of the 21st century offers a wider range of technology, ideas and opportunities for the teaching-learning interaction.

In many of the more recent social media approaches to Internet use and WWW interaction, there are few controls, varying "learning intents," and many broad-based (and at times outrageous) examples of self-indulgent "postings." Even the political scene has now begun to make major use of online postings, question-and-answer sessions and video clips to influence voting and promote candidacy. What people are learning in these contexts remains an open question most of the time.

Web Developments: Web 1.0 and Web 2.0

In the "online learning world," that genre of writing, research, theory and applications that now holds such a prominent position across the world of education, the initial introduction and operation of computers, then the Internet and the World Wide Web, offered, in the second half of the last century, potential for educational application. As mentioned earlier, early models and usage of IT (as the whole area became known) tended to reproduce former teaching practices and use technologies in a transmission mode more than interactive learning.

The World Wide Web (Web 1.0) developed as more of a "read-only Web" where a wide range of material could be accessed and exciting (in their time) elements such as encyclopaedic "sites" allowed information to be sought and downloaded. The early development of what became known as "browsers" such as Mosaic at the University of Illinois in the United States around 1994 (later to become Netscape and even later Mozilla) opened a new and exciting world where one could "visit" other places and engage in a range of actions at the touch of a keyboard or via a mouse click.

Web 1.0 or e-learning 1.0, according to the German scholar in the field, Ehlers (2009, p. 299), "follows a *broadcasting logic*" in which "information and materials are distributed, presented and made available to students." Ehlers goes on to argue that for Web 1.0 or e-learning 1.0, "Learning in this view can be described using the metaphor of 'acquisition' of learning content."

In contrast Web 2.0 or e-learning 2.0 (to adopt Ehlers's usage) offers more participation and interaction than e-learning 1.0. The term (Web 2.0), which was first used in 2004, marked a transition from mainly read-only Web 1.0 to read-and-write Web 2.0 (Greenhow, Robelia, & Hughes, 2009). This allowed for a greater level of participation and ownership of the content on the Web. Web 2.0 includes social networking Web sites such as Twitter and Facebook, media sharing such as YouTube, and blogs and micro-blogging (e.g., Twitter and more recently micro-vlogging such as Keek). Such technologies seem to result in decentralising knowledge, allowing for collective construction of knowledge based on a combination of facts and range of human experiences. This also means that knowledge is validated through peers and community members who are the readers and writers of the content in the first place (Dede, 2008). A good example of the advancement of Web 2.0 over the previous Web 1.0 is in the area of encyclopaedias. Web 1.0 opened up the way such mainstays as the *Encyclopaedia Britannica* could be consulted and people (especially students) could find and "mine" knowledge embedded in the work. Web 2.0 led to Wikipedia, where anyone can add, edit and develop entries (this of course led to a need for monitoring and authentication, as many entries may be flawed). The change, however, made the encyclopaedia an interactive and "alive" idea rather than a chronicle of the past, as the printed versions had become.

Given the rapid and ongoing changes of technology, it is difficult to make clear boundaries between different generations of the Web – e.g., Web 1.0, Web 2.0 and any forthcoming generation. Indeed, today's technology is a result of the evolvement of older technologies, and so is the ways it is conceived and used.

Some of the applications of Web 2.0 technology and ideas have seen rapid shifts in ideas about the way people learn and interact. In higher education, for example, most of the modern universities and colleges offer blended courses in all areas. It has been pretty well documented that in the US, UK and Australia, to name just a few, there are fewer and fewer "full time" university students who attend campuses all day or most of the week (Cairns, 2012). Learning through face-to-face lecture and tutorials has, in many instances, been replaced by podcasts and online activities. Much of the traditional work is completed offsite, and library usage is now more and more online with electronic books, journals and on-screen reading. Some students in universities never visit the physical library and operate totally online for library usage.

Web 3.0 and Beyond?

Over the past few years there has been an online suggestion that there has emerged, as a possible development, what has been described as Web 3.0. This development is also often termed the "semantic Web." Whilst most explanations of just what this evolution of the Web might entail are somewhat vague and even confusing (try a search of the Web using a search engine such as Google and see what we mean!), the World Wide Web Consortium (headed by the originator of the WWW) suggests that Web 3.0 will involve machines being able to interact on the Web in ways we can only currently imagine. It should be a personalised and very advanced and different experience from what we know today.

We are not sure, at this time, if it is in the interests of learners' learning for the advances to follow the apparent direction of Web 3.0. Faster and more personalised information and interaction will no doubt be welcomed, although the potential, like so many of the WWW developments over the last 20 years, has yet to bear fruit.

What is evident is that as access and interaction have increased at such a rapid and exponential rate across the many aspects of Web 2.0, with social media being one of the major growth and excitement aspects, the uses and applications of such technologies to learn and educate have been slow to follow and exploit the massive scale of use and interaction these approaches have generated.

Educators appear unsure as to whether some of the Web 2.0 aspects are useful and applicable, and classroom teachers are still wary of mobile phones, Facebook use, Twitter and such as educational activity possibilities. The rise of lateral uses such as "sexting" in adolescent behaviour as well as bullying on the Web and through e-mail and the uses of images and worse social deviance amongst adults have many governments and social agencies concerned. The dexterity of many users of modern technology in manipulating, hacking, maliciously faking aspects and invading privacy is a common topic in the press and other media. There is no doubt there has been rapid and sophisticated learning happening, but it is often not in line with acceptable social and community mores.

So, where will it all go, and what is beyond today's e-learning and online learning?

Some (such as Bonk and Graham, 2006) appear to see blended learning as the inevitable educational model with variations where there will be "no schools" and totally online learning systems (these already exist in many places). Others might argue that there will always be a place and space for education in face-to-face locations and interactions as the needed major form of learning.

We will see, perhaps in this 21st century, where the next educational revolution will take us.

Pedagogies and Developments in the 21st Century: Impact of Online Learning on Educational Practice

The availability of the Internet and other Web-based technologies has placed knowledge within the reach of almost everyone who can afford the basic ICT infrastructure – e.g., Internet-connected computer or mobile device. Hence, learning is no longer exclusive to certain settings or social groups. One of the recent developments of distance education programs is known as MOOC. Starting with small number of students in North American universities, free and open online courses are currently being offered by Coursera through some of the world's best-known universities (Kirschner, 2012). Universities such as Stanford University, the University of Melbourne and the University of Queensland are some current examples of universities that offer MOOCs. Despite the challenges and concerns about the quality of education in MOOC (see for example Kop, 2011), this mode of distance learning has become a reality for many universities in the world. What is fascinating about the MOOC development is that anyone with the technology available to them can undertake a course at university level in an open and "unfiltered" way, without regard to entrance requirements and prior knowledge or learning. This is a major step beyond the original open university ideas developed in the 20th century in the United Kingdom. Whether the MOOC development (which has attracted hundreds of thousands of students in a very short time) will lead to formal qualifications and challenge the exclusive university market is yet to be seen but is a concern for many in the higher education sector.

Previous studies emphasized the need for pedagogies that encourage learners to discover their learning needs and, therefore, participate in planning their own learning (Black & Wiliam, 2009; Webb & Jones, 2009). There also is a need for a teaching culture that goes beyond learning facilitation per se to a culture where teachers are encouraged to experiment and innovate in their use of online learning technologies in teaching and learning (Laurillard, 2012). Such collaboration allows both teachers and students to work together and create their own understanding of knowledge and meaning (Laurillard, 2008; Palloff & Pratt, 2010). It is the lifelong skills that learners and knowledge workers need in the current times to solve complex problems and create new knowledge (Häkkinen & Hämäläinen, 2012).

The impact of online learning on education and learning within society has a somewhat slim and shallow research base. As the U.S. Department of Education reported in January 2012 in relation to the impact of online learning on educational productivity with regard to secondary schooling in particular, the research "was found to be lacking" (2012, p. vi).

Based on findings from higher education, where the U.S. Department of Education acknowledged there was a better research base on impact, the report identified nine applications of online learning that are possible "pathways to improved productivity" (p. vi):

- Broadening access
- Engaging students in active learning
- Individualizing and differentiating instruction
- Personalizing learning
- Making better use of teacher and student time

- Increasing the rate of student learning
- Reducing school-based facilities costs
- Reducing salary costs
- Realising opportunities for economies of scale

A number of additional interesting questions arise from consideration of reports and syntheses such as the U.S. Department of Education report. These include whether the greater and wider adoption of online learning approaches might lead to the demise of educational institutions as we have known them for centuries. One implication of differentiated pace and levels of student engagement and progress might mean that age/grade grouping will become irrelevant. Another might mean that students need never attend an institutional space, already a reality in many situations and courses. Some of the largest higher education providers in the world (in terms of student enrolments) are operating as wholly online institutions (e.g., University of Phoenix), while others, such as Saudi e-University, started as a fully fledged online university providing fully accredited and recognised undergraduate and postgraduate degrees.

Certainly, the range of possible impacts on higher education has been canvassed quite recently in a study reported by the Pew Research Center in the US (PewInternet, 2012). This study surveyed 1,021 Internet experts (a non-random sample) for their views about the future impact of the Internet on higher education. The intent was to "imagine where we might be in 2020" (p. 3). Some 60% agreed with a scenario outlining change, while 39% agreed with a scenario suggesting modest change by 2020.

The majority scenario was as follows:

> By 2020, higher education will be quite different from the way it is today. There will be mass adoption of teleconferencing and distance learning to leverage expert resources. Significant numbers of learning activities will move to individualized, just-in-time learning approaches. There will be a transition to "hybrid" classes that combine online learning components with less-frequent on-campus, in-person class meetings. Most universities' assessment of learning will take into account more individually-oriented outcomes and capacities that are relevant to subject mastery. Requirements for graduation will be significantly shifted to customized outcomes. (p. 4)

The advent, in the late 20th century, of more emphasis on what has been labelled as "blended learning," where online and some forms of other face-to-face interaction take place, appears to be emerging as the main approach across higher education. Bonk and Graham in *The Handbook of Blended Learning*, 2006, suggested that in higher education and workplace education and training, blended learning was rising to be the dominant model, and they concluded their chapter (the handbook's concluding one) on the future directions with the following point:

> Most of the learning opportunities outlined in this handbook would not have been possible or even conceivable ten or twenty years ago. The authors of this book have pushed the envelop of the possible in adult learning. They are succeeding in making life a lifelong blended learning event. (p. 565)

Conclusion

While the advent of online learning has been an exciting development for many involved across the education sector from schools to higher education and has been taken up in training, business and workplaces as well, the promise or potential is what has been spoken about through much of the second half of the 20th century, rather than clear demonstrations of the educational applications and productivity impacts of adoption.

This 21st century needs to more carefully monitor, explore and demonstrate that online learning does offer learners a better way and that the often touted advantages do outweigh the lists of disadvantages (especially the social interaction and support face-to-face learning experiences can offer).

Online learning has the capability to show new insights to learners and their learning and to adopt new pedagogies to enhance and develop learner-managed learning to an extent that will produce real improvements, not just wallow in the possible excitement technology often leads to in the first instance.

References

Beetham, H., & Sharpe, R. (eds.) (2007). *Rethinking pedagogy for a digital age: designing and delivering e-learning*. London and New York: Routledge.
Black, P., & Wiliam, D. (2009). Developing the theory of formative assessment. *Educational Assessment, Evaluation and Accountability, 21*(1), 5–31.
Bonk, C. J. (2009). *The world is open: how Web technology is revolutionizing education*. San Francisco: Jossey-Bass.
Bonk, C. J., & Graham, C. R. (eds.) (2006). *The handbook of blended learning: global perspectives, local designs*. San Francisco: Pfeiffer.
Cairns, L. G. (2012). Are we reinventing the university in the 21st century or has the ultramodern university just necessarily evolved? World Universities Forum, Rhodes, Greece.
Coomey & Stephenson. (2001).
Crook, C. (2012). The "digital native" in context: tensions associated with importing Web 2.0 practices into the school setting. *Oxford Review of Education, 38*(1), 63–80. doi: 10.1080/03054985.2011.577946
Dede, C. (2008). A seismic shift in epistemology. *Educause Review, 43*(3), 80.
Devlin, M. (2006). Challenging accepted wisdom about the place of conceptions of teaching in university teaching improvement. *International Journal of Teaching and Learning in Higher Education, 18*(2), 112–119.
Driscoll, M. (1998). *Web-based training: using technology to design adult learning experiences*. San Francisco: Jossey-Bass/Pfeiffer.
Ehlers, U. D. (2009). Web 2.0 – e-learning 2.0 – quality 2.0? Quality for new learning cultures. *Quality Assurance in Education, 17*(3), 296–314.

Entwistle, N., Skinner, D., Entwistle, D., & Orr, S. (2000). Conceptions and beliefs about "good teaching": an integration of contrasting research areas. *Higher Education Research and Development, 19*(1), 5–26.

Garrison, D. R. (2011). *E-learning in the 21st century: a framework for research and practice* (2nd ed.). New York and London: Routledge.

Greenhow, C., Robelia, B., & Hughes, J. E. (2009). Learning, teaching, and scholarship in a digital age Web 2.0 and classroom research: what path should we take now? *Educational Researcher, 38*(4), 246–259.

Häkkinen, P., & Hämäläinen, R. (2012). Shared and personal learning spaces: challenges for pedagogical design. *Internet and Higher Education, 15*(4), 231–236. doi: 10.1016/j.iheduc.2011.09.001

Kember, D. (1997). A reconcepualization of the research into university academics' conceptions of teaching. *Learning and Instruction, 7*(3), 255–275.

Kirschner, A. (2012). A pioneer in online education tries a MOOC. *Chronicle of Higher Education*, n/a.

Kop, R. (2011). The challenges to connectivist learning on open online networks: learning experiences during a massive open online course. *International Review of Research in Open and Distance Learning, Special Issue – Connectivism: Design and Delivery of Social Networked Learning, 12*(3).

Laurillard, D. (2008). The teacher as action researcher: using technology to capture pedagogic form. *Studies in Higher Education, 33*(2), 139–154. doi: 10.1080/03075070801915908

Laurillard, D. (2012). *Teaching as a design science: building pedagogical patterns for learning and technology*. New York: Routledge.

Palloff, R. M., & Pratt, K. (1999). *Building learning communities in cyberspace: effective strategies for the online classroom*. San Francisco: Jossey-Bass.

———. (2010). *Collaborating online: learning together in community*. San Francisco: Jossey-Bass.

Papert, S. (1980*). Mind-storms: children, computers, and powerful ideas*. Sussex: Harvester Press.

PewInternet (2012). *The future impact of the Internet on higher education: Experts expect more-efficient collaborative environments and new grading schemes; they worry about massive online courses, the shift away from campus life*. Pew Research Center. Retrieved from http://www.pewinternet.org/Reports/2012/Future-of-Higher-Education.aspx

Rudestam, K. E., & Schoenholtz-Read, J. (eds.) (2010). *Handbook of online learning* (2nd ed.). Los Angeles: SAGE.

Selwyn, N. (2012). Bursting out of the "ed-tech" bubble. *Learning, Media and Technology, 1–4*. doi: 10.1080/17439884.2012.680212

U.S. Department of Education, Office of Educational Technology (2012). *Understanding the implications of online learning for educational productivity*. Washington, DC.

Wallace, P. (2004). *The Internet in the workplace: how new technology is transforming work*. Cambridge: Cambridge University Press.

Webb, M., & Jones, J. (2009). Exploring tensions in developing assessment for learning. *Assessment in Education: Principles, Policy & Practice, 16*(2), 165–184. FIGURE 2.2 Conceptions of Teaching (Kember, 1997, p. 264)

Part 2
Theory that Informs Practice

The main focus of the two chapters in part 2 is pedagogical in nature although both chapters are grounded in the practical experiences of online learners engaged in both individual and collaborative learning. As more and more educational programmes go online we find that learners have to take personal responsibility for parts of the learning process that are not content specific and may not have traditionally been explicitly addressed. Much has been made of the need to produce graduates with strong critical thinking skills, comfortable with problem solving and decision making in chaotic and unstructured environments – people who are capable of producing new insight and disruptive innovations, future thought leaders. It is becoming clear that these skills are more dependent upon teaching people to think through critical reflection than teaching people content. In an online world where content is ubiquitous and available 24/7, we need to ask serious questions about how we can support learners to engage productively with the available media. An examines the issues of providing support for the problem solving process and presents seven strategies that could be used to support the cognitive processes of online learners. Hee-Young Kim looks at the experience of communities of online learners and asks what can be done to build capability through better strategies for self-regulation of learning. She describes her experiences of establishing and supporting a "community of survival" for collective learning and provides a set of guiding principles that are valuable to both learners and learning designers alike. Both authors take the view that too many online learning programmes pay too little attention to the provision of guidance aimed at helping learners regulate their own learning process and learn from each other's learning efforts.

3
Strategies for Supporting Students' Metacognitive Processes in Ill-Structured Problem Solving in Online Environments

YUN-JO AN

University of West Georgia, USA

Editors' Introduction

This chapter argues that self-directed learners will inevitably be faced with problem solving in ill-structured domains and that, as yet, we have a limited understanding of how to support online learners as they engage in such processes. The author reviews current research and presents seven strategies that could be used to support the cognitive processes of online learners. She provides examples and a rich commentary on how each of the strategies could be incorporated into our online activities. Anyone who is engaged in the design or specification of online learning environments will find this chapter to be an invaluable resource.

Introduction

We encounter and solve problems all the time. Problem solving is regarded as the most important activity in our everyday and professional lives (Jonassen, 2000). In today's knowledge age, the importance of problem solving seems greater than ever before. More and more jobs are ill defined, so organisations need people who can think critically and creatively and effectively use ever-increasing amounts of data to solve problems, especially ill-structured problems, in collaboration with others around the world using appropriate digital tools and resources. Like most problems we encounter in everyday life, ill-structured problems are complex, ill-defined and open-ended. They have vaguely defined or unclear goals, and the information needed to solve them is not entirely contained in the problem statements. Unlike well-structured problems, ill-structured problems seldom have a single, correct, or best solution. They typically have several possible solutions and multiple solution paths, and the actions needed to solve them are not readily apparent. Also, they often require the integration of several content domains (Chi & Glaser, 1985; Ge & Land, 2004; Jonassen, 1997, 2000; Sinnott, 1989; Voss & Post, 1988). Thus, ill-structured problems are much more difficult to solve than well-structured problems and demand higher cognitive and metacognitive abilities (Ge & Land, 2004). However, they are much more meaningful and relevant to learners. Researchers have increasingly emphasized the importance of developing students' ability to solve ill-structured problems (e.g., Cognition and Technology Group at Vanderbilt, 1990; Jonassen, 1997; Reigeluth, 1999).

Coomey and Stephenson (2001) developed the paradigm grid for online learning (see Figure 3.1). Solving ill-structured problems in online environments falls under the SE quadrant in that learners are in control of the overall direction of the learning in the ill-structured problem-solving process. In this chapter, I first describe the four major processes for ill-structured problem solving and discuss the importance of metacognition in the ill-structured problem-solving process. Then, I briefly explain what scaffolding means and discuss the importance of scaffolding in ill-structured problem solving. Finally, I present seven research-based strategies for supporting students' metacognitive processes when they solve ill-structured problems in online environments.

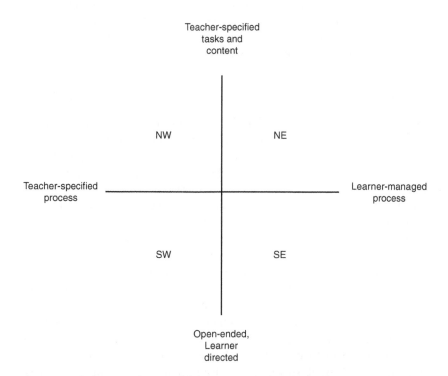

Figure 3.1 Online paradigm grid (Coomey & Stephenson, 2001)

Ill-Structured Problem Solving and Metacognition

Based on the foundational work on ill-structured problem-solving (Sinnott, 1989; Voss & Post, 1988; Voss, Wolfe, Lawrence, & Engle, 1991), Ge and Land (2004) identified the following major processes for ill-structured problem solving:

- Problem representation
- Solution development
- Argument construction
- Monitoring and evaluation

First, problem representation is a critical process in ill-structured problem solving since it determines the ease of solution development (Chi & Glaser, 1985). During this process, problem solvers define the problem, identify constraints and diverse perspectives, and select goals. Second, during the solution development process, problem solvers compare possible solutions and make decisions on the selection of the solutions. Third, constructing arguments is needed in both problem representation and solution development processes since ill-structured problems have multiple representations and solutions. Problem solvers must assess the viability of alternative solutions and construct arguments grounded on evidence to justify their proposed solutions (Jonassen, 1997). Finally, monitoring and evaluation are required throughout the ill-structured problem-solving process. Problem solvers monitor their problem-solving processes and evaluate alternative solutions (Sinnott, 1989).

In order to be successful in ill-structured problem solving, problem solvers need both domain-specific knowledge and structured or structural knowledge. Doman-specific knowledge refers to content knowledge in a specific discipline. On the other hand, structured or structural knowledge, which is described as schemata or cognitive structure, is the knowledge of how concepts within a domain are interrelated (Chi & Glaser, 1985; Ge & Land, 2004; Jonassen, 2000; Voss & Post, 1988; Voss et al., 1991). Novices, who do not possess sufficient domain-specific knowledge and structural knowledge, tend to interpret complex problems in simplified ways, overlooking critical factors; have difficulty identifying relevant information; and often fail to consider alternative solutions (Powell & Willemain, 2007; Voss & Post, 1988).

Metacognition is also important because ill-structured problem solving involves ongoing monitoring and evaluation. The term *metacognition*, coined by Flavell (1979), is often simplified as "thinking about thinking" or "cognition about cognition." Although different researchers define metacognition differently, most researchers (e.g., Flavell, 1979, Hacker, Dunlosky, & Graesser, 1998; McCormick, 2003) generally agree that metacognition consists of both metacognitive knowledge and metacognitive regulation (see Figure 3.2). Metacognitive knowledge refers to declarative knowledge about and awareness of one's own cognitive processes. Flavell (1979) further divides metacognitive

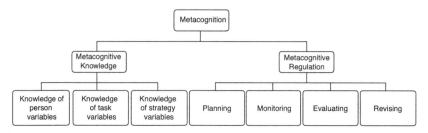

Figure 3.2 Components of Metacognition

knowledge into three categories: knowledge of person variables, task variables and strategy variables. Metacognitive regulation, on the other hand, refers to one's procedural knowledge for regulating cognitive processes and consists of the following four components (Brown, 1987):

- Planning
- Monitoring
- Evaluating
- Revising

Problem solvers need to analyse the problem and develop appropriate plans. Planning involves setting goals, identifying problem-solving strategies and allocating resources. They also need to monitor and evaluate their problem-solving processes and revise their plans, goals and strategies. When domain-specific knowledge and structural knowledge are absent or limited, metacognition is necessary for solving ill-structured problems. Wineburg (1998, 2001) found that metacognitive knowledge could compensate for absence of relevant domain knowledge.

Scaffolding

Many students are unfamiliar with the ill-structured problem-solving process and are not well prepared to effectively manage cognitive and metacognitive challenges posed by ill-structured problems (An, 2010). Studies show that students do not always engage in the planning activities and rarely use metacognitive monitoring processes (Azevedo, Cromley, & Seibert, 2004; Azevedo, Guthrie, & Seibert, 2004). Researchers have increasingly emphasised the importance of scaffolding students' cognitive and metacognitive processes during ill-structured problem solving.

Scaffolding refers to support provided by human and computer tutors, teachers, or more capable peers that enables learners to solve a problem or carry out a task they cannot accomplish independently (Vygotsky, 1978; Wood, Bruner, & Ross, 1976). Scaffolds can take a variety of forms, including expert modelling, expert advice, prompts, learner guides and tools. Saye and Brush (2002) distinguished between hard scaffolds and soft scaffolds. Hard scaffolds refer to "static supports that can be anticipated and planned in advance based on typical student difficulties with a task" (p. 81). In contrast, soft scaffolds provide dynamic and spontaneous support based on learner responses. Further, Hannafin, Land, and Oliver (1999) identified four types of scaffolding: conceptual, metacognitive, procedural and strategic. First, conceptual scaffolding guides learners regarding what to consider and helps them reason through complex problems. Second, metacognitive scaffolding provides guidance on how to think during learning. It supports planning, monitoring and evaluation. Third, procedural scaffolding emphasises how to utilize resources and tools. Finally, strategic scaffolding provides guidance on how to approach learning tasks or problems. Relatively little attention has been given to metacognitive scaffolding, and we currently do not have sufficient guidance on how to scaffold students' metacognitive processes when they solve ill-structured problems, especially in online environments.

Supporting Metacognitive Processes in Online Ill-Structured Problem Solving

In this section, I will present seven research-based strategies for supporting students' metacognitive processes in ill-structured problem solving in online environments. Figure 3.3 summarizes the seven strategies.

Metacognitive Training

Research shows that metacognitive training helps students develop deeper conceptual understanding as well as metacognitive skills. For example, Azevedo and Cromley (2004) investigated the effectiveness of self-regulated learning (SRL) training in facilitating college students' learning with hypermedia. Undergraduate students (N = 131) were randomly assigned to either a training condition or a control condition and used a hypermedia environment to learn about the circulatory system in 45 minutes. Students in the training condition received 30 minutes of training on the different phases and areas of regulation, a simplified model of SRL and specific SRL variables. Students in the control condition received no training. The results indicate that students in the training condition gained a deeper conceptual understanding compared to the control group students. Also, the training group students deployed the SRL processes more frequently to effectively regulate their learning with hypermedia.

In a similar vein, Mevarech and Kramarski (1997) designed a metacognitive instructional method called IMPROVE to promote students' mathematics knowledge and reasoning. In IMPROVE, students are trained to use a series of self-addressed metacognitive questions, including comprehension questions (e.g., What is the problem all about?), connection questions (e.g., What are

1. Metacognitive Training

- Provide online training on the ill-structured problem-solving process and metacognitive strategies.
- Provide a rationale for each metacognitive strategy that is taught (informed training).

2. Metacognitive Prompts

- Provide question prompts that support metacognitive processes, including planning, monitoring, evaluation, and revising.
- Keep in mind that students may not use the prompts provided and fail to take advantage of them.

3. Soft Scaffolding

- Pay extra attention to making students' thinking and problem-solving processes visible using various digital tools and media, including blogs, wikis, discussion forums, video conferencing tools, online mind mapping and brainstorming tools, and online diagramming tools.
- Carefully monitor the progress students are making and provide tailored support and timely feedback based on an ongoing diagnosis of students' problem solving processes.

4. Problem-Solving Plans and Progress Reports

- Have students collaboratively write a problem-solving plan and progress reports using wikis or Google Docs to engage them in metacognitive activities and to make their problem solving processes visible.

5. Process Visualization and Metacognitive Maps

- Make the entire problem-solving process explicit and visible using online mind mapping or diagramming tools so that students can see the big picture.

6. Peer Interaction

- Create a supportive social environment where metacognitive activities are valued.
- Use effective communication and collaboration tools (e.g., online brainstorming and planning tools, Web 2.0 tools) to support students' collaborative planning, monitoring, and evaluation processes.
- Make both synchronous and asynchronous communication and media available.

7. Role-Playing

- Have students play metacognitive roles (e.g., planning manager, monitoring manager, evaluation manager, revision manager) in online small groups.

Figure 3.3 Seven Strategies for Supporting Students' Metacognitive Processes in Online Ill-Structured Problem Solving

the similarities and differences between the given problem and problems you have solved in the past, and why?), strategic questions (e.g., What strategies are appropriate for solving the problem, and why?) and reflection questions (e.g., What am I doing here? Can I solve it differently?). Mevarech and Fridkin (2006) examined the effects of the IMPROVE method on students' mathematical knowledge, mathematical reasoning and metacognition. Participants were 81 precollege students who studied an advanced course in mathematical functions. Students were randomly assigned into one of two groups, and groups were randomly assigned into one of two conditions: IMPROVE versus traditional instruction (the control group). The IMPROVE students were explicitly trained to use the self-addressed metacognitive questions while solving mathematical problems. The control group was exposed to traditional instruction with no explicit exposure to metacognitive training. The findings of the study indicate that the IMPROVE students significantly outperformed their counterparts on both mathematical knowledge and mathematical reasoning. In addition, the IMPROVE students developed a higher level of metacognition compared to their counterparts.

Although these studies were not conducted in the ill-structured problem-solving context, they still provide important insights. To facilitate students' ill-structured problem solving in online environments, the instructor may consider providing online training on the ill-structured problem-solving process and metacognitive requirements. Further, using the IMPROVE idea, the instructor can develop and provide a variety of modules that train students to use specific metacognitive strategies. Research suggests that students who are aware of the value and usefulness of metacognitive activities in problem solving are more willing to engage in these activities (Brown & Campione, 1996; Coleman, Brown, & Rivkin, 1997; King, 1992; Zimmerman, 1998). So it is important to provide a rationale for each strategy that is taught. "Informed" training, in which students are informed of the conditions that are most appropriate for the use of the new strategies, is much more powerful than "blind" training. Without understanding why, when and how they are useful, students have difficulties in using the learned strategies in new settings (Brown, Bransford, Ferrara, & Campione, 1983; Lin, 2001). After learning new metacognitive strategies, students must be given opportunities to practice them.

Metacognitive Prompts

Literature reveals that question prompting is an effective strategy for scaffolding ill-structured problem solving. Research studies show that question prompts direct students to the most important aspects of a problem, help them become more metacognitively aware of the problem situations and their cognitive activities, and encourage self-explanation and elaboration (Bransford & Stein, 1993; Bulu & Pedersen, 2010; Chi, Bassok, Lewis, Reimann, & Glaser,

1989; King, 1991, 1992; Ge & Land, 2003, 2004; Ge, Chen, & Davis, 2005). Ge and Land (2003) found that students who received question prompts performed significantly better than those who did not receive question prompts in the processes of problem representation, developing solutions, making justification, and monitoring and evaluation, using the question prompts as a checklist to monitor their problem-solving processes, to make sure they were on the right track and to check their courses of action. Specifically, students who closely followed the question prompts demonstrated significantly better problem-solving skills in metacognitive activities, including planning for the problem-solving process, monitoring the problem-solving progress, evaluating the effectiveness of the solutions and justifying the viability of the proposed solution against alternatives. Examples of questions that can be used to support metacognitive processes, including planning, monitoring, evaluation and revising, are provided in Table 3.1.

Some of the questions are from Bulu and Pedersen (2010); Ge and Land (2004); Jonassen (2011); and King (1991).

Recently, Bulu and Pedersen (2010) investigated the effects of domain-general and domain-specific prompts on learning of scientific content and problem solving. Domain-general prompts (e.g., What information do you need to find in order to solve this problem?) were designed to support the processes of ill-structured problem solving. In contrast, domain-specific prompts (e.g., What does Akona need to survive?) were designed to support students' understanding of the specific content area. The findings of the study revealed that domain-general scaffolds facilitated monitoring and evaluation better than domain-specific ones, while domain-specific scaffolds facilitated learning of the scientific content and problem representation better than domain-general scaffolds.

Some other studies point out that students may not use the prompts provided and thus fail to take advantage of them. Greene and Land (2000) found that students sometimes omitted questions or answered superficially, thereby failing to engage in deeper thinking. Similarly, Ge and Land (2003) found that some students ignored the question prompts provided, which resulted in a lack of attention to important aspects of the problem. It is important to note that the effective use of question prompts relies on students' prior knowledge (King, 1992). If students don't have relevant prior knowledge, they may be less likely to be prompted by questions and thus may not benefit from them. One way to guide students to use question prompts mindfully is to force them to provide answers to the question prompts embedded in the computer-based learning environments. Research studies show that prompts embedded in computer-based instruction facilitate metacognition. For example, Davis and Linn (2000) found that self-monitoring prompts embedded in the Web-based Knowledge Integration Environment (KIE) helped students think carefully about their activities and facilitated their planning and reflection.

Strategies for Supporting Students' Metacognitive Processes • 43

Table 3.1 Examples of Metacognitive Question Prompts

Metacognitive Processes	Question Prompts
Planning	• What is the problem? • What kind of problem is this? • How is it similar to, or different from, those problems that I have solved? • What do I know about the problem? • What do I need to learn to solve the problem? • What information do I need to find in order to solve the problem? • What is the most effective way to solve the problem? • Is there another way to solve the problem? • What steps and activities should be completed to solve the problem? • How much time should I spend on each activity or goal?
Monitoring, Evaluating and Revising (during problem solving)	• Am I on the right track? • Am I making progress toward my goals? • Am I making good use of my time? • Have I identified all the factors and constraints? • Have I considered different perspectives of different stakeholders? • What other perspectives should I consider? • What evidence do I have to support the proposed solution? • Have I considered other alternative solutions? • Can I justify the viability of the proposed solution against alternatives? • Are my problem-solving strategies effective? • Do I need to change my goals, plans, or strategies? How?
Evaluating and Revising (after problem solving)	• What are the pros and cons of the solution? • Is it the most viable solution? • Was the problem solved within the constraints identified earlier? • How cogent was my argument for the proposed solution? • Was my problem solving process effective? • What worked? • What didn't work? • What could have been done differently or better? • What would do I do differently next time?

Soft Scaffolding

Well-designed hard scaffolds, such as question prompts, can not only support students' ill-structured problem solving, but also reduce the amount of soft scaffolding online instructors need to provide in an ill-structured problem-solving environment. However, as Saye and Brush (2002) noted, "there are limits to gains that may be achieved through hard scaffolds" (p. 93). Student support needs in the ill-structured problem-solving process are so complex and unpredictable that it is difficult to successfully support students' problem solving through hard scaffolds alone. To effectively support students' ill-structured problem solving, the instructor needs to provide tailored soft scaffolding based on an ongoing diagnosis of students' problem-solving processes (An, 2010).

Researchers have demonstrated the effectiveness of human adaptive tutoring in facilitating students' learning with hypermedia. For example, Azevedo and colleagues (Azevedo et al., 2004; Azevedo, Cromley, Winters, Moos, & Greene, 2005) conducted two studies to determine whether adaptive scaffolding was effective in facilitating students' ability to regulate their learning with hypermedia. The students were randomly assigned to one of three conditions: adaptive scaffolding (AS), fixed scaffolding (FS) and no scaffolding (NS). Results indicated that students in the adaptive scaffolding condition developed a significantly deeper conceptual understanding and deployed key self-regulatory processes related to planning, monitoring activities and effective strategies. Similarly, Azevedo, Moos, Greene, Winters, and Cromley (2008) found that students who had access to a human tutor gained significantly more declarative knowledge than their counterparts and more frequently deployed key self-regulatory processes. Specifically, they regulated their learning by activating their prior knowledge, metacognitively monitoring their cognitive system and their progress towards goals, deploying effective learning strategies and engaging in help-seeking behaviour. These findings provide evidence that soft scaffolding is effective in facilitating metacognitive and self-regulatory processes. However, there has been little research examining the effects of soft scaffolding in the ill-structured problem-solving context. More research is needed in this area.

Different students with various levels of prior knowledge and skills have different support needs. To effectively support students' metacognitive processes during problem solving, the instructor should carefully monitor the progress students are making and provide tailored support and timely feedback based on an ongoing diagnosis of students' problem-solving processes. In the beginning, the instructor should help students analyse the problem and make an effective problem-solving plan. Some students tend to jump right to the solution process without trying to interpret the given problem (Ge & Land, 2003). To assist students in planning, the instructor may encourage them to do the following:

- Analyse major factors and constraints
- Reflect on how much they already know about the problem domain

- Relate various problem aspects to their prior knowledge
- Identify what they do not know or learning issues
- Set specific goals by dividing the problem task into different components
- Determine how much time to spend on each goal (Ge & Land, 2004)

As Ge and Land (2004) noted, students do not necessarily monitor and evaluate their problem solving. Using various strategies, including modelling, coaching and question prompting, the instructor should help students periodically reflect on what they are doing to ensure they are on the right track; evaluate their problem-solving processes; modify their goals, plans and strategies if necessary; and use time and resources effectively. Also, the instructor should help students consider various perspectives and constraints and compare and evaluate alternative solutions before selecting a solution (Ge & Land, 2004; Voss et al., 1991). Students often propose solutions without considering different perspectives and constraints. They also do not voluntarily construct arguments to justify their proposed solutions without being prompted to do so (Ge & Land, 2003) and have difficulty supporting their arguments with evidence (Bell & Linn, 2000). It is important to communicate the importance of iteratively restricting alternatives and refining arguments before selecting a solution (Jonassen, 1997) and to provide appropriate support to engage students in the processes of gathering evidence and justifying the selected solution against alternatives.

Students' problem-solving processes are often invisible in online environments. In order to effectively monitor their problem-solving progress and to provide appropriate soft scaffolding, the instructor should pay more attention to making students' problem-solving processes visible. The instructor may have students periodically record their problem-solving processes or write reflective journals. Blogs, wikis, or other similar tools can be used for recordings of the problem-solving processes and reflections. Providing a discussion forum is another way to make students' problem-solving processes visible. If students communicate in a chat room or using a video conferencing tool, the instructor may ask them to save and archive their messages. Digital graphic organisers, online mind mapping and brainstorming tools (e.g., MindMeister, bubbl.us, SpiderScribe, Edistorm) and online diagramming tools (e.g., Gliffy, Cacoo, Creately, Lucidchart) can also be used to make students' thinking visible. For example, in the solution development process, the instructor may ask students to use a compare/contrast matrix to compare and contrast multiple alternative solutions.

Problem-Solving Plans and Progress Reports

Using Hannafin and colleagues' (1999) scaffolding classification, An (2010) designed conceptual, metacognitive, procedural, and strategic scaffolds and explored their effectiveness in supporting students' wiki-based, ill-structured problem solving in an online graduate-level course. For metacognitive scaffolding, she developed templates for a project plan and progress reports in an attempt to support student groups' planning, monitoring and evaluation in their ill-structured problem-solving processes. In the project plan, which was designed to facilitate the student groups' initial planning process, students were required to include their team name and wiki URL, project scope, tasks and activities to be completed, timeline, and team communication and collaboration strategies. The progress reports were designed to help the student groups monitor their collaborative problem-solving processes, assess what they had done, and make critical group decisions accordingly. In the progress reports, the students were required to include their project title, team name, date, overall project status, project risks and issues, evaluation and lessons learned, and next steps and timeline.

Overall, the project plan and progress reports turned out to be effective in supporting student groups' metacognitive processes. The students reported that writing the project plan helped them make initial project plans effectively. They also reported that writing the progress reports helped their groups avoid procrastination, make progress, monitor and evaluate their progress, and make necessary changes to improve their problem-solving process. The project plan and progress reports made the student groups' plans, strategies, progress, reflections and evaluations visible, and it allowed the instructor to understand what was going on in each group and to provide appropriate feedback and guidance. Although they were designed for metacognitive scaffolding, they also helped the instructor better understand the student groups' conceptual needs and provide tailored conceptual scaffolding.

As noted earlier, students' problem-solving processes are often imperceptible, especially in online environments, and it makes it harder for the instructor to provide appropriate support. Having students collaboratively write a problem-solving plan and progress reports using wikis or Google Docs can be one way to facilitate their metacognitive processes in ill-structured problem solving since they not only force students to engage in metacognitive activities, including planning, monitoring, evaluating and revising, but also enable the instructor to provide more adaptive scaffolding by making the students' problem-solving processes visible. However, it is worth noting that writing a problem-solving plan and progress reports might not be effective when there is a lack of communication among group members (An, 2010).

Process Visualization and Metacognitive Maps

The Digital IdeaKeeper is a scaffolded software environment that supports middle school learners with online inquiry. A "process visualization" scaffolding strategy, in which information analysis is decomposed into its constituent tasks, was used to support metacognitive aspects of online inquiry (Quintana

& Zhang, 2004). Quintana, Zhang, and Krajcik (2005) argue that making the entire online inquiry process explicit and visible can help learners see the "big picture" and monitor and regulate their work more effectively. In a similar vein, Lee and Baylor (2006) provided guidelines for designing a metacognitive map for Web-based learning, which consists of two sub-maps (global and local tracking maps) and a planning space. First, the global map provides an overall structure of the learning content and guides learners to plan their learning activities more effectively. Second, the local tracking map helps learners check what they have already completed and judge what they need to do next. With the local tracking map, learners can evaluate their learning processes and performance. Finally, the planning space supports learners' premediated planning of the learning tasks. Learners can check their learning goal, learning strategies and expected learning time, and revise them based on their ongoing monitoring and evaluation of their learning.

The process visualization approach and Lee and Baylor's (2006) metacognitive map idea provide practical strategies for metacognitive scaffolding. By making the entire problem-solving process explicit and visible using online mind mapping tools (e.g., MindMeister, SpiderScribe), online diagramming tools (e.g., Gliffy, Cacoo, Creately, Lucidchart), or other similar tools, the online instructor can help students understand that ill-structured problem solving involves a range of activities, aid students in developing a problem-solving plan from a holistic perspective, and monitor and evaluate their problem-solving progress more effectively.

Peer Interaction

Peer interaction, a form of collaborative learning, can facilitate metacognitive processes in ill-structured problem solving by making students' thinking visible and by exposing them to multiple perspectives. Working collaboratively gives students a chance to ask questions, explain their ideas or positions, elaborate thinking and provide feedback. Through the cycles of questioning, explaining, elaborating and feedback, students articulate their ideas and make their thinking process visible and available for examination and reflection (Ge & Land, 2003). Also, peer interaction creates a context for students to share different ideas and challenge one another's thinking. By exposing students to multiple perspectives, peer interaction can help them consider things they might otherwise have overlooked (Lin, Hmelo, Kinzer, and Secules, 1999) and build upon each other's ideas. Ge and Land (2003) found that students who worked with peers tended to consider a wide range of factors and constraints. By comparing and contrasting different ideas, strategies and perspectives, students can come up with more effective problem-solving strategies and plans and monitor and evaluate their problem-solving processes more effectively. However, peer interactions may not lead to effective metacognitive activities if students are not actively engaged in high-level peer discourse. As King (1999) noted, students do not always engage in high-level discourse spontaneously unless they are prompted to do so. Without appropriate guidance, students may interact with each other at very basic levels. Ge and Land (2003) suggest that peer interaction must be guided and monitored with various strategies in order to maximize its benefits.

It is important to create a supportive social environment where metacognitive activities are valued (Lin, 2001). If the environment does not value and support metacognitive activities, students will have a hard time engaging in them. Students need to understand why metacognitive processes are important for their problem solving and feel comfortable acknowledging what they do not know, asking questions, sharing their ideas and giving constructive feedback to one another. They should be encouraged to consider multiple perspectives throughout the problem-solving process and to take advantage of each other's knowledge and skills. Question prompts can be used to facilitate constructive peer interaction during the ill-structured problem-solving process. The questions in Table 3.1 can serve as a script or a starting point for students to practice asking each other questions that support metacognitive processes. The instructor may encourage students to create their own questions by using the question prompts as examples as their competence increases (Ge & Land, 2004).

To support students' collaborative planning, monitoring and evaluating processes in an online environment, it is important to use effective collaboration and communication tools. Online brainstorming tools such as Edistorm can be useful for collaborative brainstorming and planning. Web 2.0 tools, such as wikis and Google Docs, can be useful for collaborating writing. Students may use them to collaboratively develop their problem-solving plan and to record their progress and reflections. By making group members' thinking visible and public, those tools enable students to reflect on different ideas and perspectives and to build upon each other's ideas. They also keep everyone on the same page.

For effective communication and collaboration, students need to use both synchronous and asynchronous communication media since synchronous communication is more effective and efficient for group decision making while asynchronous communication allows students to have more time to reflect on the content and to work at their convenience (An & Reigeluth, 2008). An (2010) explored how online students use wikis in the ill-structured problem-solving process. The results of the study indicate that although wikis are effective for collaborative writing and editing, they are not effective as a communication tool in the ill-structured problem-solving process. The students in her study depended on synchronous communication tools, such as Skype and phone calls, to make major group decisions efficiently. Collaborative planning, monitoring, evaluation and revising require a lot of discussions and decision making. Student groups should be guided to have synchronous meetings on a regular basis to discuss their progress and make group decisions efficiently. Online video conferencing tools, such as Adobe Connect, WebEx, Skype and ooVoo, can be used for synchronous meetings.

Role-Playing

Having students play metacognitive roles in a small group is another way to facilitate metacognitive processes. White and Frederiksen (2005) describe four metacognitive roles students can play while engaged in a collaborative inquiry task: planning manager, productivity manager, revision manager and reflection manager. The planning manager gets the group to set its goals, develop a plan for achieving them and decide who will do what. The productivity manager stops the group from time to time and gets the group to assess its progress. If there is any problem, the revision manager gets the group to fix it. The reflection manager gets the group to reflect on what they have done.

Similar metacognitive roles can be used to support students' ill-structured problem solving in online environments. For example, students can play the roles of planning manager, monitoring manager, evaluation manager and revision manager in online small groups. The numbers and names of the roles can vary depending on problem-solving situations. To maximize the benefits of the role-playing, it is important to provide them with role guides, as per White and Frederiksen (2005). The role guides can include the goals of each role and question prompts as discussed earlier.

Conclusion

Ill-structured problem solving is not a linear, straightforward process. Rather it is an iterative and cyclical process (Jonassen, 1997) and involves ongoing monitoring and evaluation. Therefore, metacognition is critical for successful problem solving. Metacognition is necessary especially when domain-specific knowledge and structural knowledge are absent or limited. However, students do not always engage in metacognitive activities without appropriate support. In an attempt to help online instructors better support students' metacognitive processes in ill-structured problem solving, this chapter presents seven strategies, including metacognitive training, metacognitive prompts, soft scaffolding, problem-solving plan and progress reports, process visualization and metacognitive maps, peer interaction and role-playing.

Multiple strategies can be integrated into an online problem-solving situation. For example, in the initial stage of problem solving, the instructor may provide a brief online training on metacognitive processes and strategies along with a visual representation of the entire problem-solving process and encourage students to collaboratively write a problem-solving plan using a template in which metacognitive prompts are embedded. Then the instructor may provide question prompts to facilitate monitoring and evaluation processes. To provide more adaptive scaffolding, the instructor may have students collaboratively write progress reports periodically and provide tailored feedback. However, the integration of a number of strategies might be unnecessary for students with high levels of prior knowledge and metacognitive skills who do not need much guidance from the instructor. It is important to choose appropriate strategies based on students' skills and needs. Also, it is important to adapt support based on an ongoing diagnosis of students' problem-solving processes.

To provide appropriate support in online environments, the instructor should pay extra attention to making students' thinking and problem-solving processes visible. There are a variety of digital tools and media that have significant potential to make students' thinking and problem-solving processes visible and to facilitate online communication and collaboration, including Web 2.0 technologies, online brainstorming and mind mapping tools, online diagramming tools and video conferencing tools. However, we should keep in mind that the potential of technologies can be realised only when they are properly used.

References

An, Y. J. (2010). Scaffolding wiki-based, ill-structured problem solving in an online environment. *MERLOT Journal of Online Learning and Teaching, 6*(4), 723–734.

An, Y. J., & Reigeluth, C. M. (2008). Problem-based learning in online environments. *Quarterly Review of Distance Education, 9*(1), 1–16.

Azevedo, R., & Cromley, J. (2004). Does training on self-regulated learning facilitate students' learning with hypermedia? *Journal of Educational Psychology, 96*(3), 523–535.

Azevedo, R., Cromley, J. G., & Seibert, D. (2004). Does adaptive scaffolding facilitate students' ability to regulate their learning with hypermedia? *Contemporary Educational Psychology, 29,* 344–370.

Azevedo, R., Cromley, J. G., Winters, F. I., Moos, D. C., & Greene, J. A. (2005). Adaptive human scaffolding facilitates adolescents' self-regulated learning with hypermedia. *Instructional Science, 33,* 381–412.

Azevedo, R., Guthrie, J. T., & Seibert, D. (2004). The role of self-regulated learning in fostering students' conceptual understanding of complex systems with hypermedia. *Journal of Educational Computing Research, 30,* 87–111.

Azevedo, R., Moos, D. C., Greene, J. A., Winters, F. I., & Cromley, J. G. (2008). Why is externally-facilitated regulated learning more effective than self-regulated learning with hypermedia? *Educational Technology Research and Development, 56,* 45–72.

Bell, P., & Linn, M. C. (2000). Scientific arguments as learning artifacts: designing for learning for the Web with KIE. *International Journal of Science Education, 22*(8), 797–817.

Bransford, J. D., & Stein, B. S. (1993). *The IDEAL problem solver: A guide for improving thinking, learning, and creativity* (2nd ed.). New York: W. H. Freeman and Company.

Brown, A. L. (1987). *Metacognition, executive control, self-regulation, and other more mysterious mechanisms.* Hillsdale, NJ: Lawrence Erlbaum.

Brown, A. L., Bransford, J. D., Ferrara, R. A., & Campione, J. C. (1983). Learning, remembering, and understanding. In J. H. Flavell & E. M. Markman (eds.), *Handbook of child psychology: Vol. 3. Cognitive development* (4th ed., 77–166). New York: John Wiley and Sons.

Brown, A. L., & Campione, J. C. (1996). Psychological learning theory and the design of innovative environments: on procedures, principles and systems. In L. Shauble & R. Glaser (eds.), *Contributions of instructional innovation to understanding learning.* Hillsdale, NJ: Erlbaum.

Bulu, S. T., & Pedersen, S. (2010). Scaffolding middle school students' content knowledge and ill-structured problem solving in a problem-based hypermedia learning environment. *Educational Technology Research and Development, 58*(5), 507–529.

Chi, M., Bassok, M., Lewis, M., Reimann, P., & Glaser, R. (1989). Self-explanations: how students study and use examples in learning to solve problems. *Cognitive Science, 13,* 145–182.

Chi, M.T.H., & Glaser, R. (1985). Problem-solving ability. In R. J. Sternberg (ed.), *Human abilities: an information processing approach* (227–250). New York: W. H. Freeman and Company.

Cognition and Technology Group at Vanderbilt (1990). Anchored instruction and its relationship to situated cognition. *Educational Researcher, 19*, 2–10.
Coleman, E. B., Brown, A. L., & Rivkin, I. D. (1997). The effect of instructional explanations on learning from scientific texts. *Journal of the Learning Sciences, 6*(4), 347–367.
Coomey, M., & Stephenson, J. (2001). Online learning: it is all about dialogue, involvement, support and control – according to the research. In J. Stephenson (ed.), *Teaching and learning online: pedagogies for new technologies* (37–52). Sterling, VA: Kogan Page.
Davis, E. A., & Linn, M. (2000). Scaffolding students' knowledge integration: Prompts for reflection in KIE. *International Journal of Science Education, 22*(8), 819–837.
Flavell, J. H. (1979). Metacognition and cognitive monitoring. *American Psychologist, 34*, 906–911.
Ge, X., Chen, C., & Davis, K. A. (2005). Scaffolding novice instructional designers' problem-solving processes using question prompts in a Web-based learning environment. *Journal of Educational Computing Research, 33*(2), 219–248.
Ge, X., & Land, S. M. (2003). Scaffolding students' problem-solving processes in an ill-structured task using question prompts and peer interactions. *Educational Technology Research and Development, 51*(1), 21–38.
Ge, X., & Land, S. M. (2004). A conceptual framework for scaffolding ill-structured problem-solving processes using question prompts and peer interactions. *Educational Technology Research and Development, 52*(2), 5–22.
——— (2000). A qualitative analysis of scaffolding use in a resource-based learning environment involving the World Wide Web. *Journal of Educational Computing Research, 23*(2), 151–180.
Hacker, D. J., Dunlosky, J., & Graesser, A. C. (1998). *Metacognition in educational theory and practice.* Hillsdale, NJ: Lawrence Erlbaum Associates.
Hannafin, M., Land, S., & Oliver, K. (1999). Open learning environments: Foundations, methods, and models. In C. Reigeluth (ed.), *Instructional-design theories and models: a new paradigm of instructional theory* (115–140). Mahwah, NJ: Lawrence Erlbaum Associates.
Jonassen, D. H. (1997). Instructional design models for well-structured and ill-structured problem-solving learning outcomes. *Educational Technology Research and Development, 45*(1), 65–94.
——— (2000). Toward the design theory of problem solving. *Educational Technology Research and Development, 48*(4), 63–85.
——— (2011). *Learning to solve problems: a handbook for designing problem-solving learning environments.* New York: Routledge.
King, A. (1991). Effects of training in strategic questioning on children's problem-solving performance. *Journal of Educational Psychology, 83*(3), 307–317.
——— (1992). Facilitating elaborative learning through guided student-generated questioning. *Educational Psychologist, 27*(1), 111–126.
——— (1999). Discourse patterns for mediating peer learning. In A. M. O'Donnell & A. King (eds.), *Cognitive perspective on peer learning* (87–115). Mahwah, NJ: Lawrence Erlbaum Associates.
Lee, M., & Baylor, A. L. (2006). Designing metacognitive maps for Web-based learning. *Educational Technology & Society, 9*(1), 344–348.
Lin, X. D. (2001). Designing metacognitive activities. *Educational Technology Research and Development, 49*(2), 23–40.
Lin, X. D., Hmelo, C., Kinzer, C., & Secules, T. (1999). Designing technology to support reflection. *Educational Technology Research and Development, 47*(3), 43–62.
McCormick, C. B. (2003). Metacognition and learning. In W. M. Reynolds & G. E. Miller (eds.), *Handbook of psychology: Vol .7.* (79–102). New York: Wiley.
Mevarech, Z., & Fridkin, S. (2006). The effects of IMPROVE on mathematical knowledge, mathematical reasoning and metacognition. *Metacognition and Learning, 1*(1), 85–98.
Mevarech, Z., & Kramarski, B. (1997). IMPROVE: a multidimensional method for teaching mathematics on students' mathematical reasoning. *British Journal of Educational Psychology, 73*, 449–471.
Powell, S. G., & Willemain, T. R. (2007). How novices formulate models. Part I: qualitative insights and implications for teaching. *Journal of the Operational Research Society, 58*(8), 983–995.
Quintana, C., & Zhang, M. (2004). *The Digital IdeaKeeper: Extending digital library services to scaffold online inquiry.* Paper presented at the annual meeting of the American Educational Research Association, San Diego, CA.
Quintana, C., Zhang, M., & Krajcik, J. (2005). A framework for supporting metacognitive aspects of online inquiry through software-based scaffolding. *Educational Psychology, 40*(4), 235–244.
Reigeluth, C. M. (1999). What is instructional-design theory and how is it changing? In C. M. Reigeluth (ed.), *Instructional-design theories and models: a new paradigm of instructional theory: Vol. 2* (5–29). Mahwah, NJ: Lawrence Erlbaum Associates.

Saye, J. W., & Brush, T. (2002). Scaffolding critical reasoning about history and social issues in multimedia-supported learning environment. *Educational Technology Research and Development, 50*(3), 77–96.

Sinnott, J. D. (1989). A model for solution of ill-structured problems: Implications for everyday and abstract problem-solving. In J. D. Sinnott (ed.), *Everyday problem-solving: theory and application* (72–99). New York: Praeger.

Voss, J. F., & Post, T. A. (1988). On the solving of ill-structured problems. In M. H. Chi, R. Glaser, & M. J. Farr (eds.), *The nature of expertise* (261–285). Hillsdale, NJ: Lawrence Erlbaum Associate.

Voss, J. F., Wolfe, C. R., Lawrence, J. A., & Engle, R. A. (1991). From representation to decision: an analysis of problem solving in international relations. In R. J. Sternberg & P. A. Frensch (eds.), *Complex problem solving: principles and mechanisms*. Hillsdale, NJ: Lawrence Erlbaum Associates.

Vygotsky, L. S. (1978). *Mind in society.* Cambridge, MA: Harvard University Press.

White, B., & Frederiksen, J. (2005). A theoretical framework and approach for fostering metacognitive development. *Educational Psychology, 40*(4), 211–223.

Wineburg, S. (1998). Reading Abraham Lincoln: an expert-expert study in the interpretation of historical texts. *Cognitive Science, 22*, 319–346.

Wineburg, S. (2001). *Historical thinking and other unnatural acts: Charting the future of teaching the past.* Philadelphia: Temple University Press.

Wood, D., Bruner, J., & Ross, G. (1976). The role of tutoring in problem-solving. *Journal of Child Psychology and Psychiatry, 17*, 89–100.

Zimmerman, B. J. (1998). Academic studying and the development of personal skill: a self-regulatory perspective. *Educational Psychologist, 33*(2/3), 73–87.

4
Coping Together: Collective Self-Regulation in a Web-Based Course

JACKIE HEE-YOUNG KIM

Armstrong Atlantic State University, USA

Editors' Introduction

This chapter examines the challenges facing the online learner, particularly the self-directed learner. The author suggests that the most successful online learners adopt the skills of "strategic learning"; this is characterised by having developed high levels of self-regulation and having the ability to consistently deploy these skills. She points to communal factors as being a key determinant in the development of self-regulating strategies through modelling of peers and the instructor and through heightened self-awareness of their own self-regulation. The chapter reports on the findings from a learning design that transformed her online class into a "community of survival"; the detailed findings compare and contrast individual and collective self-regulation strategies, and from this emerges a set of guiding principles that learning designers can use to bring a sharper focus on the promotion of self-regulated learning strategies.

Introduction

Because the Internet requires a high level of autonomy to be used effectively, it is a double-edged sword that can assist or impede students struggling to become self-directed learners. On the one hand, some students enjoy the flexibility of learning at their own pace when engaging in Internet-based learning activities. On the other, the demands of self-regulated learning can be challenging and even overwhelming for students who are not well prepared for this kind of approach (Azevedo & Cromley, 2004; Smith, Torres-Ayala, & Heindel, 2008).

Students who lack sufficient self-regulatory skills tend to struggle with online learning environments; they submit low-quality assignments, earn failing grades and drop out before the semester is over. One of the more challenging tasks of any online instructor is to help students improve the quality of their work in order to complete the course successfully. I have witnessed a drastic worsening

53

in the quality of students' work as assignments become longer and more complex and require more research. I hypothesise three factors underlying the fact that students submit poor-quality assignments and subsequently fail their online classes: (a) students' failure to understand course requirements; (b) students' procrastination; and (c) students' poor time management and/or study habits (Solomon & Rothblum, 1994). The failure to submit quality assignments, or any assignments at all, results in low grades and, subsequently, students drop out.

While seeking solutions to the issues raised here, I found self-regulation theory to be of value (at least on an experimental level) in trying to meet the aforementioned challenges of online classrooms. All learning environments present challenges, but online learning environments are unique because students bear considerably more responsibility for their own progress than they would in a face-to-face classroom. Therefore, students need to develop better self-regulatory skills in order to increase their academic motivation, learn more and procrastinate less.

Why Collective Self-Regulation?: The Dual Needs of Self-Regulation

This research project found its genesis in my professional curiosity: I wondered if it was possible to promote self-regulation in online environments. If so, what would be the best approach? I found an answer in Kagitcibasi's (1994, p. 276) argument that autonomy and social relatedness are co-occurring human needs. In other words, self-regulation and personal control are strongly influenced by communal factors (Mills & Clark, 1982, p. 283). It is therefore critical to synthesise both autonomy and social relatedness in order to promote optimal human functioning. Accordingly, this research project explores self-regulation in the communal context of online learning. This approach is highly correlated to Vygotsky's work (1978, 1986, 1987, 1997). I used the students, peers and the instructor (myself) as models of self-regulation based on the belief that self-regulated learning strategies are best addressed through modelling (Paris & Winograd, 2001; Perels, Gurtler, & Schmitz, 2005). Peers play a key role in supporting their classmates' development of self-regulation skills (Schunk & Zimmerman, 1998). Therefore, these principles must play a central role in the creation of a course designed to help students develop as self-regulated learners. To enhance the incorporation of self-regulation in course design, this study will consider how online students self-observe their current study practices, how they compare their practices with the strategies of others and how study methods are better learned online with peers as part of a community of learners.

The course design in this study emphasized the behavioural aspects of self-regulation in online learning rather than focusing on cognitive aspects of self-regulation. By making students' learning methods a focus of the online discussion and by helping them to self-observe their learning strategies, instructors can convert their online classroom into collaboratively self-regulated learning environments. The ultimate psychological advantage of an emphasis on learning methods (rather than on content alone) is profound because improvement in one's approach to online learning precedes improved learning outcomes (see Bandura, 1986; Schunk & Schwartz, 1993; Zimmerman & Bandura, 1994). The role of an online instructor who assists online students in developing self-regulatory strategies is quite different than that of the traditional online instructor who only emphasises subject, content and goals. Therefore, the goal of this course design was to transform my class into a "community of survival" where students could become smart learners by becoming models for their peers and by learning from both their peers and their instructor.

Little is known about how online instructors of Web-based courses promote self-regulated learning strategies in a collective way. Therefore, I used Zimmerman's (1986, 1989, 1998, 2000) social cognitive model of SRL as a theoretical framework for my practice. Zimmerman's model not only outlines key discussion topics for the "community of survival" (which I adapted for the online discussion of self-regulation), it also offers a way to look at the motivational and environmental factors that influence enactment of SRL strategies. The "community of survival" sessions allowed me to investigate how online graduate students create a self-regulated sharing community and how they use self-regulated learning strategies to complete tasks and cope with challenges in a Web-based introductory course about teaching.

The forum on self-regulation strategies was included as part of weekly discussion postings and was titled "Community of Survival Discussion." The main goal of this discussion activity was to encourage students to create, share and reflect on their self-regulation strategies. Topics were carefully constructed to promote lively discussion and were based on variables drawn from Zimmerman's social cognitive model of self-regulation (1986, 2000, 2002). (Sample discussion topics include the following: Do you have anxiety about taking an online course? How might you overcome your anxiety? Please conduct a task analysis for the final assignment and share in the discussion board.)

The following variables formed the basis for discussion topics:

1. Forethought
    a. Goal Setting and Planning
2. Performance and Self-Observation
    a. Organizing and Transforming Instructional Materials
    b. Structuring the Learning Environment
    c. Help Seeking
    d. Self-Monitoring and Record Keeping
3. Self-Reflection

To raise the quality of assignments, a "mental representation task analysis" was adopted to model how complex assignments could be broken into small

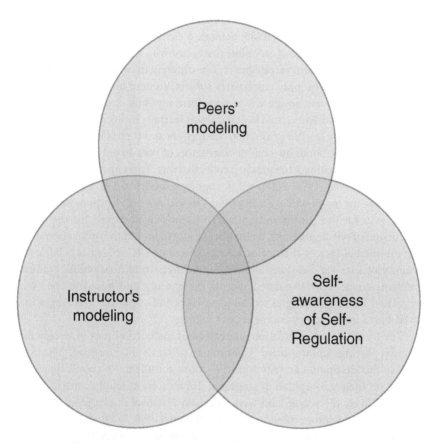

Figure 4.1 Elements of Adaptive Self-Regulation

steps. This task analysis used a heuristic and procedural approach in which each student was both aware of the instructor's objectives and set his or her own goals for the assignment. In addition to the specific strategies of self-regulation design provided at the end of this section, four general guiding principles are discussed here for the benefit of online course instructors and designers who want to create a self-regulation (SR) forum:

- SR is promotable.
- SR is social.
- SR should be customized.
- SR should be internalized.

The Mental Representation-Based Task Analysis

Understanding an assignment involves analysing the learning task, setting goals and planning or refining learning strategies. Initially, when students are assigned an unfamiliar topic, they have little ability to break the task into small steps and often fail to set specific goals for themselves or develop an effective task analysis. Online faculty can model for students how to analyse a task, set effective goals and choose correct strategies. Students tend to underestimate the difficulty of tasks and overestimate their degree of preparation; this leads to assignments that are of poor quality. Therefore, the project used the mental representation-based task analysis to create an integral planning and management skill matrix that allowed students to become self-regulated learners in a Web-based course.

The mental representation-based task analysis matrix developed for online self-regulation encourages students' mastery orientation. One of the characteristics of online students is that they are highly task oriented. In other words, they are highly performance oriented and only focus on completing their work to "get it done" or to get the highest grade. This type of performance orientation is not conducive to self-regulated learning. The mental representation-based task analysis matrix encourages students to create their own goals in addition to being aware of the objective of the assignments as written in the syllabus. Often students complete the assignment just to meet the instructor's expectations. It is not unusual for instructors to have students ask them, "Is this what you want?" It is not only critical for instructors to have clear expectations for each assignment, but also that students create their own personal goals for the assignment. Therefore, another objective discussed in this section is increasing online students' self-regulated learning by creating a task analysis matrix.

The analysis table uses a grid format and contains the following variables:

- Assignment objective
- Student's own goals for completing the assignment (performance orientation/mastery orientation)
- Value of assignment for student's career or life (mastery orientation)
- Task analysis
- Date to complete
- Monitoring check box
- Reflection

This matrix functions just like a professor who is modelling self-regulation. The systematic analysis of the assignment, the requirements and the expectations for the assignment are described in the matrix and provide a useable example for promoting self-regulated learning.

Findings

In this report I compare my findings with pre-service teachers and with the findings of Whipp and Chiarelli (2004), who conducted SR strategy research with in-service teachers. It is interesting to compare how individuals learn SR strategies and how groups learn SR strategies together. The differences in the contexts are revealing.

Goal Setting and Planning

According to Zimmerman (1998, 2000), SRL begins in a forethought phase that includes goal setting and strategic planning and which is implemented largely on the basis of beliefs about self-efficacy. Common strategies used by both my students and those of Whipp and Chiarelli included the following: (a) daily log-ons; (b) use of a weekly planner; (c) coordination of online and offline work; (d) a plan to deal with the inevitable technical problems that arise in a Web-based course; and (e) self-administered deadlines.

In the students' interviews and in their discussion postings, the most important concern expressed regarding taking an online class was the need to stay on top of assignments and not fall behind. Students understood the importance of organisation and time management to successfully remaining current with their assignments. They based their study plan and time management on their previous analysis of their personality, family issues, learning preferences and personal issues. Some students were overwhelmed by a heavy workload and found that in order to decrease stress they had to complete assignments far ahead of the actual due date. However, some students enjoyed the last-minute pressure and believed it even increased their creativity. Other students had a tendency to be very detail oriented and hyper-focused, which required them to spend more time studying than their peers. Some had a reading disability or attention deficit disorder which required them to make a greater time commitment to complete tasks. Still others had personal issues such as pregnancy, depression and so forth which affected the time spent on assignments. It is interesting to note that students were very aware of their learning environment, their needs and how best to overcome the learning barriers presented by various life circumstances.

The most common stumbling block in the students' planning phase was the lack of time to study. Most of the students had to juggle a full- or part-time job and/or family responsibilities and other commitments, which required tremendous amounts of time. The ambiguity of the online setting, where face-to-face time is removed, influenced them to adopt the mind-set that they had to finish early to avoid any conflicts due to work or technical difficulties. It was imperative that they plan their work and academic schedules as far in advance as possible in order to complete their work on time and avoid major conflicts. Students diligently marked their calendars with the due dates shown on the syllabus for important papers and exams. Some students committed certain times of the day for study while others planned to use every free minute of time to study. If students' jobs afforded them downtime, they planned to use that time to get caught up on schoolwork, whether it be reading, completing assignments, or jotting down thoughts. Further, some students had a more developed understanding of the nature of online learning, and they applied that understanding to their planning. They acted as if they were taking an independent study with no instructor to remind them of deadlines.

Organizing and Transforming Instructional Materials

Our research showed that to improve performance students tended to utilize the same kinds of study methods used in a traditional face-to-face class such as highlighting, note taking, outlining, underlining, concept mapping, diagramming, brainstorming, free writing, keeping index notes and annotated journal articles, labelling reference articles with letters and numbers, reading summaries of chapters, using various Web-based search engines for academic articles and using sorting binders and chunking tasks.

To meet the course requirements, these students also adhered to every recommended guideline. They used the rubric and student sample essays as a basis to outline, brainstorm and collect the necessary articles. Before they collected and organised the instructional materials, they tried to clarify the instructor's expectations for each assignment by reviewing the syllabus, rubrics and guidelines and by using the student sample assignments provided by the instructor as a blueprint. Online, students used adaptive strategies such as printing copies of course and discussion materials so they could be read at any time and composing their thoughts as a Word document before transferring their comments to the discussion board. Some preferred offline composing and editing while some wrote directly on an iPad.

Structuring the Learning Environment

As students became more aware of the independent nature of online learning and more accustomed to the lack of boundaries found in conventional classrooms, they "selected and arranged the physical setting to make learning easier" (Zimmerman & Martinez-Pons, 1986, p. 618) based on their learning styles, study habits and work schedule. Three dominant foci in selecting and arranging their study areas were the following: (a) maximizing the amount of time to study; (b) minimizing distractions; and (c) creating comfortable and relaxing learning environments. As nontraditional students with many other social and professional commitments, they had to be able to study anytime, anywhere, which, interestingly enough, is a fundamental characteristic of online learning itself. Strategic online students found places and time to study either at work or at home and had study devices and materials accessible at all times. Their notebooks and textbooks were either on their person or in their vehicles so they were ready to prepare for assignments anywhere they went and anytime they were free.

Strategic learners used systematic distraction management. Their primary sources of distractions were phone, TV and Internet. Many left their phones unanswered and kept the TV turned off. One of the most difficult distractions to eliminate was the Internet itself, especially Facebook and Pinterest, since they were working on computers.

Help Seeking

Most strategic online learners were not hesitant to seek direct assistance from teachers, other students, or friends and family. Whom the students turned to depended on the importance of the issue and the time available. If the matter was important enough to warrant it, students tended to call or e-mail the instructor, whom, they believed, was the most reliable source of information. If they were short on time, they sought help from any family members or friends who were immediately available. They also asked for help from other students in the class by sending e-mails and posting questions on the discussion board. Students who were inclined to solve problems on their own sought help from Internet sources.

Self-Observation and Record Keeping

Students tracked their performance at both micro and macro levels. On a macro level, they made sure they submitted all required assignments and took all quizzes by marking their calendars. At the same time, on a micro level, they made sure all components of assignments were included in their submissions by checking the syllabus, rubric and student examples on the class Web site. Students made sure they executed all the goals in their planners by creating bulleted items according to class requirements. Students were especially concerned about the accuracy of their self-observations because if they misinterpreted their performance they would not be able to make the appropriate corrections (Zimmerman, 2000, p. 20). They made sure they understood the assignment correctly by checking the comments of their peers and by comparing their work to the student examples. All of the students used organised, systematic methods to keep track of their performance, including planners, to-do lists, even a colour-coordinated poster board.

Self-Reflection

Strategic students' performance standards for self-evaluation were derived from a variety of sources. They asked self-check questions, compared the quality of their work against student examples and used the assignment rubric to evaluate their performance on various tasks.

When asked about adopting the strategies employed by their peers, many admitted that others' strategies sounded good, but that they did not want to adopt them or they lacked sufficient time to experiment. As Zimmerman, Bonner, and Kovach (2009) argued, each learner's strategy choice depends on previously used strategies. Often, as students begin to implement a new strategy, they will lapse into more familiar methods.

Motivational Influences on SRL Strategy Use

According to Zimmerman's (2000) model of self-regulation, various motivational beliefs such as self-efficacy underlie each phase of the self-regulatory process. If students possess a strong sense of efficacy about their SRL skills, they tend to be less anxious about academic demands. Interestingly, sharing SRL strategies as part of a community of learners reinforced a strong sense of efficacy about their SRL skills. Surveying others' SR strategies reaffirmed the value of their own SRL strategies, which resulted in a higher level of self-efficacy and decreased anxiety about learning online.

Self-Efficacy and Social Reinforcement

According to social cognitive theory (Bandura, 1986, 1997), self-efficacy has a strong relationship with anxiety. Individuals experiencing anxiety embody apprehension and avoidant behaviours that often interfere with performance both in everyday life as well as in academic situations. Anxiety is also one of several sources of self-efficacy (Bandura, 1997) so it serves as both a source and effect of self-efficacy beliefs. Therefore, it is critical to ascertain the sources of anxiety in online learning environments. In interviews and survey results, collective SR group students had a variety of anxieties about online learning quite similar to those found by Whipp and Chiarelli (2004). The following, drawn from the reports of online students, are the causes of anxiety:

- Being first-time online students
- Potential procrastination
- Missing social contact and interaction
- Lack of technical expertise
- Missing important deadlines
- Disbelief in technology and the submission process
- Ambiguous and unfamiliar expectations
- Assuming complete responsibility for self-discipline and staying on top of assignments
- Time constraints and unexpected issues with their jobs

The forum of "community of survival" per se played a key role in reducing anxiety and consequently promoting self-efficacy. According to the students' narratives, hearing the strategies of their peers eased their anxiety and gave them a feeling of confidence. The fact that others used similar SR strategies made them "more confident of their own strategies" (Jeff), reassured them that "what they were doing was okay" (Elian), became a positive "reinforcement of what they do" and increased confidence that they were "on the right track" (Derrick). Sharing SR strategies helped them realise that other people have similar worries and concerns. As students became more familiar with the situations of other students, they began to feel they were all in the same boat struggling with similar concerns and worries. In this way they were better able to relate to others and increasingly felt they were not all alone in working out problems. In addition, according to student comments, it seemed that the communal aspects of discussion also reduced the fear of failure (Onwuegbuzie & Jiao, 2000; Solomon & Rothblum, 1994), which is one of the causes of procrastination.

Environmental Influences on SRL

Social Support: Task Analysis

It is assumed that the framework of the task analysis assignment played a key role either as a blueprint of how to complete the assignment or as a reference of what was needed to fully meet the requirements. Further, the framework provided a template for students to construct their own task analysis for each assignment.

The task analysis assignment gave students who might otherwise have been lost a better understanding of the size of the workload required by each assignment. After completing the task analysis, they were less frightened by the size of the assignment. Conducting the task analysis helped students create a to-do list and allocate their time more effectively to completing the assignment, thereby avoiding procrastination. Students confessed that when they did not complete the task analysis they were likely to spend far less time on their assignments. They found it beneficial to break assignments down into small steps so they could better estimate how detailed they needed to be and how long it would take to complete the work.

The Table 4.1 shows that there is a large area of common ground between the kinds of strategies students adopted as individuals using SR learning and the kinds of strategies groups used to work on SR together. However, the differences in the research contexts may account for some of the differences in strategies used to develop SR skills. While Whipp and Chiarelli's (2004) study focused on looking at individual students' SR skills, the current study's approach was to look at how SR could be promoted to a group. The course design laid out features to promote online SR strategies such as having students share their ideas and installing tools that led students to become better strategic online learners using such methods as the task analysis matrix, rubrics and self-celebration techniques. Thus, there were more frequent uses of instructor-initiated SR strategies evident in the findings of this study than found in the work of Whipp and Chiarelli (2004).

The Role of the Instructor

This study showed that there are two levels to the instructor's promotion of SR strategies. In the first, the instructor designs a course of study to promote SR skills, and in the second, the instructor waits for a student to articulate his or her needs before responding with techniques to improve SR skills. In this study it proved critical to simultaneously present students with the tools necessary to improve their SR skills while also responding conscientiously to students' requests for assistance with SR skills.

One by-product of this experimental online self-regulation activity was that it helped me, as the instructor, to discover my role as a responder. Surprisingly, reading all these very personal accounts of how students met challenges and trained themselves to be strategic online learners made me more engaged in reading the discussion postings than I had been in previous semesters. I found myself having more empathy for my students' situations, emotions, struggles, fears, anxieties and aspirations. I read the students' discussions more often and more closely. (After teaching this same course for six years, reading students' postings had become a very mundane task.) I was gratified to find ways to ease their worries and to help them solve errors. In instances where students posted comments saying they did not like a particular feature of online learning, or complained that no one reminded them of assignment deadlines, or felt that the lack of auditory input created a barrier for their self-regulation, I responded with an avatar (see Figure 4.2). I created a talking avatar with voki.com. (I copied HTML codes from voki.com and pasted codes into the source view mode of the e-mail message box instead of the what you see is what you get, or WYSIWYG, mode). Thus, students could hear assignment reminders through their e-mail. If a student posted that she was concerned she had submitted an assignment incorrectly, I could reply right away either confirming her error or reassuring her she had submitted successfully. I tried to consistently respond to the students' worries with active interest and care. Students appreciated my initiatives and gave me a high rating on the course evaluation.

I found that this collective online self-regulation activity created significant reciprocity among students as well as between students and the instructor. Student behaviour was influenced by the modelling of both their peers and the instructor, and in turn, the instructor's responses were influenced by students' feedback (see Figure 4.3).

Discussion and Implications

Using Zimmerman's social cognitive model of SR learning, this study uncovered a number of SR learning strategies used by online students including planning, organizing and self-monitoring; environmental structuring; social solicitation; and self-judgement and self-reflection. In addition, this study addresses how a

Table 4.1 Comparison of Two Groups: Traditional and Adapted Self-regulated Learning (SRL) Strategies used by online learners

SRL Strategies		Traditional	Online Adaptation
Forethought Goal setting and planning	Whipp & Chiarelli (2004)	Calendars and organisers; self-imposed deadlines; chunking work	Daily log-ons; coordination of online and offline work; planning for tech problems
	Collective SR Strategy Group	Colour-coded calendar; having a separate calendar for the class; creating to-do lists; planning to use slow time at work; setting aside dedicated time for study; creating a reward system for successful completion of assignments; completing the task analysis matrix provided by the instructor; creating a mind-set to stay on top of every task; talking to someone who has already taken the course to ease anxiety	Morning log-ons for mental preparation of tasks; synchronization of calendars among iPad, iPhone, computer, or Google calendar; multiple back-up plans; plan to submit assignment in advance of the deadline in case of technical problems; setting a regular time in their schedule to devote to online class (treating an online class like a face-to-face class); computerizing the schedules
Performance and self-observation	Whipp & Chiarelli (2004)	Note taking; outlining; underlining or highlighting course texts; graphic organisers	Printing out course materials and discussions; offline composing and editing of postings; sorting discussion threads
Organizing and transforming instructional materials	Collective SR Strategy Group	Note taking; colour coding; outlining; underlining/highlighting; concept map/diagram; brainstorming (write down all main ideas then revisit next day); writing rough draft on the paper or computer before typing final; keeping index notes and annotated journal articles nearby; understanding guidelines, rubrics and syllabus before beginning; creating summaries of readings; analysing the sample essay; breaking the task into parts; labelling reference articles with alphabets and numbers; getting clear instructions from the instructor about the assignment; locating Web search engines for academic articles; using sorting binder; chunking the task	Printing out course materials and discussion; composing on a Word document first before transferring to discussion post; offline composing and editing; typing initial notes on iPad; using student examples provided by instructor as a blueprint for doing the assignment
	Whipp & Chiarelli (2004)	Reducing distractions; relaxation techniques	Finding faster computer and Internet connections; creating a psychological space for class

Structuring learning environment	Collective SR Strategy Group	Reducing distractions; creating every environment as study environment to earn time (e.g., carrying a textbook and notebook on them or in their vehicles); finding a designated study area suitable for their learning styles; doing assignments when there is slow time at work; finding time for mental preparation; letting their spouse and family know what assignments they have and when they are working on it; incense and essential oils; yoga, meditation, walking, martial arts; working while children are sleep; posting reminders on the refrigerator, on computers and in the bathroom; setting tentative deadlines for completing assignments; leaving TV off and phones unanswered in a different room; buying a comfortable desk and chair	Buying better technology equipment; having access to the Internet at any time; locating free public WiFi in case of technical emergency
Help seeking	Whipp & Chiarelli (2004)	Using phone, e-mail, or in-person contact to get help from instructor or peers	Accessing technical expertise; peer contacts to reduce loneliness; Web-based helpers; using student postings as models
	Collective SR Strategy Group	Phone, e-mail or text messages to get help from professor, peers, family members, technical service at school, colleagues who have been or are in graduate school; friends who already have taken the course	Posting a question on the general discussion list; seeing how other students approach the assignment preparation; surfing online to find the answers; Skyping with husband in Kuwait
	Whipp & Chiarelli (2004)	Keeping charts and records of completed assignments and grades	Multiple back-ups; tracking reading and writing for discussions; frequent checks of online grade book

(*Continued*)

Table 4.1 Continued

SRL Strategies		Traditional	Online Adaptation
Self-monitoring and record keeping	Collective SR Strategy Group	Creating bulleted items according to requirements; constantly reading syllabus and rubric both during and after completion of assignments; colour-coordinated list on poster board; using task analysis matrix to check; continuous check on planners	Frequent check of grade book on class Web site; using class Web site calendar to stay on task
Self-reflection Self-judgement	Whipp & Chiarelli (2004)	Using checklists and rubrics; using instructor comments and grades	Using audience of peers to shape discussion postings
	Collective SR Strategy Group	Asking self-check questions to make sure they are on the right track with the task; checking over the rubric	Comparing work with the student examples provided by the instructor
	Whipp & Chiarelli (2004)	Success based on academic performance	Success based on technical, social, academic performance
Self-reactions	Collective SR Strategy Group	Satisfaction with own SR strategies (65%); adapted peers' SR strategies (30%); needed more time to modify their SR strategies to suit to their learning styles and study habits and personality (5%); appreciated the methods of full-time working students who invented ways to study with less time and increase their motivation	Coping strategy of others became reinforcements for following their own strategy; learning the problem solving approach of others was helpful; community of survival discussion helped develop skills required to be a strategic online learner

Coping Together: Collective Self-Regulation in a Web-Based Course • 67

Figure 4.2 Talking Avatar: Assignment Reminder

design incorporating collaborative/collective student discussion of SR learning can positively impact student attempts to become better strategic learners. Although limited by the number of students studied and by the fact that they were graduate students who might be more accustomed to self-regulating their online learning, this study nonetheless proves that the increased use of SR learning strategies can be encouraged when students share their own SR learning strategies in online settings. In particular, we found that novice online learners benefited more from a shared SR forum than seasoned online learners. Of particular note, the study found that ideally before assigning tasks the instructor should analyse them in order to scaffold students' planning for and completion

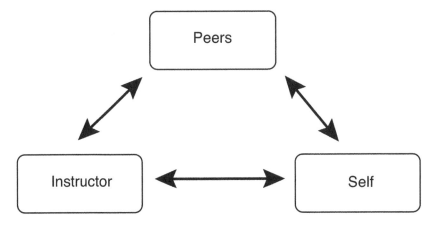

Figure 4.3 Social Interaction Paths of Online Self-Regulation

of assignments. Task analysis was converted into a strategic tool for every phase of SR from planning to self-reflection. Students used the task analysis matrix to plan, execute, monitor, evaluate and reflect. Significantly, this prevented procrastination, which is a major cause of student failure in online classes.

General Guiding Principles of SR Learning

This study found that teaching self-regulation skills in online learning environments could be as effective as teaching SR skills in traditional settings. Experimentation with the "community of survival" activity uncovered the following useful approaches for improving learning in an online context:

- SR is promotable.
- SR is social.
- SR should be customized.
- SR should be internalized.

This study revealed that SRL strategies could be promoted in an online learning setting by letting students share their own strategies and by having them model how they analyse tasks. It should be noted that not all students reported having learned from the strategies of others. For some students SR strategies are acquired more internally and need to be taught. Even students who had previously learned and applied strategies sometimes failed to continue using them either because they needed more time to make them their own or because the strategies no longer fit their learning styles. Sometimes the instructor is not aware that his or her description of an assignment is unclear to students. The fact that the instructor knows the materials well sometimes obscures the fact that the same materials are new and very unfamiliar to the students. These various missteps in the process of online learning emerged as sources of student anxiety, which in turn decreased students' sense of self-efficacy and limited their online learning success. Online instructors should conduct a preliminary task analysis for each assignment and provide a task analysis matrix that will help students understand the size and complexity of the assignment and the amount of time they will need to complete their work. Faculty modelling of task analysis strengthens the social support system for increasing self-regulation.

In addition, the self-regulation strategies shared by students also add to the social support system. We found that students acquired SR strategies by observing and reading about the performance of their more skilled peers. The strategies used by high-achieving students for online learning are particularly valuable as models for students who are newcomers in an unfamiliar learning environment. High-achieving students track themselves more efficiently and are able to make more fine-grained adaptations than can novices. The study also found that even experienced strategic online learners benefit from simply listening to the strategies of other students. Hearing strategies similar to theirs reminded them to religiously follow their own. The listening and sharing process reassured them about the effectiveness of their own strategies and reminded them to continue their use.

Time constraints and the organisational demands of online courses make it difficult to include formal training about online SR learning strategies as part of the curriculum of online classes. Therefore, modelling of task analysis and creating a forum to share SR strategies can compensate online learners for the lack of formal SR training.

There is no one-size-fits-all approach to learning or teaching SR strategies. Some online learners did have a common set of SR skills such as keeping organised calendars, using rubrics and so on, but different students used a variety of different strategies as well. Many students found the strategies used by others were not a good fit for their personality and learning preferences. Strategic students seemed to be more aware of their learning preferences and deficiencies in their study habits. Self-regulation derives from a gradual process in which a student's knowledge about "self-as-learner" becomes internalized through a combination of experiences involving both the instructor's teaching and modelling and the student's own use of internal speech to guide behaviour and provide self-feedback about his or her performance or practice (Meichenbaum, 1972. Students sometimes recognised that a strategy might be beneficial for them but were unable to adopt it because they lacked sufficient time to complete the necessary levels of skill acquisition: emulation, self-control and self-regulation (Meichenbaum, 1972, 1977).

Specific Strategies for SR Learning

Listed here are specific recommendations based on lessons learned from the "community of survival" activity and from student feedback on its benefits. These strategies will allow online instructors and instructional designers to bring a sharper focus to the promotion of self-regulatory skills in online environments.

- Use a discussion forum for SR strategies.
- Use student examples.
- Use clear rubrics.
- Provide a sample task analysis matrix.
- Have students create their task analysis matrix and share with peers.
- Organise the class calendar in a consistent way.
- Provide the self-check questions to monitor student progress.
- Encourage students with full-time jobs to share their time-saving strategies.
- Share the SR strategies used by former students.

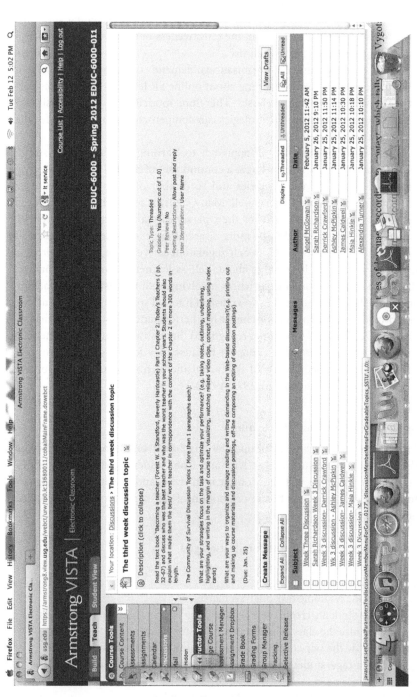

Figure 4.4 Screenshot of Community of Survival Discussion Board

- Encourage self-celebration of small accomplishments (Zimmerman and Martinez-Pons [1986] called it "self-consequences").

Conclusion

This study suggests that online instructors can promote SRL strategies in their online classroom and thereby mitigate the fact that students typically receive little advice on how to study for online classes or how to negotiate the particular demands of online learning. Collective discussions of SR strategies have the potential to help students gain new SR strategies as well as to reinforce strategies students may have previously developed but use only sporadically. There is every reason to believe that this model of SRL strategy promotion can be an important addition to any online course design. The proposed model, as exemplified by Figure 4.4, should be relatively easy to implement as it builds upon the collective discussion.

Clearly the SR forum is a valuable mechanism to encourage group cohesiveness and other social benefits of online discussions. Through the experience of sharing their SR strategies, students build a sense of belonging and feel linked to one another in a way not previously possible. Many theorists believe that group cohesion results from a deep sense of "we-ness," or belonging to a group as a whole. By recognizing the similarities that exist among group members, individuals tend to develop a closer connection with their peers (Bollen & Hoyle, 1990). Our students found similarities with their peers in terms of limited financial resources, a lack of time to study, demanding jobs and family issues. As students became more aware of similarities between members of their group, they began to see their classmates as companions who shared similar difficulties with online learning and could also share strategies for success. Eventually they felt, "I am not alone. We are in the same boat. We are doing this together." This kind of group cohesion increases students' motivation and self-efficacy, and these, in turn, are major attributes of higher self-regulation. Course designers might consider including in Web-based courses more tools and study aids that specifically focus on assisting and encouraging students to use SRL strategies. The current chapter provides online instructors with a set of practical, empirically based guidelines that emerged from this study and encourages online instructors to consider and address explicitly their students' needs for self-efficacy and self-regulation as they strive to provide engaging and effective instruction.

References

Azevedo, R., & Cromley, J. G. (2004). Does training on self-regulated learning facilitate students' learning with hypermedia? *Journal of Educational Psychology, 96*(3), 523–535.

Bandura, A. (1986). *Social foundations of thoughts and action: A social cognitive theory*. Englewood Cliffs, NJ: Prentice Hall.

Bandura, A. (1997). *Self-efficacy: The exercise of control*. New York: W. H. Freeman.

Bollen, K. A., & Hoyle, R. H. (1990). Perceived cohesion: a conceptual and empirical examination. *Social Forces, 69*(2), 479–504.

Kagitcibasi, C. (1994). A critical appraisal of individualism and collectivism: Toward a new formulation. In U. Kim, H. C. Triandis, C. Kagitcibasi, S. Choi, & G. Yoon (eds.), *Individualism and collectivism: theory, method, and applications* (52–65). Thousand Oaks, CA: Sage.

Meichenbaum, D. (1972). Cognitive modification of test-anxious college students. *Journal of Consulting and Clinical Psychology, 39*, 370–380.

Mills, J., & Clark, M. (1982). Exchange and communal relationships. In L. Wheeler (ed.), *Review of personality and social psychology: Vol. 3* (121–144). Beverly Hills, CA: Sage.

Onwuegbuzie, A.J., & Jiao, Q. G. (2000). I'll go to the library later: the relationship between academic procrastination and library anxiety. *College & Research Libraries, 61*(1), 45–54.

Paris, S. G., & Winograd, P. (2001). The role of self-regulated learning in contextual teaching: principles and practices for teacher preparation. Washington, DC: U.S. Department of Education. Retrieved from http://www.ciera.org/library/archive/2001-04/0104parwin.htm

Perels, F., Gurtler, T., & Schmitz, B. (2005). Training of self-regulatory and problem solving competence. *Learning and Instruction, 15*(2), 123–139.

Schunk, D. H., & Schwartz, C. W. (1993). Goals and progress feedback: effects on self-efficacy and writing achievement. *Contemporary Educational Psychology, 18*(3), 337–354.

Schunk, D. H., & Zimmerman, B. J. (1998). *Self-regulated learning: from teaching to self-reflective practice*. New York: Guilford Press.

Smith, G. G., Torres-Ayala, A. T., & Heindel, A. J. (2008). Disciplinary differences in e-learning instructional design. *Journal of Distance Education, 22*(3), 63–88.

Solomon, L. J., & Rothblum, E. D. (1994). Procrastination Assessment Scale-Students (PASS). In J. Fischer and K. Corcoran (eds.), *Measure for clinical practice: Vol. 2* (446–452). New York: Free Press.

Vygotsky, L. (1978). *Mind in society: the development of higher psychological processes*. Cambridge, MA: Harvard University Press.

Vygotsky, L. S. (1986). *Thought and language* (rev. ed.). Cambridge, MA: MIT Press.

Vygotsky, L. S. (1987). *Thinking and speech*. Ed. and trans. N. Minick. New York: Plenum. (Translation of Vygotsky, 1982).

Vygotsky, L. S. (1997). *Educational psychology*. Trans. R. Silverman. Boca Raton, FL: St. Lucie Press. (Orig. 1926).

Whipp, J. L., & Chiarelli, S. (2004). Self-regulation in a Web-based course: a case study. *Educational Technology Research and Development, 52*(4), 5–22.

Zimmerman, B. J. (1986). Becoming a self-regulated learner: what are the key subprocesses? *Contemporary Educational Psychology, 16*, 307–313.

Zimmerman, B. J. (1989). A social cognitive view of self-regulated academic learning. *Journal of Educational Psychology, 81*(3), 329–339. doi:10.1037//0022–0663.81.3.329

Zimmerman, B. J. (1998). Academic studying and the development of personal skill: a self-regulatory perspective. *Educational Psychologist, 33*, 73–86.

Zimmerman, B. J. (2000). Attaining self-regulation: a social cognitive perspective. In M. Boekaerts, P. R. Pintrich, & M. Zeidner (eds.), *Handbook of self-regulation* (13–39). San Diego, CA: Academic.

Zimmerman, B. J. (2002). Becoming a self-regulated learner: an overview. *Theory Into Practice, 41*(2), 64–70. doi:10.1207/s15430421tip4102_2

Zimmerman, B. J., & Bandura, A. (1994). Impact of self-regulatory influences on writing course attainment. *American Educational Research Journal, 31*, 845–862.

Zimmerman, B. J., Bonner, S., & Kovach, R. (2009). *Developing self-regulated learners*. Washington, DC: American Psychological Association.

Zimmerman, B. J., & Martinez-Pons, M. (1986). Development of a structured interview for assessing students' use of self-regulated learning strategies. *American Educational Research Journal, 23*, 614–628.

Part 3
Researchers

Not surprisingly, when dealing with anything that increasingly owes its existence to an electronic network of connectivity, online learning generates a great deal of innovation and research with regard to the technological aspects of the art but remarkably little research or evidence about how learners actually engage with the materials or the level of efficacy with regard to producing learning. Online learning is renowned for its ability to present a "shiny new penny" at regular intervals, and currently one wave of interest appears to be around the area of open educational resources (OERs). Two of the three chapters in part 3 deal specifically with this topic. Bacsich and Pepler report on an extensive pan-European initiative to draw together what is currently known about the use of OERs. They deal with questions such as why students look for OERs, how they find them, if they are the principle source of learning or a valuable supplement, and if the seekers are engaged in formal education or are free-range learners. Finally, they review the implications of the use of OERs for teachers and institutions. In the following chapter Reedy looks specifically at this last issue as he investigates how early career academics approach the selection, use and generation of OERs with regard to their teaching commitments. In the final chapter, Weyers appeals for a more learner-centric approach to our design efforts. He reviews the evolution of our thinking about the learning process and shows how learning design can be shaped to better map the complexity of the knowledge schemas learners mentally construct.

5
Learner Use of Online Content

PAUL BACSICH AND GILES PEPLER

Sero Consulting Ltd., UK

Editors' Introduction

The open educational resources movement is conventionally dated from the time in 2001 when the Massachusetts Institute of Technology (MIT) announced it would put its complete programme catalogue online – thus it has been underway for around 12 years. However, until recently the focus across the world has been on provision of resources: even in the last few years the only other focus was on provision-related issues such as quality, accreditation and usability. Apart from the major (but specific) studies of user needs and behaviour done by MIT and a few open universities there has until recently been little else that focused on issues of learners and how (and why) they use OER. This chapter aims to fill that gap. It is based largely on a survey of the OER literature, linked to a survey of the wider literature on online resources where one can draw conclusions relevant to OER.

Introduction

In early 2011 a team at Sero Consulting was contracted by the Higher Education Academy as part of the JISC/Higher Education Academy OER Programme (JISC, 2009b) to carry out a rapid study of learner use of online resources (including but not only OER) for learning. This project rapidly became known as LUOERL and has its own wiki where all results are stored (LUOERL, 2012).

JISC (2011) noted that the project was the following:

> a short literature review to provide a greater understanding of the ways in which learners, whether or not in formal education, use online resources to aid their learning experiences and the factors which influence the selection of resources. The resultant report provides a basis for additional work being commissioned by the [Higher Education] Academy and JISC to examine the potential contribution open educational resources can make to the student learning experience. It is hoped that collectively this

work will enable practitioners, policy makers and researchers to adopt more effective evidence-informed or research-informed approaches to their decision-making, research and practice on matters relating to the use of open-educational resources in learning and teaching.

Twelve areas of interest for the research were proposed by the Higher Education Academy: learners' rationale for searching for online resources; types of online resources being sought; complexity/granularity of resources being sought; how resources found are used; whether learners in some subject areas appear to conduct more searches for online resources than others; educational level of resources being sought; location of resources; extent to which resources are the principal or a supplementary source of learning materials; whether or not learners are in formal education; enablers and barriers to use of online resources; how learners retain access to the resources; and provenance information and copyright status of resources being used.

During the course of the study a small number of additional topics forced themselves to the researchers' attention, and these have been added to the following analysis.

The topic of learner use was picked up again when the POERUP project, part financed by the Lifelong Learning Programme of the European Commission, started in November 2011. POERUP, Policies for OER Uptake (POERUP, 2013), is a collaborative project stretching until spring 2014 that is carrying out a survey of countries' approaches to OER, creating a global database of OER initiatives and piloting a range of ideas on institutional and national policies which would tend to foster the uptake of OER. POERUP partners include Sero (who leads the project), the University of Leicester, Dutch Open University and Athabasca University (Canada), along with other partners in France, Italy and Hungary. Involvement in POERUP led to a process of reflection on the earlier LUOERL report, in the much more international context of POERUP. The POERUP wiki contains specially written reports on OER in UK, Canada, Mexico, Argentina, Thailand, France, Belgium, Spain and around 10 other countries.

Our conclusions from our studies on learner use of OER (and online resources more generally) can be summarised as follows.

There is clear evidence to confirm the gut feeling of many academics (especially those engaged in distance teaching) that students' rationales for searching are dominated by assessment requirements, explicit or implicit. When they come to select relevant resources, students lack understanding of provenance and quality aspects of resources.

Students tend to prefer audio to video (confirming what many devotees of podcasting and critics of video have been saying for years). Despite the need to be competitive and private when it comes to assessment (as traditionally constructed), students demonstrated positive attitudes to sharing.

There are lessons also for how academics should organise material. The studies demonstrated learner need for structure in or above the resources and thus the importance of a task-based pedagogy to guide learner use. Students use multiple methods for discovery (browsing, search engines, tutor and peer guidance), but their particular approach is more shaped by pedagogical task context than by subject area differences or other contextual variables.

The research literature gives no answer or only weakly evidenced answers to a number of perennial questions:

- Is there any link between OER and student attainment? Only one key study could be found to demonstrate that.
- Is there any information on how students store and "curate" (not a word they would use) resources they have found? Only one key study addressed how learners retain access to resources.

It was rather clearer that a more nuanced approach to digital literacy than the "digital natives/digital immigrants" discourse was now gaining traction in the literature.

There is a little bit of evidence, confirming the beliefs of many academics involved in resource-based learning, that there is a substantial challenge in designing resources for users with unknown characteristics – it is much easier to do this when characteristics are known.

The Major Theoretical Insights That Guide and Have Arisen From the Research

These headings have been taken from a 12-item classification first proposed by the Higher Education Academy and extended for this chapter as new research came into play.

Learners' Rationale for Searching for Online Resources

There seem to be no "meta studies" of students' motivation for searching specifically for OER resources. However, there are a number of surveys of individual OER projects – some of which (such as Carson's MIT surveys) are of sufficient scale to be usable. Carson (2009) observes that the following:

- Of students using OER, 44% said it was to enhance personal knowledge, 39% said it was to complement a course and 12% said it was to plan a course of study.
- Of self-learners using OER, 41% said it was to explore interests outside of the professional field, 20% said it was to plan future study, 17% said it was to review basic concepts in their field and 11% said it was to remain current in their field.

The Open Universiteit Nederland (OUNL) OpenER project was aimed specifically at those who had not "successfully attended higher education" (Schuwer et al., 2007). Reasons given for visiting the site are as shown in Figure 5.1 (respondents were allowed more than one choice):

Slightly less identifiable as the "rationale" for visiting but still of interest is the student ranking of the Open University's OpenLearn (Godwin and McAndrew, 2008) features. The authors' findings suggest that while some learners seek stronger communication tools, there is a need to refrain from promoting social networking as desirable to all learners. Perhaps key among their conclusions is that consideration should always be given to providing links to assessment and accreditation. Responses in order of importance to students range from "a large choice of content" (1st in importance) down to "to be able to interact with other learners" (10th).

In the wider context the literature surveyed typically addresses the search for online resources in relation to isolated research tasks performed within a traditional course context (e.g., to complete one's homework or perform an isolated in-class task), and thus motivators are considered in this light. This is consistent with the general belief among experts that student learning is substantially driven by assessment, perhaps increasingly so with full-time students at campus universities (it has been true for part-time students at open universities for many years).

"Research content" is moreover typically seen as a source for assignments, with students' perception of research very much led by the context of their assignments (Hampton-Reeves et al., 2009). Some authors suggest that, in light of this, research assignments should include details about expectations for conducting quality research (Head, 2007).

More generally, students' rationale for seeking online resources over other options boils down to ease of use/access (i.e., anytime, anywhere); efficiency; and streamlined searchability (i.e., ability to search thousands or even millions

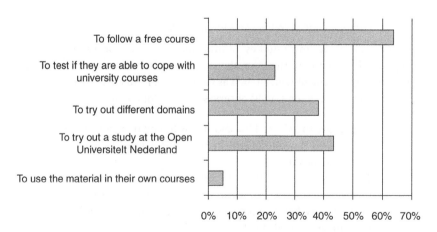

Figure 5.1 Reasons for accessing OER's

of resources at once). It is generally taken for granted that the contemporary student's research projects will begin with a simple Google-type search for online resources (see chapter 6).

Types of Online Resources Being Sought

It appears that the desire to provide OER has initially been driven by the supply side and rarely, yet, in response to learner preferences. However, this should not undermine the value of student surveys – in fact, considering the dearth of research, such studies possibly assume greater importance.

The University of Oxford Listening for Impact research (a JISC-funded study) into podcasting (Geng, Marshall, and Wilson, 2011) found that the resources produced were popular among students and external users (learners and teachers) alike. This popularity was growing considerably (from 7% who had listened to podcasts from the Oxford portal in November 2010 to 33% in February 2011) and is expected to continue on an upward trend. Students reported they particularly valued the podcasts because the lectures were "related" to their own course or subject, they had supporting resources linked and they could be played in-line (i.e., in the location where they had been accessed/discovered).

The podcasts were made available via iTunes, and the authors noted the significant external influence exerted by Apple – e.g., the boost when iTunes entered new educational markets such as China.

In the US, OER videos from the Kahn Academy were used to explain to students the sub-prime lending crisis, and the collected student responses demonstrated very high levels of satisfaction with the assignment. It should be noted that the videos that comprise the Kahn collection are relatively short (10–20 minutes) and are designed to be appropriate for students to view on a computer (McDowell, 2010).

In the wider context, findings suggest that today's learners utilise numerous types of OER and non-OER media including not only the obvious ones (e-books, Web sites, images) but also the following:

- Wikipedia articles (Field, 2006; Lim, 2009; Chandler & Gregory, 2010; Menchen-Trevino & Hargittai, 2011; Clark, Haygood, & Levine, 2011).
- Videos, e.g., Khan Academy/YouTube (Johnson, Levine, Smith, & Stone, 2010; Wong et al., 2010; Winn, 2010; Brownell, 2011).

Complexity/Granularity of Resources Being Sought

There seem to be apparent tensions and contradictions in relation to the granularity that may be sought by students, and the need for contextualising and the "pedagogic wrapper," reflected throughout the wider research. Lane's (2007,

p. 5) studies of OpenLearn led him to conclude the following: "The effectiveness of open educational material is usually improved where there is a clear sense making structure."

This is supported by the findings of the University of Nottingham team, which looked at reusable learning objects for health studies. While they acknowledged that increasing the "specificity" of the objects can significantly reduce the potential for reuse, they found that this was a necessary trade-off.

At the OUNL it was found that the OpenER courses were considered of much greater appeal if they contained not simply content but also "learning guidance and exercises" and if they could be completed with a test or exam (Mulder, 2007).

How Resources Found Are Used

Lane, McAndrew, and Santos (2009, p. 5) found similar evidence that users appreciated "the chance to dip in and take bits out of courses without having to worry about doing the whole thing."

They also found that these users, and indeed others who were already United Kingdom Open University (UKOU) students, also valued the opportunity to make contact with peers. Notwithstanding these caveats with regard to "social networking" (Godwin & McAndrew, 2008) it appears that some students use OpenLearn as an additional communication tool. The resources may initially draw them in, but they then have access to a new group of peers (Lane et al., 2009).

Wilson surveyed students prior to OpenLearn starting with responses revealing a hunger for assessment (90%), qualifications (89%) and tutorials (64%) (Wilson, 2008).

The Open Nottingham Project surveyed undergraduates about how they had used the repurposed geographical data handouts – with 67% saying to better help them understand the topic, 56% as a revision resource and 44% reporting they had "cited them in an assignment" (Stapleton, Horton, & Beggan, 2011). With specific regard to podcasts, the Listening for Impact survey found that the resources were considered of most use to catch up when a lecture had been missed, to stimulate interest in that subject, and/or as an aid to revision (Geng et al., 2011).

This topic is well worth revisiting in the future, as OER begins to blend with the world of MOOCs. A massive open online course is a type of online course aimed at large-scale participation and open access via the Web (Wikipedia, 2013). Many researchers believe that MOOCs are a fundamentally new paradigm. In contrast, many distance learning theorists do not believe that MOOCs are new, or better. One of the most senior such theorists is Sir John Daniel: his paper (Daniel, 2012) is required reading and has an extensive bibliography. A useful review and contextualisation of this paper can be found in McAndrew and Jones (2012), which adds a perspective from the Open University. Bacsich (2012a) provides a brief introduction to the strategic aspects of MOOCs in a wider perspective of "archetypal" models of online education.

Whether Learners in Some Subject Areas Appear to Conduct More Searches for Online Resources Than Others

There seem to be no substantial studies of disciplinary difference with regard specifically to OERs. However, the findings from the wider context may well have considerable read-across. Prefacing their report of Caledonian University students, Margaryan, Littlejohn, and Vojt (2011) note that previous studies into technology use by students have shown considerable variations: with higher usage among technology and business studies students and lower among the arts, languages, social and health care. However, they counsel caution in analysing such data since the previous studies were concerned with what are now increasingly redundant technologies such as CD-ROMs. Their study supports the view that the "digital natives and digital immigrants" thesis may distort perceptions of students and that a much more nuanced discussion is now required. It would appear from the study that there may still be some distinctions between younger and older students but that these must be seen in much wider contexts.

Surveys of student search behaviour are examined elsewhere within single subjects (e.g., physics, nursing and English composition), but not in a comparative – or quantitative – context (Dee & Stanley, 2005; Jamali & Nicholas, 2008; McClure & Clink, 2008).

Educational Level of Resources Being Sought

Most of the more substantial studies have concentrated on undergraduates, or the use of undergraduate-level materials to engage nontraditional students.

There is evidence that users at all academic levels are (on a basic search level) engaged in nearly identical search methods despite their differing requirements as learners – that is, commencing with a simple Google search. Studies trace the search patterns of students as young as primary school age, as well as those of PhD students, and all levels of resource are pursued along the way. As undergraduate students are the subject of most studies located, though, in this case the majority of resources being sought are indeed at the undergraduate level.

There are also many studies asserting that high-level postsecondary students do spend a good deal of time in search of journal articles (Nicholas et al., 2006, 2009, and 2011).

Location of Resources Most Likely to Be Used

This chapter has focused largely on English-language papers and thus mostly deals with education in the English-speaking world (and largely on higher education). This will clearly have an influence on where the resources are used. The vast majority of resources reviewed (via the papers on them) have been hosted in the US and the UK.

McAndrew and colleagues (2008) reported that access to OpenLearn had been "truly global" with access from 225 "domains" (countries/territories). UK access over the duration of the two-year period was approximately 30%. The 2009 annual MIT survey (Carson, 2009) illustrated a similarly international perspective with 54% of the traffic coming from outside the US including 11% from Western Europe.

Podcasts created and released for the Listening for Impact project at the University of Oxford were accessed, and in some cases reused, by listeners from around the globe. Feedback received indicates these listeners came from a broad spectrum of backgrounds from the professions (education, law, medicine) to current students as well as the retired (Geng et al., 2011). The project was seen as particularly successful in attracting students "new to Oxford."

Given the population and number of universities in the US – and the breadth of the OER activities now underway in that country across the educational and public sectors – it seems likely that most resources are hosted in the US.

On the other hand, in relation to general penetration of OERs in an organised effort across the entire higher education sector, the UK would be in the lead.

However, since many students seem now to use Wikipedia articles in their studies (not to mention YouTube, etc.), the concept of "which country" an item is hosted in is rather elusive, an interesting twist on the "globalisation" of learning.

Many postsecondary students use (via automatic authentication) full-text journal articles from a wide variety of publishers and repositories; the issue of the host country for such material is not clear, nor – we suspect – of great interest to students.

Extent to Which Resources Are the Principal or a Supplementary Source of Learning Materials

From the existing research this question remains impossible to answer with any certainty or clarity. OERs range from the smallest level of granularity to entire course modules or courses. These may be used in a variety of ways depending on the context of the learner. In the majority of studies, OERs have apparently been designed as supplementary materials – which may not be the same as how they have been used.

For an investigation of OER as the principal source of learning materials see the Carnegie Mellon Open Learning Initiative (Lovett, Meyer, & Thille, 2008).

Recent developments such as the OER University (WikiEducator, 2012a) and the first of the accredited courses launched from this by the University of Southern Queensland (WikiEducator, 2012b) imply that OER as the principal source of learning materials will be an increasingly important issue for at least some universities. Of course this puts much more pressure on the usability and quality of the OER. Such aspects of OER can be benchmarked in the same way as other aspects of online learning (Pick&Mix, 2011).

Whether or Not Learners Are in Formal Education

It is difficult to make an accurate assessment since one of the driving forces for those involved in OER creation and release is to broaden participation – particularly among nontraditional learners.

The OpenER at OUNL was one such project, but it is still noteworthy that 43% had not participated in higher education before; 75% of the survey respondents were at the time "not involved in any formal learning trajectory" (Schuwer et al., 2007, p. 101); and – exploring a separate issue – "60% were female" (Schuwer et al., 2007, p. 100). At MIT 43% of visitors describe themselves as "self-learners" (as opposed to students or educators) (Carson, 2009).

In the earlier period at OpenLearn the dominant age group was 35- to 54-year-olds. Unlike the other studies, other characteristics of the visitors included "well-educated" and "confident," and many already had an "existing connection" with the UKOU (Godwin, 2008).

Of course it often seems to be the case that learners may be in formal education "somewhere" but not necessarily at the institution providing the resources. In some countries with well-developed credit transfer systems (US and Sweden in particular) students may be taking courses from several institutions simultaneously.

Enablers and Barriers to Use of Online Resources

Most relevant OER research seems to be on barriers rather than enablers. (This is more extensively explored in chapter 6). The wider research implies that most of the barriers to the use of OER are either the same as or consequences of more generic barriers to accessing and using technologies for learning. However, the issues of designing learning for the "unknown user" and the tensions between granularity and the need for scaffolding permeate much of the research – even if they do not achieve the profile we may have imagined.

> In its (OER) current level of deployment, however, does it necessarily support "meaningful learning"? (Esslemont, 2007, p. 44)

In the wider context, the literature review identifies numerous enablers and barriers to use of online resources. An obvious enabler is access to simple search engines like Google, directing users to simply displayed results. This accommodates what is seen as a contemporary learner preference for quick fact extraction and brief viewing, as opposed to continuous reading, as noted by the e-Books Observatory (JISC, 2009a). Today's students favour brevity, consensus and currency in the information sources they seek (Head & Eisenberg, 2009); resources easily accessed, interacted with and departed from make all the difference. Today's young learners have often expressed a desire that digital libraries should, generally speaking, be "more like Google" (Bell, 2004).

Researchers warn that young people are seen to rely overly heavily on search engines, to "view rather than read," and to be lacking the critical and analytical skills to assess the information they find on the Web. In this sense they are not truly "web literate" (Nicholas et al., 2008). Many students use Google but are bewildered by the number of responses it generates and will rarely look beyond the first few pages of search results (Hampton-Reeves et al., 2009); hence any Web site that asks them to engage deeply feels disruptive to their learning (Nicholas et al., 2006). Connaway and colleagues (2008) find that in some situations, information seekers will "readily sacrifice content for convenience"; issues of time and levels of difficulty in obtaining information are usually of more concern to students than issues of accuracy (Weiler, 2005).

A surprising number of authors point out that today's student is more amenable to "the human touch" than is typically presumed (Connaway et al., 2008; Hampton-Reeves et al., 2009). Guidance in search methodology, personalised training sessions and uses for "human resources" (i.e., mentors, tutors, even parents) as key enablers are recommended by numerous authors – though several note an intriguing reluctance by students to work with librarians (Head & Eisenberg, 2009).

On the other hand, an oft-identified barrier is publishers' embargoes on various materials; students are frustrated when a promised resource is suddenly unavailable and lose trust in the resources they are using (Wong et al., 2010). There is also evidence that a single bad experience – e.g., "no results found" – with a resource can put a user off it permanently (Matusiak, 2006).

How Learners Retain Access to the Resources

The only systematic study of how learners retained access to the resources appears to be Lim's (2009) study of Wikipedia. Wikipedia was used more frequently (for accessing resources) than library databases – which comprised the smallest frequent user group. However, slightly more than half of the respondents accessed Wikipedia through a search engine, while nearly half accessed it via their own bookmarks.

It is tempting to move on from this research to a wider discussion of the validity of Wikipedia. However, I see this as just one example of the wider problem of ensuring that students make value judgements on the quality and reliability of all sources of information. It is quite reasonable for students – and researchers – to use heuristics to make these value judgements, but not ones as crude as "Britannica good, Wikipedia bad." There is a particular onus on academics: it is just not good enough to "ban" Wikipedia or to say that one never uses it so one cannot make judgements. In reality, many researchers use Wikipedia. External examiners (in countries like the UK which have them) should be a key influence, especially when it comes to final year and master's dissertations.

One should not conflate Wikipedia with wikis in general. Wikipedia is a wiki, but there are many other wikis with relevant information, and most of them are managed in very different ways from Wikipedia. The examples I am familiar with might be called "professional wikis" – these are wikis, such as VISCED, where only professionals in the subject are allowed to edit (Re.ViCa, 2013). Perhaps not surprisingly, this is conducive to higher quality, but no guarantee of it.

Returning to the safer ground of the topic of this subsection, students have various approaches to the issue of retaining access. Some still like paper: several contemporary surveys show that, if given the option, students will opt to print out longer texts (Sweat-Guy, Elobaid, & Buzzetto-More, 2007). Other students like to use a Web browser's tabs as an organisational tool. They may then bookmark their findings or copy and paste them as notes into a Word document, e-mail items to themselves and so forth. Some use more sophisticated features such as RefWorks, EndNote and so on (Wong et al., 2010).

Provenance Information and Copyright Status of Resources Being Used and Learners' Awareness of This

Much of the wider research backs up a finding of students' inconsistent attitudes to provenance. The experience of the OUNL OpenER project is overwhelmingly that students expect the courses to be of a suitable academic level and that the university is the guarantor of quality. Elsewhere, many students seem content to trust the validity of resources found on the Web. Lim's study of students' use of Wikipedia suggested that students tend to use it for rapid fact checking and background information and that they had generally had good experiences of it as a resource. However, their perceptions of its "information quality" did not reflect this (see the prior subsection).

In the wider context, Menchen-Trevino and Hargittai (2011), Hampton-Reeves and colleagues (2009) and others examine this issue, finding that students are not generally sophisticated in their understanding of things like peer review or currency: "There is a common view that if something is published it must be reliable" (Hampton-Reeves et al., 2009). Lorenzen (2001) finds that students are weak at determining the quality of the information they found on a Web site and may in fact judge the validity of a Web site based on "how elaborate it looks."

How Do Learners Search for/Discover Online Resources?

As with much of the thematic analysis of OER, the literature here militates against comparative study. The key variables concern whether the users of OER

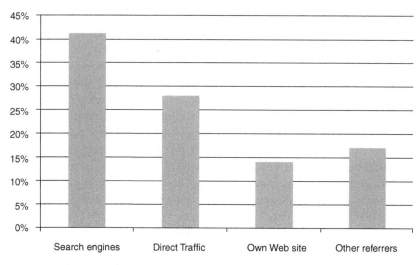

Figure 5.2 Common ways of finding OER's (MIT study)

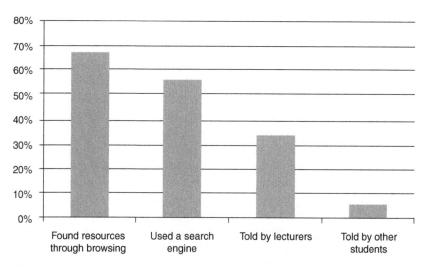

Figure 5.3 Common ways of finding OER's (Open Nottingham study)

are already informal learners, are enrolled students and/or whether they have been directed to resources by lecturers.

The 2009 Carson MIT survey reports the statistics in Figure 5.2 for how the visitors arrived (Carson, 2009).

In the Open Nottingham project survey, 35% of respondents said they had previously used OER (Stapleton et al., 2011). Of these, they found the resources in various ways as follows in Figure 5.3.

Does OER Influence Selection of Courses or Institutions?

There was evidence from some JISC/HEA OER projects that availability of OER content was having a positive influence on students' choice of course – in cases such as the University of Westminster MSc in multimedia this was seen "strong" and, if integrated into the institutional marketing strategy, has the potential to yield immediate returns (Stannard, 2010).

Elsewhere, evidence on a more significant scale is presented by the Massachusetts Institute of Technology Open CourseWare (OCW) initiative where 35% of freshmen said they were aware of OCW before making the decision to attend MIT and had been influenced by its availability (Carson, 2006, 2009).

Does OER Have an Impact on Students' Attainment?

This is a very hard question, and the "no significant difference" debates are as intense as those over the "digital natives" issue.

The Open Learning Initiative at Carnegie Mellon began in 2002 and, as such, is one of the few OER programmes of sufficient maturity and stability to test the impact on student learning. OLI undertook three studies of the statistics course with the aims of (a) investigating whether students could learn as much from stand-alone OER course as a "traditional" instructor-led course and (b) investigating the potential for accelerated learning using the OER course in "hybrid" mode. The studies involved "class size" groups measured against peer control groups over a single-semester statistics course.

The results demonstrated that the students working on the stand-alone OER course achieved almost identical scores to those on the traditional instructor-led course and outperformed the national average – thus meeting the "no harm done" test. The accelerated learning study revealed that the students using the hybrid model learnt 15 weeks' worth of material "as well or better" than the traditional learners in just 8 weeks. Both groups of students were shown to have spent the same amount of time actually studying, and retention of knowledge was roughly equal – with perhaps a slight edge to the hybrid learners group. On all other measures the hybrid group was at least the equal of the traditional learners.

The researchers suggest that the reason for this accelerated learning is that (due in no small part to the OER course design) the OER learners engaged more meaningfully with the materials, used their time more effectively and were better prepared for the classes (Lovett et al., 2008).

Role of University Libraries

Libraries are a critical conduit to digital resources, just as they were for print resources. A number of stereotypes of student use (non-use) of libraries are not borne out by the research.

Interestingly, undergraduates and postgraduates are the largest group of users of university library links to access scholarly databases, suggesting an important "hot link" role for libraries (Nicholas et al., 2009) for them and not only for researchers. Students use libraries often and consider both reference librarians and library databases extremely helpful (Head, 2007). Students are (still) very reliant on library catalogues (Hampton-Reeves et al., 2009).

In one study, 9 out of 10 students turned to libraries to conduct course-related research via online scholarly research databases (Head & Eisenberg, 2009).

In terms of more modern approaches libraries tend to guide e-book selection and retrieval (JISC, 2009a).

Learners' Choice of Digital Resources and Choice of Tools

Insights into the learners' choice of digital resources and choice of tools were surprising and noteworthy.

Knowledge that a system is free and has worthwhile contents apparently makes a substantial contribution to reducing abandoned-access attempts (Peterson Bishop, 1998).

Resource selection is based on prior knowledge and experience – for example, a belief (whether or not true) that resources provided by Google and Google Scholar are reliable and relevant (Wong et al., 2010).

Respondents employ a consistent and predictable research strategy for finding information, whether they are conducting course-related or everyday-life research (Head & Eisenberg, 2009). Too much so – sadly, students repeatedly select the method that initially provided them with successful results and almost never try to explore other options (Matusiak, 2006). In fact, preference for digital tool types is predictable by gender/age (JISC, 2009a), but there is a correlation to subject matter (Pan et al., 2006).

Role of Google

Almost all users start with Google, and want their digital library to be more like it, rather than to have less familiar search tools. Google (and a few similar commercial Internet search engines) dominate students' information-seeking strategy: 45% of students use Google when first locating information, with the university library catalogue used by 10% (Griffiths & Brophy, 2005). Almost all students use course readings and Google first for course-related research (Head & Eisenberg, 2009).

More experienced researchers link to publication gateways via Google/Google Scholar, then stay on a journal site only long enough to collect the article (Nicholas et al., 2011).

All end users (students and researchers) want the following: direct links to online content; text and media formats; evaluative content, such as summaries/

abstracts, tables of contents and excerpts; relevant search results; item availability information; and simple keyword search with an advanced, guided search option. Thus libraries need to offer "Google-like" functionality and availability (i.e., be open 24 hours a day) and familiar search modes to meet user expectations (Connaway et al., 2011).

Use of library-supplied databases may in fact be increasing due to the ubiquity of full-text and the ease with which it can be associated with online indexes (Medeiros, 2009) – in other words, the library is becoming more like Google. The evolution of the library is explored in the literature on Library 2.0, which is understood as the following:

> A loosely defined model for a modernized form of library service that reflects a transition within the library world in the way that services are delivered to users. The focus is on user-centred change and participation in the creation of content and community. The concept of Library 2.0 borrows from that of Business 2.0 and Web 2.0 and follows some of the same underlying philosophies. This includes online services like the use of OPAC systems and an increased flow of information from the user back to the library. (Wikipedia, 2012)

For those who are concerned about citing Wikipedia, see Chad and Miller (2005), which covers similar ground, and if that seems too commercial there is a recent research study for JISC (Adamson, Bacsich, Chad, Kay, & Plenderleith, 2008) – one of

> several studies [that] have been done to put flesh on the bones of the Library 2.0 concept. Furthermore, many librarians are experimenting with blogs, wikis and other web 2.0 systems including social networking, to better track and gain feedback from their users. There are even a few innovative Library 2.0 systems in operation. (Bacsich, 2012b, p. 183)

Implications for Teachers and Institutions

We make the following recommendations, phrased primarily in terms of staff engaged in the teaching process, but also as follows:

- Staff should pay more attention to student views and experience of OER and online resources. Quality and benchmarking schemes and associated survey instruments can easily be updated to accommodate a greater focus on content. In addition to EU work especially from OPAL (2011), the benchmarking e-learning scheme Pick&Mix has an OER mode (Pick&Mix, 2011).
- Institutions with their academic staff should consider how best to foster judicious use of resources (including OER) by students, especially

in their project and dissertation work. Ideally a guide to good practice is required. This would be particularly fruitful to foster in the UK context because of the External Examiner system and the roles of the Quality Assurance Agency and Higher Education Academy. The structure for this guide could draw on a number of sources including the Pick&Mix (2011) version mentioned earlier.
- In course redesign, staff should aim to make more use of OER and externally provided free-of-charge, non-open resources in future programmes.
- Staff should ensure when providing public information about their courses that descriptions of "study time" and "contact hours" for courses do not get trapped into a classroom-based narrative that does not provide a realistic description of the learner experience in relation to OER and online systems. This is becoming particularly relevant as the recommendations in the Higher Education White Paper for England titled *Students at the Heart of the System* (Department of Business Innovation and Skills, 2011) come to pass. This is a particular issue in some European countries where the current regime at ministry level is suggesting a "back to tradition" approach towards learning and teaching.

Open Questions and Directions for Future Research and Implications for OER Practice

Overview

In a nutshell, there is still a great deal to be researched about learner views and use of OER and online resources generally. The literature on learner use of online educational resources is very immature. There are significant gaps in the literature: there are almost no meso-level studies, no international comparisons and very little on learners other than university undergraduates. It would be very useful to see if the findings were similar for postgraduates and for corporate staff undergoing professional development. The overwhelming majority of published studies do not generalise beyond their particular contexts of study, and there is no consistent research approach.

Despite the large amount of activity in the UK on the creation of OER, there is still a large gap on learner experience work related to OER, especially in relation to larger-scale studies. There is a significant research opportunity.

Suggested Research Work

Learner Use Projects

There is still a widespread lack of learner-focused evaluation projects in specific techno-pedagogic areas, such as student use of Wikipedia (including search and quality judgement) and student study-time issues for students accessing OER and online resources. (Time is a vastly under-researched topic, of course.)

There is a clear need to have more research on student experience of formal learning using OER at campus-based universities.

Extending the Language Coverage

It would be prudent for appropriate researchers to check the own-language literature on learner use from the Netherlands and Sweden, even though the number of hits is not likely to be large. There appears to be a more substantial literature in Spanish and to a lesser extent in French.

There is across the European Union a surprising disconnect between the OER community and the "elite" of e-learning research (perceived or self-styled) – judged in relation to such metrics in the UK as the Research Excellence Framework, EU Framework Programme and Lifelong Learning Programme grant holders, grant holders and committee members of the UK Economic and Social Research Council Technology Enhanced Learning research programme, Association for Learning Technology Research Committee, e-learning journal editors and so forth. There is the exception of the UK Open University in particular and some key individuals there and at a few other locations. It may possibly be an artefact of our perspective on these countries, but this seems a little less the case in the Netherlands and Canada.

In an ideal world, in order to establish the area of OER as a research activity worthy of the attention of the best scholars in e-learning, a comprehensive open, editable and re-purposable bibliography of papers and other literature on OER should be generated – an open educational bibliography. This needs an international consortium. Some European developments like POERUP, the EU project on Policies for OER Uptake, touch on this, but international and in particular transatlantic collaboration is needed.

Acknowledgements

This work was initially supported by the UK Higher Education Academy (HEA), who funded the initial literature search project LUOERL, and more recently by the European Commission's Lifelong Learning Programme, who part funded its revising and updating under the project POERUP. We are grateful to other Sero colleagues and consultants for their assistance in this work.

References

Adamson, V., Bacsich, P., Chad, K., Kay, D., & Plenderleith, J. (2008). *JISC & SCONUL Library Management Systems Study: an evaluation and horizon scan of the current library management systems and related systems landscape for UK higher education by Sero Consulting Ltd.* Retrieved from http://www.jisc.ac.uk/media/documents/programmes/resourcediscovery/lmsstudy.pdf

Bacsich, P. (2012a). *Alternative models of education delivery. Policy brief.* UNESCO Institute for Information Technologies in Education. Retrieved from http://iite.unesco.org/pics/publications/en/files/3214709.pdf

Bacsich, P. (2012b). Impact of e-learning in the 21st century university. In T. Kerry (ed), *International perspectives on higher education: challenging values and practice*. New York: Continuum Books.
Bell, S. J. (2004). The infodiet: how libraries can offer an appetizing alternative to Google. *Chronicle of Higher Education, 24*. Retrieved from http://chronicle.com/article/The-Infodiet-How-Libraries/4458
Brownell, G. (2009, October 28). iPod University. *Newsweek (Atlantic Edition)*, 29–30. Retrieved from http://www.newsweek.com/2009/10/28/ipod-university.html
Carson, S. (2006). *MIT OpenCourseWare 2005 program evaluation findings report*. Cambridge, MA: MIT. Retrieved from http://ocw.mit.edu/ans7870/global/05_Prog_Eval_Report_Final.pdf
Chad, K., & Miller, P. (2005). *Do libraries matter? The rise of Library 2.0*. Retrieved from http://www.talis.com/applications/downloads/white_papers/DoLibrariesMatter.pdf
——— (2009). *MIT OpenCourseWare 2009 program evaluation findings summary*. Cambridge, MA: MIT. Retrieved from http://ocw.mit.edu/ans7870/global/09_Eval_Summary.pdf
Chandler, C. J., & Gregory, A. S. (2010). Sleeping with the enemy: Wikipedia in the college classroom. *History Teacher, 43*(2), 247–257.
Clark, N., Haygood, D., & Levine, K. (2011). Trust me! Wikipedia's credibility among college students. *International Journal of Instructional Media, 38*(1), 27–36.
Connaway, L. S., Radford, M. L., Dickey, T. J., De Angelis Williams, J., Confer, P. (2008). Sense-making and synchronicity: information-seeking and communication behaviors of millennials and baby boomers. *Libri, 58*(2), 123–135. Retrieved from http://www.oclc.org/research/publications/library/2008/connaway-libri.pdf
Daniel, J. (2012). Making sense of MOOCs: musings in a maze of myth, paradox and possibility. *Journal of Interactive Media in Education (JIME) 2012*. Retrieved from http://www-jime.open.ac.uk/jime/article/view/2012-18
Dee, C., & Stanley, E. E. (2005). Information-seeking behavior of nursing students and clinical nurses: implications for health sciences librarians. *Journal of the Medical Library Association, 93*(2), 213–222. Retrieved from http://www.ncbi.nlm.nih.gov/pmc/articles/PMC1082938/
Department of Business Innovation and Skills (2011). *Students at the heart of the system. White paper*. BIS. Retrieved from https://www.gov.uk/government/uploads/system/uploads/attachment_data/file/31384/11-944-higher-education-students-at-heart-of-system.pdf
Esslemont, C. (2007). "Bridging the abyss": open content to meaningful learning. In P. McAndrew & J. Watts (eds.), *Proceedings of OpenLearn* (44–46). Retrieved from http://kn.open.ac.uk/public/getfile.cfm?documentfileid = 12174
Field, K. A. (2006). Why engineering students love Wikipedia. *Design News, 61*(7), 11. Retrieved from http://www.designnews.com/article/1033-Why_Engineering_StudentsLove_Wikipedia.php
Geng, F., Marshall, C., & Wilson, R. (2011). *Listening for Impact: final report*. Oxford: JISC. Retrieved from http://www.jisc.ac.uk/media/documents/programmes/digitisation/listeningforimpactfinalreport.pdf
Godwin, S. (2008). *OpenLearn questionnaire report part A1-1*. Open University. Retrieved from http://kn.open.ac.uk/public/document.cfm?docid = 10857
Godwin, S., & McAndrew, P. (2008). *Exploring user types and what users seek in an open content based educational resource*. ED-MEDIA 2008 World Conference on Educational Multimedia, Hypermedia and Telecommunications. Vienna, Austria: Open University. Retrieved from http://oro.open.ac.uk/27399/1/godwin-mcandrew-edmedia2008.pdf
Griffiths, J. R., & Brophy, P. (2005). Student searching behavior and the Web: use of academic resources and Google survey of existing search engine use research. *Library Trends, 53*(4), 539–554. Retrieved from http://academic.research.microsoft.com/Publication/6952998/student-searching-behavior-and-the-web-use-of-academic-resources-and-google
Hampton-Reeves, S., Mashiter, C., Westaway, J., Lumsden, P., Day, H., Hewertson, H., Hart, A. (2009). *Students' use of research content in teaching and learning*. JISC. Retrieved from http://www.jisc.ac.uk/media/documents/aboutus/workinggroups/studentsuseresearchcontent.pdf
Head, A. J. (2007). Beyond Google: how do students conduct academic research? *First Monday, 12*(8). Retrieved from http://firstmonday.org/htbin/cgiwrap/bin/ojs/index.php/fm/article/view/1998/1873
Head, A. J., & Eisenberg, M. B. (2009). *How college students seek information in the digital age. Project Information Literacy progress report*. Retrieved from http://projectinfolit.org/pdfs/PIL_Fall2009_Year1Report_12_2009.pdf

Jamali, H. R., & Nicholas, D. (2008). Information-seeking behaviour of physicists and astronomers. *Aslib Proceedings, 60*(5), 444–462. Retrieved from http://eprints.rclis.org/handle/10760/13096

JISC (2009a). *JISC national e-books observatory project*. Retrieved from http://www.jiscebooksproject.org/

JISC (2009b). *Start-up meeting: OER programme*. Retrieved from http://www.jisc.ac.uk/whatwedo/programmes/elearning/oer/startupmeeting090609.aspx

JISC (2011). *Learner Voice literature review*. Retrieved from http://www.jisc.ac.uk/whatwedo/programmes/elearning/oer2/LearnerVoice.aspx

Johnson, L., Levine, A., Smith, R., & Stone, S. (2010). *The 2010 horizon report*. Austin, TX: New Media Consortium. Retrieved from http://www.nmc.org/pdf/2010-Horizon-Report.pdf

Lane, A. (2007). *Open content: when is it effective educationally?* Open Education 2007: Localizing and Learning. Logan, UT: Utah State University. Retrieved from http://oro.open.ac.uk/17830/

Lane, A., McAndrew, P., & Santos, A. (2009). *The networking effects of OER*. 23rd ICDE World Conference, the Netherlands. Retrieved from http://oro.open.ac.uk/17827/

Lim, S. (2009). How and why do college students use Wikipedia? *Journal of the American Society for Information Science and Technology, 60*(11), 2189–2202. Retrieved from http://portal.acm.org/citation.cfm?id = 1656292

Lorenzen, M. (2001). The land of confusion?: High school students and their use of the World Wide Web for research. *Research Strategies*, 18(2), pp.151-163.

Lovett, M., Meyer, O., & Thille, C. (2008). The Open Learning Initiative: measuring the effectiveness of the OLI statistics course in accelerating student learning. *Journal of Interactive Media Education (JIME)*, Special issue on researching open content in education. Retrieved from http://jime.open.ac.uk/2008/14

LUOERL (2012). *LUOERL*. Retrieved from http://luoerl.referata.com/wiki/LUOERL

Luyt, B., Zainal, C. Z., Mayo, O. V. P., & Yun, T.S. (2008). Young People's Perceptions and Usage of Wikipedia. *Information Research*, 13(4). Retrieved from http://informationr.net/ir/13-4/paper377.html

Margaryan, A., Littlejohn, A., & Vojt, G. (2011). Are digital natives a myth or reality? University students' use of digital technologies. *Computers & Education, 56*(2), 429–440. Retrieved from http://linkinghub.elsevier.com/retrieve/pii/S0360131510002563

Matusiak, K. K. (2006). Information seeking behavior in digital image collections: a cognitive approach. *Journal of Academic Librarianship, 32*(5), 479–488. Retrieved from http://linkinghub.elsevier.com/retrieve/pii/S0099133306000942

McAndrew, P., & Jones, A. (2012). Editorial: massive open online courses, a perspective paper by Sir John Daniel. *Journal of Interactive Media in Education (JIME)*. Retrieved from http://www-jime.open.ac.uk/article/2012-17/pdf

McAndrew, P., Inamorato dos Santos, A., Lane, A., Godwin, S., Okada, A., Wilson, T., Connolly, T., Ferreira, G., Buckingham Shum, S., Bretts, J., & Webb, R. (2008). *OpenLearn: Research Report 2006-2008*, Milton Keynes: OpenLearn, The Open University. Retrieved from http://www3.open.ac.uk/events/6/2009727_62936_o1.pdf

McClure, R., & Clink, K. (2008). How do you know that?: an investigation of student research practices in the digital age. *portal: Libraries and the Academy, 9*(1), 115–132. Retrieved from http://muse.jhu.edu/content/crossref/journals/portal_libraries_and_the_academy/v009/9.1.mcclure.html

McDowell, E. A. (2010). Using open educational resources to help students understand the subprime lending crisis. *American Journal of Business Education, 3*(11), 85–91. Retrieved from http://journals.cluteonline.com/index.php/AJBE/article/view/66

Medeiros, N. (2009). Researching the research process: information-seeking behavior, Summon, and Google Books. *OCLC Systems & Services, 25*(3), 153–155. Retrieved from http://www.emeraldinsight.com/journals.htm?articleid = 1810661&show = html

Menchen-Trevino, E., & Hargittai, E. (2011). Young adults' credibility assessment of Wikipedia. *Information, Communication & Society, 14*(1), 24–51. Retrieved from http://webuse.org/p/a35/index.html

Mulder, F. (2007). *The advancement of lifelong learning through open educational resources in an open and flexible (self) learning context*. ICDE Standing Conference of Presidents (SCOP). Heerlen, the Netherlands: Open Universiteit. Retrieved from http://www.ou.nl/Docs/Campagnes/SCOP/OER_paper_by_Fred_Mulder.pdf

Nicholas, D., Huntington, P., Monopoli, M., & Watkinson, A. (2006). Engaging with scholarly digital libraries (publisher platforms): the extent to which "added-value" functions are used. *Information Processing & Management, 42*(3), 826–842. Retrieved from http://portal.acm.org/citation.cfm?id = 1131990.1710774

Nicholas, D., Rowlands, I., Williams, P., Huntington, P., Fieldhouse, M., Gunter, B., Withey, R., Jamali, H. R., Dobrowolski, T., & Tenopir, C. (2008). The Google generation: the information behaviour of the researcher of the future. *Aslib Proceedings, 60*(4), 290–310. Retrieved from http://www.emeraldinsight.com/journals.htm?issn = 0001-253X&volume = 60&issue = 4&articleid = 1733495&show = pdf

Nicholas, D., Huntington, P., Jamali, H. R., Rowlands, I., & Fieldhouse, M .(2009). Student digital information-seeking behaviour in context. *Journal of Documentation, 65*(1), 106–132. Retrieved from http://www.emeraldinsight.com/journals.htm?articleid = 1766885&show = pdf

Nicholas, D., Rowlands, I., Williams, P., Brown, D., & Clark, D. (2011). *E-journals: their use, value and impact – final report.* Research Information Network. Retrieved from http://www.rin.ac.uk/our-work/communicating-and-disseminating-research/e-journals-their-use-value-and-impact

OPAL (2011). *Open Educational Quality Initiative (OPAL): final report (public part).* Retrieved from http://eacea.ec.europa.eu/llp/projects/public_parts/documents/ict/2011/ict_mp_504893_opal_final.pdf

Pan, B., Gay, G., Saylor, J., & Hembrooke, H. (2006). One digital library, two undergraduate classes, and four learning modules: Uses of a digital library in classrooms. *Journal of the American Society for Information Science and Technology,* 57(10), pp.1315-1325.

Peterson Bishop, A. (1998). Logins and bailouts: measuring access, use, and success in digital libraries. *Journal of Electronic Publishing, 4*(2). Retrieved from http://quod.lib.umich.edu/cgi/t/text/text-idx?c = jep;view = text;rgn = main;idno = 3336451.0004.207

Pick&Mix (2011). OER benchmarking – mood ω of Pick&Mix. Retrieved from http://www.scribd.com/doc/120864476/Pick-Mix-for-OER-uptake-in-institutions

Re.ViCa (2013). *VISCED/Virtual schools and colleges index.* VISCED. Retrieved from http://virtualcampuses.eu/index.php/VISCED#Virtual_schools_and_colleges_-_Index

Schuwer, R., Kirschner, P. A., Hendriks, M., & van der Baaren, J. (2007). Impact of open educational resources in the Netherlands. In P. McAndrew & J. Watts (eds.), *OpenLearn: researching open content in education, proceedings of the OpenLearn2007 Conference.* Milton Keynes, UK: OpenLearn, Open University (99–101). Retrieved from http://kn.open.ac.uk/public/getfile.cfm?documentfileid = 12197

Stannard, R. (2010). *University of Westminster MMTV OER. JISC project final report.* London. Retrieved from http://www.heacademy.ac.uk/assets/York/documents/ourwork/oer/OER_1_Westminster_final_report.pdf

Stapleton, S., Horton, J., & Beggan, A. (2011). *OER Re-use Student Survey* (January 2011), Nottingham. Retrieved from http://webapps.nottingham.ac.uk/elgg/cczss1/files/-1/869/Open+Nottingham+Re-use+SurveyV1.0.doc

Sweat-Guy, R., Elobaid, M., & Buzzetto-More, N. (2007). Reading in a digital age: e-books are students ready for this learning object? *Interdisciplinary Journal of Knowledge, and Learning Objects, 3*. Retrieved from http://citeseerx.ist.psu.edu/viewdoc/summary?doi=10.1.1.102.8235

Weiler, A. (2005). Information-seeking behavior in Generation Y students: motivation, critical thinking, and learning theory. *Journal of Academic Librarianship, 31*(1), 46–53.

WikiEducator. (2012a). OER university. Retrieved from http://wikieducator.org/OER_university/Home

WikiEducator. (2012b). Australia's University of Southern Queensland launches the first OERu prototype. Retrieved from http://wikieducator.org/Australia's_University_of_Southern_Queensland_launches_the_first_OERu_prototype

Wikipedia (2012). *Library 2.0.* Retrieved from http://en.wikipedia.org/wiki/Library_2.0

Wikipedia (2013). *Massive open online course.* Retrieved from http://en.wikipedia.org/wiki/Massive_open_online_course

Wilson, T. (2008). New ways of mediating learning: investigating the implications of adopting open educational resources for tertiary education at an institution in the United Kingdom as compared to one in South Africa. *International Review of Research in Open and Distance Learning, 9*(1), 1–19. Retrieved from http://www.irrodl.org/index.php/irrodl/article/view/485

Winn, J. (2010). *ChemistryFM OER project final report.* University of Lincoln. Retrieved from http://www.heacademy.ac.uk/assets/York/documents/ourwork/oer/OER_1_Lincoln_Final_Report.pdf

Wong, W., Stelmaszewska, H., Bhiman, N., Barn, S., & Barn, B. (2010). *User behaviour in resource discovery: final report.* London: Middlesex University. Retrieved from http://www.ubird.mdx.ac.uk/wp-content/uploads/2009/11/ubird-report-final.pdf

6
Open Educational Resources: Understanding Barriers to Adoption and Use

GABRIEL REEDY

King's College London, UK

Editors' Introduction

This chapter looks at the challenges faced by academics in traditional higher education in the adoption and use of open educational resources. The author reports on an extensive study conducted with a range of early career academics in anticipation that this group would likely be the most open to innovative approaches to teaching and that they also may be most in need of proven teaching materials. Are OERs a saviour for these hard-pressed academics or an additional burden at a time when proving teaching capability is the most pressing issue? Reedy provides a fascinating account of the challenges inherent with the selection and use of any third-party resource and rounds out the chapter with a set of key pointers that have emerged to guide would-be adopters in overcoming common barriers.

The open educational resources movement has gone from a small, grass-roots effort to a global mission supported by powerful educational, nonprofit and nongovernmental organisations around the world (Wiley & Gurrell, 2009). As the number of available resources continues to increase, problems of developing high-quality resources have been surpassed by others: how can the use of OERs be encouraged and barriers to their use be slowly broken down, so that a truly sustainable cycle of use and production can be obtained (D'Antoni, 2007)? Though originally envisaged primarily as an extension of traditional learning environments such as schools, colleges and universities, formalised education has been relatively slow to adopt innovative teaching practices and technology-enhanced learning; as such, OERs are frequently not reflected in teaching or formalised curricula (Atkins et al., 2007). The corporate sector, which due to a number of driving forces has been quicker to adopt technology-enhanced learning, is now beginning to explore OERs for use in training and professional development activities.

Among the many pressures on new online tutors and trainers, some of whom have little or no previous teaching experience, is the now-widespread requirement of achieving a teaching qualification or certification recognised by industry (e.g., Certified Membership of the Association for Learning Technology or CMALT). However, many such programmes, while providing an initial exposure to teaching or online tutoring practice, often focus more on tools, tips and teaching theory, rather than on innovative pedagogies and new technologies for the benefit of student learning.

Background Research: OER Use in Academic Settings

This chapter is based in research that set out to explore in some depth the ways in which OERs could be used for innovative teaching and learning in various fields and disciplines. These can also be adapted and applied to a commercial training context. It was conceived as a design-based research project to help tutors and trainers adapt practice through the use of OERs (Design-Based Research Collective, 2003).

Using a combination of e-mail networking and personal networking with colleagues around the UK, early career university teachers from various fields and disciplines in traditional university settings were recruited to participate in the research project. In an effort to make the project particularly useful to new teachers – those who most need OERs and who are most likely to approach teaching from an innovative perspective – participants were part of a postgraduate teaching qualification scheme for early career university teachers (Postgraduate Certificate in Higher Education or Postgraduate Certificate in Academic Practice).

Though they represent a relatively recent innovation, these HEA-governed programmes are a central pillar of attempts to improve teaching in the higher education sector. At most universities, early career academics are now required to complete these programmes as part of their probationary contract. As the experience is now becoming ubiquitous for early career academics, it is an ideal point at which to encourage innovative practices like the use of OERs. Similarly, among training professionals in industry, corporate, nonprofit and professional development training, certification programmes offer an ideal opportunity to encourage the use of OERs.

Participants in this project included six early career academics in various fields, including mental health, nursing, education, classics and computer science. Initial contact with potential participants was made by e-mail and followed up by a telephone screening interview to explain the project and determine whether the participant was interested in participating. Following participants were interviewed about their experiences with OERs, the nature of their teaching responsibilities, what they hoped to achieve by participating in the project and what they hoped OERs could add to their teaching.

After this initial interview, an e-mail was sent to participants containing links to potentially applicable OER materials for them to peruse and explore in their own time. This list of resources included background material on OER use in teaching, Creative Commons licensing and links to both general and subject-specific repositories. Participants were encouraged to contact the researcher with any questions or assistance while exploring these links, and in most cases a series of additional telephone and e-mail conversations was conducted, focused on helping participants explore the available resources and evaluate their potential for use in their own teaching.

Finally, a second follow-up interview was conducted, focusing on what participants found in their search, how they went about evaluating its fitness for their own teaching or tutoring, and how they found (or did not find) OERs that could be implemented in their own teaching practice. In most cases, although not all, it was this second interview that was most enlightening about the nature of OER as a potential tool in traditional university settings.

The resulting data, which consisted of interview transcripts, field notes, notes of telephone conversations and e-mail conversations, was analysed for emergent themes, and analytical codes were refined over the course of the data collection and analysis. The final set of codes were representative of an inductive analytical process and pointed to emergent themes across all the data that related to the questions posed by this research. These themes, which generally fell under two broad categories, will be explored in the next section, and the implications for e-learning professionals, tutors, trainers and teachers follow.

Teachers, Tutors, Trainers and Educators Need High-Quality, Innovative, Interesting and Engaging Learning Resources

Regardless of the discipline or mode of teaching, participants discussed how they faced a shortage of materials for teaching and new ideas for how to teach particularly difficult subjects. Interestingly, though all the participants were appointed at "traditional" universities, they each were responsible for teaching in various modes:

- Seminars and lectures
- Clinical face-to-face teaching
- Online teaching consisting of local and distance-learning students
- Self-directed online tasks and blended activities supporting face-to-face teaching

Online tutor G described the many different kinds of teaching she was responsible for and her optimism for OERs in this way: "I hope that, whether it's in terms of the e-learning, or something in terms of seminars or lectures, that we can use resources in a way that allows students to engage in the learning while they're there, rather than just try to cram the information that we're giving them."

Participants discussed the need for resources they use in their teaching to have a clear and traceable provenance, and OERs were appealing to them in the sense that they promise resources from trusted academic sources that are usable without worrying about licensing issues. In many cases, participants had already used other OER or "nearly-OER" resources without having any association with the concept. Among the list of sources that were named included items from the following:

- The BBC
- The British Library
- Several universities in the UK including the Open University, Nottingham, Manchester and Oxford
- Professional licensing bodies such as the Nursing and Midwifery Council (NMC)
- Many other sources

Additionally, every participant mentioned searching for resources using search engines like Google and using non-OER resources like YouTube videos, TED talks and similar resources in their teaching.

Across disciplines and fields, participants spoke of their willingness to use resources that came from reputable sources, and there was a recognition that such use could potentially save significant time while providing a valuable learning experience for students. As tutor R explained:

> There is no need for me to recreate what is already out there, probably in a better format than I myself can do. So, you know, there's . . . That's a waste of time . . . I'm not a technophobe, but I'm certainly not somebody who's very well versed in all the details of e-learning and how you do it and things like that. So, if I can find something that's been done before and that suits my needs, that's absolutely fine with me.

But teachers in several fields were clear that a reputable provenance was no guarantee of high-quality content. Tutor N said:

> What I have found looking at some of the content is . . . even those that have come from very good sites – because obviously there is always a danger when using something that's out there as open source – that it's not quite the quality that you want it to be. But even those coming from very reputable sources, I've found it's very dangerous to assume that the

quality of the information, or indeed the way that things are demonstrated, are the ways that we would want students to learn.

In discussing the benefits of searching for OERs, one tutor went on to explain that she enjoyed the "hunt" for other resources and that it gave her ideas for what to incorporate into her online and face-to-face teaching. Many educators echoed this notion, pointing out that they often went looking online for ideas:

> I may have ideas about what I want to include in content, and sometimes you'll search for that and you may find something that suits very well. Other times, you're doing a general search and actually what is out there gives you ideas about what you can use. You may see something that's quite innovative or quite different and you think, actually, that could be quite useful for students in certain contexts. So that's really useful.

There was also a clear sense of pedagogical needs that arose among participants in this project. They discussed various ways in which the resources they were looking for needed to help them accomplish some very specific learning goals. These goals were often specific to disciplinary contexts, but in other ways they could be conceived of as transcending those contexts. Tutor G from classics, for instance, discussed the value of having high-quality images as reusable resources but pointed out that these were especially useful when they could be placed in a context that helped students make sense of their social and cultural significance – something the images on their own were less useful for. Tutor R, an academic in nursing, however, expressed an almost identical concern over OER images she found. An image, she noted, had to have a contextual significance in order for it to be useful in her teaching:

> One thing I did find was some very good pictures in terms of wounds, which I thought would be very useful for my wound healing lecture next year, but again, what was interesting . . . [navigates to resource] Now, I wouldn't use that because, first of all, I'm not absolutely convinced that it's a real arm . . . there's nothing to contextualise what you're seeing. There's no information there to go with it, and also it may be that they're demonstrating this for an immune-neutropenic or a very immunocompromised patient, but there's no reason you would have full gown and gloves on for removing, for taking blood . . . And it may be that, actually, in some situations it may be perfectly appropriate, but given the fact that there's no information there to contextualise what they're seeing, that would be particularly difficult.

In practice-based fields (computer science, education, nursing and mental health), academics discussed various perspectives on the theory-practice gap:

their pedagogical aims often centred around bridging that gap in some way and helping students make sense of theory as it pertains to their practice. Tutor Y shared the following:

> It would be quite nice if we had something... which would help speed up that process. Kind of, think about evidence-based mental health, think about treatments, think about patients and how that might apply to real people. I think it's ... because it's very theoretical, and you're looking at the evidence of what treatment works, we need to link it in a bit more with practice, so it's not all theory.

Another tutor, from computer science, explained that his goal was to use OERs as a way of embedding the world of practice into the classroom experience. "The idea," he explained, "is that when they go into industry, they have to write code and work with existing code. If they have some experience with playing with existing code, then that will be really helpful."

Many tutors took the pedagogical aims further in discussing the kinds of resources that might be useful and retreated to the epistemological bases of their fields in discussing what they needed from OERs. Tutor G explained that there were quite different ways to explore particular topics within her field but that often those perspectives were incompatible with each other. Resources produced from one perspective, therefore, were less useful to her practice:

> You might be looking at a site about children with additional needs, but it's got a very medical model way of looking at disabilities, whereas our philosophy is far more inclusionary, kind of a social model of disability. So there are those kinds of philosophical things around the resource that, you know ...

Tutors also discussed how, ideally, online learning could support classroom discussion in a blended mode, setting students up for the more limited time in the classroom and potentially scaffolding new concepts or ideas. Studying images of classical artefacts, for example, was a way one participant encouraged her students to prepare for the seminar portion of their course – where discussions would focus on how to make the connections between the artefact and the historical and cultural relevance.

In explaining their needs for high-quality resources, however, tutors, teachers and trainers from across all fields discussed the specific needs of their student population, their particular programme or module, and their ways and means of teaching. In a sense, the theme centred on a recurring theme among academics: the peculiarity of their contexts. The educators explained, in their own ways, how their teaching was unique and different from what their colleagues did, both within and outside their institutions and organisations. As such, what they needed more than anything else were resources suitable for their peculiar teaching requirements. In the words of one educator, tutor R:

> I remember finding what potentially was a very good source on the use of PCA, patient controlled analgesia, which when I read the description sounded fantastic. It looked at all the different aspects of care that you may need to consider for these patients, but when I actually accessed the resource itself, I found it too busy. There was too much going on, and as a nurse very experienced with the use of patient controlled analgesia, I found it difficult to follow what was happening. And whatever I put out there for students has to be easily accessible . . . Some of our students, especially, without wishing to stereotype, but some of our older students may not be as experienced with IT as some of the others and they may struggle to access some of these resources. So it needs to be almost point and click, really, for a lot of them.

Significant Barriers to OER Use Exist Across Educational Settings

The other significant theme that arose, perhaps not surprisingly, within the data were the number of barriers that tutors and teachers faced in attempting to find, evaluate and use OERs. In the main, these educators found that they were not able to successfully complete the cycle of implementation or reuse of OERs in their own teaching practice. The barriers were diverse in the sense that they did not all emerge in the same ways for each participant; however, similar barriers frequently emerged across multiple tutors' experiences with OERs.

The most significant barriers to OER use for tutors and teachers in this study remained technological ones. Though they frequently played down their own technological expertise, in the main, they proved to be quite capable and comfortable with technology. Indeed, most of them tutored at least partly in online environments. However, even the most technologically savvy educator (a computer sciences lecturer) experienced problems accessing, downloading and working out how to use resources from well-known repositories that were clearly packaged for academics. During one session, for instance, a package downloaded from the Jorum site that purported to be examples of Java code ended up being a Flash video, which could not be opened by software on the participant's computer. Another package, which was supposed to be example code, generated an error message when it was opened in an appropriate programming package.

Incompatibility of technologies, even supposedly Web-standard technologies, was a problem for many educators. Two of them enlisted the help of learning technologists, whom they happened to have access to, in an attempt to work out how to access and utilise an OER package they found interesting based on our initial searches. However, even these more technical colleagues were not able to make the package usable. As one articulates the problem:

> Now one of the issues for us, on some of the sites, was iTunes. Some of the things only played in iTunes, and talking to [our learning technologist] . . . I can't open iTunes at all on my computer, which was annoying because there was actually some really good . . . little snippets of lectures and all sorts that would have been good . . . that we probably would want to use at some point, if I could open them.

Tutor R reported a well-known repository being unavailable over the Christmas holiday period, which was when she had "downtime" to do some curriculum design and planning.

> Which of course actually, is an issue! At that time of year they were under development, so there were bits you couldn't actually get in and see anything . . . that's the time of our downtime, which of course is their downtime when they build the site, but it is a time when people like myself are reviewing what will be useful and picking up [resources].

In describing her own difficulties attempting to use various OERs she had located, tutor G explained the difficulty she had in downloading and trying to unzip a package from a well-known repository and put it into her VLE environment for further testing. During one of our sessions, we walked through it together, and indeed, the package seemed not to be usable without further specialist knowledge:

> In terms of a couple of practical things, there were some resources that I tried to download from Jorum, that when I downloaded them came as a zipped file, but then wouldn't open properly . . . Let me show you what I got . . .

Later, after consulting with her learning technologist, one of the resources was finally able to be loaded onto the VLE, but when accessed it did not display properly:

> So, I mean, in terms of usability, it needs to be not just usable for the students, but it needs to be usable for me, because if I get completely lost in the technology then I'm not going to use it. [Our learning technologist] eventually managed to get this to go with the Blackboard, but couldn't download it on to other local machines. So let me just open up e-learning. [Pause]
> So we got this, which in terms of . . . that is great and we looked at the scenarios which may be suitable, but none of the pictures came up, none of the actual interactive bits. As I say, there were two of these that I

attempted to download, one around learning disabilities, and I couldn't get that to sit at all. So I think one of the challenges is that maybe some of the technology that is used to produce some of these educational resources isn't as compatible with the technology we have available in the university, which presents particular problems.

Tutor Y explained that her frustration with the technology, while not a new or unique problem, needed to be addressed in order for OERs to move into the mainstream among academic educators and industry training professionals.

I would imagine that most lecturers or teachers who are going to use open education resources are going to be pretty similar to me. They're going to be probably quite enthusiastic about the idea, but actually in terms of their tech know-how, very limited. So we either need to get a degree in IT, or we need people available who can deal with these kinds of problems for us. And I know we are very lucky, we have our learning technologists, but they're also very, very busy with many other things.

Finding and Evaluating Open Educational Resources is Difficult

Further frustration occurred when tutors tried to access and utilise resources that, although seemingly appropriate based on the associated description and metadata, proved to be less useful than they expected. Searching for and evaluating resources is a time-consuming task, and it was made more difficult for participants in this project who had to go to great lengths to determine whether an OER was potentially suitable for their use. This was a common complaint, and it was especially frustrating among packaged OERs that had no "preview" ability or clear list of included items. As Tutor R explained her experience and response, which was echoed across the project, "So in this case, it doesn't seem like it has given you either the details or the information that you need in order to make sense of how to use it."

As educators moved on from an initial evaluation of a resource into a more substantive one, they frequently found other, more serious pedagogical concerns about the material. In some cases, it was philosophical or epistemological – a concern that was highlighted in advance for some participants based on their previous experiences using other online resources. However, in other cases, these concerns were less ethereal: resources had no clear learning goals or outcomes, for instance; they were too busy or difficult for students to understand; materials needed to be reordered or revised in order to be explanatory for students; or they were not current or accurate in terms of being representative of good practice. One participant explained that she felt the bar, in terms of pedagogical fitness, was higher for an online resource than it was for something you might use in the classroom. In the classroom, she noted, you could explain away elements and guide students' focus to particular aspects of the resource. But in an online setting, there is much less control of the student experience:

> But what I found quite interesting was, I would never put, just stick that up there. I would always want to have something in my material that explained it more. And some of them really didn't, and I was quite surprised, actually, that some university sites didn't have that explanation ... That matters. That matters very, very much, and so that's ... because I mean some video out there is a student project. It's not, you know, I've got nothing against student projects, but it's not necessarily somebody highlighting it in the way you'd want it to come across to students.

The frustrations that arose for participants in the project invariably meant they spent much more time trying to find, assess, evaluate and test OERs than they anticipated. As such, time associated with the reuse of OERs was a major barrier outlined by participants in this project. Tutors and teachers reported that they felt the time spent on the project to be useful in terms of their learning, but as one person pointed out, the amount of time necessary for a teacher or tutor to come to terms with OER use and to implement it in their practice had to be seriously considered. As she put it, "There's a kind of a cost-benefit analysis stuff around this, I think, isn't there?"

> I am sure every single person ever says this; it's time consuming, isn't it? I mean, probably if I totted up the number of hours, looking [for resources on one subject], sort of, at least a day's work probably. I mean, it's useful ... but it's hugely time consuming, but everyone says that, I'm sure.

The tutors and teachers in this project who had access to learning technologists found that they needed them and made frequent contact with their colleagues for help during the project. Others, who did not have access to learning technologists, attempted to get along without them but noted that it was difficult.

Further barriers noted by participants in this project were rather more to do with the nature of their own work as academics in a UK higher education system currently experiencing an unprecedented amount of change. As academics and institutions move towards the government's stated goal of a more marketised system, the potential gains and downsides of participation in OER can change. Indeed, though not part of this data corpus, one potential participant in this project was so disturbed at the thought of being asked to share any repurposed material back to the OER community that she withdrew from the project, citing her fear that the university management would not look kindly on her giving her work away for free.

In a sense, then, teachers and tutors beginning their careers in more traditional educational settings are starting to feel some of the pressures that have existed for some time in the private and commercial training sector, if not also in the world of professional development training. Many business models have already been piloted, from the idea that free online content generates improved market visibility and public esteem, to the "taster" model used by Google, which gives some initial content or services for free (to the user, often supported by advertising) and then charges the user for additional content and services.

One teacher discussed these very tensions, which are inherent in bringing a market to what has traditionally been a relatively collaborative sector. In particular, she discussed the need for her course offering to be unique and differentiated from the offerings of others, in order to provide value for her students, and she pointed out that using material produced in other institutions would be problematic in terms of students' perceptions of the course's value for money. In a stratified and differentiated marketplace, the relative value provided to students by various institutions or educational providers will certainly come into more relief. Far removed from the intentions of the original OER movement, this market perspective brings to light the issue that students might perceive they are paying an institution or organisation for something they could potentially get for "free" from the Internet. The teacher also highlighted the tension in terms of using a "competitor's" material in your own "product," which is problematic in a market economy:

> As we move to, let's face it, it's a very marketised model of university education, it seems. I think the idea that we collaborate and share knowledge between universities, etc . . . I mean, I'd like to think that kind of thing will carry on, but . . . the concern I have is that in this kind of marketised model, to make use of materials like that and embed them within our own programme . . . you know, in effect they are our competitors . . . That is the world that we are moving towards.

Conclusion

Several related themes emerged from the data gathered during the course of this project, and these themes appeared across different tutors and teachers, regardless of discipline and teaching role. These themes have been outlined in turn here, but they cannot and should not be considered as wholly discrete: they are, of course, intricately intertwined in the experiences of each participating educator.

When interpreting these results, it is important to remember that the educators in this project are not what could be described as reticent to use OERs; indeed, they volunteered to participate in this extensive project focused on OERs. As early career academics, they are interested in innovation in their teaching and in providing an optimal learning environment within their respective disciplines and fields. The barriers faced by these teachers are not driven by lack of desire to use OERs. And indeed, because they arose during the course of this project, they are not barriers related to having support or guidance in approaching OER use in their teaching. They are legitimate concerns and documented barriers from motivated educators who would like to use to OERs as innovation in their teaching. If these highly motivated participants have difficulties bringing OERs into their practice, then these and similar barriers are likely to be faced by teachers, tutors, trainers and educators throughout formal educational settings and in industry.

The approach taken in this project, and indeed the approach most OER processes are based upon, is a teacher-centred approach to learning: the learning experience is created by the tutor, trainer, or teacher for the benefit of the student. However, in some areas, teachers are encouraging students to create their own OERs, for their own learning benefits, thus tapping into the distributed potential power of online learning. An even more common experience noted anecdotally by teachers, tutors and trainers in various settings is the increasing frequency by which students are finding their own learning resources in order to supplement their formal learning. While potentially frightening for some educators, the potential here for OERs is huge: by unleashing students to find and access these learning resources on their own, teachers and tutors engage students as active participants in their own learning.

Although it was not a theme that echoed across all participants, there was some success in terms of implementing OERs in teaching; two tutors in particular, both of whom had access to dedicated learning technologists in their departments, found resources they went on to use in their own teaching and attributed that use to the support provided by this project.

Among those who were able to overcome the barriers and find material they decided would be useful in their teaching was a nursing academic, tutor R. She described finding an OER that had a powerful impact on her work, leaving her reflective about her own practice as a nurse, as well as reflective about her teaching.

> I mean, this is a poem about, I think it's a little girl, who goes to see her very tiny little baby brother in neonatal intensive care, and you're reading through and absolutely dreading the moment that it says, you know, baby brother didn't come home, or something like that . . . Being a nurse or a doctor, I suppose you're always waiting for the worst to happen. But actually the ending is really lovely, and it really made me think about that experience and what I got out of that and how I thought about it. So actually something like this [resource], maybe rather than just the interactivity in terms of the technology, but actually putting information or resources up there that students can really engage with at a deeper level,

rather than just learning how to do hand hygiene . . . just really having an emotional connection.

And being critically aware of your feelings and thoughts about that helps you then to interact more successfully with your patients, your peers, your colleagues. And using something like this, where actually you look at reflection in terms of looking at the self, may be more useful. I really liked that bit of this activity and I liked the activity as a whole, but it needs some reordering.

In that sense, then, the reality is that in some circumstances OERs can be beneficial in what is a highly dynamic environment of higher education and corporate training, where often even face-to-face teaching now is accompanied by significant elements of online study. It is this success that is most interesting in terms of future work; the fact that traditional universities are continuing to migrate to Virtual Learning Environments (VLEs) and to expand their blended and distance-learning options means that the potential for OERs to be useful to so-called "traditional" academics will continue to grow. Likewise, among corporate and industry training professionals, many of whom are much further down the road to e-learning adoption, there is a huge potential for OERs to change the landscape. To the extent that these resources can be made useful and viable for educators, they will be reused and the cycle will continue; however, to the extent that the barriers remain high enough to keep educators from using OERs, the problem of OER reuse will continue.

Overcoming Barriers to OER Use and Reuse

Based on the results of this research, the following guidelines may help academics, trainers, learning technologists, graphic designers and others interested in developing, using and reusing OERs to overcome the barriers identified in this chapter.

Finding OERs

When an OER, online resource, or artefact is created (e.g., video, graphic, text, etc.), identifiable metadata (tags) are needed to help others locate and access the resource. Adding the resource to any of the large OER repositories is, by itself, not enough. Additionally, audio and video files can have associated text transcripts which will also help with finding things relevant to your search. Voice-to-text software (e.g., Adobe Soundbooth) can automatically create a transcript from an audio or video file.

When searching for OERs, don't stop with Google and the main OER repositories. Remember to look to institutions and commercial providers, who may have OER material that can be reused or used under creative commons licensing.

Open Educational Resources • 109

Avoiding Compatibility Problems With OERs

When an OER, online resource, or artefact is created, use Internet-standard technologies that can be easily used by others regardless of platform, browser, device, or operating system.

When using OERs, consider asking a learning technologist to help extract the content from nonstandard or incompatible technologies so that the object becomes reusable starting with your own use. In this way, you can encourage the cycle of reuse for OERs.

Considering OERs in Pedagogical or Instructional Design

When an OER, online resource, or artefact is created, consider and document where and how it might be used as part of a broader instructional design or highlight the learning outcomes intended for the resource. Include detailed cases of how it was successfully used, including the mode (face-to-face, online, blended).

When using OERs, think about the various ways that resources can contribute to the learning experience, rather than searching only for very specific "holes" in your own teaching. Consider building the learning experience around the OER, rather than the other way around.

Dealing With Commercial Issues

When an OER, online resource, or artefact is created, remember the potential value of OERs to promote your organisation and yourself within various markets and professional social networks. Consider consulting with your legal department about the practicalities of releasing material under creative commons licensing.

When using OERs, consider ways in which your reuse of openly available resources for commercial gain may be problematic or cause commercial issues. Will your customers or students recognise the material as an OER and react negatively, or will they perceive the OER as being just a part of a learning experience that has a high overall value?

Inducting New Educators Into OERs

When an OER, online resource, or artefact is created, remember to consider how to make it easy for relatively novice educators to find, access and use it in their own teaching.

When using OERs, actively induct new tutors, trainers and teachers into the use of OERs so they have a supportive environment in which to learn about using OERs.

References

Atkins, D.E., Seely Brown, J., & Hammond, A.L. (2007). *A review of the open educational resources (OER) movement: achievements, challenges, and new opportunities. Report to the William and Flora Hewlett Foundation.* Retrieved from http://www.learn.creativecommons.org/wp-content/uploads/2008/03/areviewoftheopeneducationalresourcesoermovement_bloglink.pdf

D'Antoni, S. (2007). *Open educational resources: the way forward. Deliberations of an international community of interest.* Paris: UNESCO-IIEP. Retrieved from http://oerwiki.iiep-unesco.org/images/4/46/OER_Way_Forward.pdf (or open this file in Google Books).

Design-Based Research Collective (2003). Design-based research: an emerging paradigm for educational inquiry. *Educational Researcher, 32*(1), 5–8.

Wiley, D., & Gurrell, S. (2009). A decade of development . . . *Open Learning: The Journal of Open and Distance Learning, 24*(1), 11–21.

7

Designing Dynamic Online Learning Environments That Support Knowledge Construction

MARK WEYERS

International Institute of Academic Development (IIAD)

Editors' Introduction

This chapter provides a brief overview of the various theories of learning that have shaped current approaches to instructional design as applied to online learning environments. Weyers introduces the SOLO taxonomy (the structure of the observed learning outcomes) and describes how a learner's understanding of a knowledge domain increases through four levels of complexity over time from a surface to a deep understanding. Weyers goes on to argue for a move from a focus on instructional design – which he sees as being teacher centric – towards a more learner-centric style of design. Taking a connectionist view, Weyers goes on to offer a set of design principles for a more dynamic model of online learning, principles that recognise and are adaptive to the complexity and depth of the mental knowledge schemas the learner already possesses. He closes the chapter by showing how this new model could be applied to a higher education curriculum.

Introduction

This chapter argues for the need of a new qualitatively different way of modelling learning design. It will outline some of the educational theories that have formed the basis for past and contemporary approaches to learning design and point out their limitations. It will then outline some principles that draw from dynamical systems theory to provide a more flexible and dynamic framework for designing learning environments that support knowledge construction and higher-level understanding.

Information and knowledge have always been key resources for a developing and evolving society. Knowledge has a value associated with it – innovation and the creation of new knowledge; how to harness it and how to apply it are crucial to modern-day society. Thus, the link between research and teaching is becoming increasingly important in a world that demands graduates who

111

have the critical skills of intellectual flexibility, analysis and enquiry. Learning environments that allow students to engage in higher-level cognitive tasks such as critical thinking, analysis and problem solving (Jenkins, Healey, & Zetter, 2007) are becoming increasing important. Barnett (2000, p. 163, cited in Jenkins et al., 2007) argues that in a knowledge society an understanding of how knowledge is developed (i.e., researched to create understanding) and transmitted (i.e., taught and learned) is critical. Courses need to be restructured so that students understand how knowledge is created within academic disciplines through research. The ability to "do" and understand research will be a fundamental skill for people within the new "knowledge economies" as graduates will be expected to have the abilities to analyse and contribute to research.

The emergence of the global knowledge society has been influenced strongly by the increase in information and communication technologies. The new knowledge society is changing dramatically how we learn and use knowledge. Our academic disciplines, even 50 to 100 years ago, lacked the kind of complexity and cross-disciplinary approaches of modern-day academic disciplines. Modern-day knowledge is flexible, reflexive and continues to expand and increase. The futurist Ray Kurzweil argues that this phenomenon follows Moore's Law, which posits that the rate of innovation in computer technology is increasing at an exponential rate, and because science and technological development are dependent on computing power, this continual increase translates into exponentially more frequent advances in other dependent academic fields of study (e.g., biotechnology, nanotechnology). Kurzweil calls this the Law of Accelerating Returns.

Similarly, Gonzalez (2004) describes the challenges of the rapid depreciation of the value of knowledge thus:

> One of the most persuasive factors is the shrinking half-life of knowledge. The "half-life of knowledge" is the time span from when knowledge is gained to when it becomes obsolete. Half of what is known today was not known 10 years ago. The amount of knowledge in the world has doubled in the past 10 years and is doubling every 18 months.

This rapid depreciation in value and exponential increase in the complexity of new knowledge is radically affecting human capability and is having a fundamental impact on shaping our future. This has massive implications for our learning architects and designers. Contemporary learning is no longer dependent on the accumulation of knowledge, as technology has made information available to anyone with a computer and access to the Internet. What is now critical is one's ability to find it, assess its importance, process it, apply it and most importantly create new knowledge (i.e., innovate). Therefore, the learning environments of the 21st century need to support this reality. They need to be flexible and adaptable, and they need to allow the learner to generate content and continually add content as information expands within a knowledge domain. Unfortunately, a fundamental assumption that underlies a great deal of the instructional design literature is that the acquisition of knowledge is a linear process with a clear beginning and end point for the learner.

The Impact of Traditional Learning Theories on Instructional Design

Behaviourist psychology focuses on how behaviour changes in relation to positive and negative reinforcement. Behavioural change happens through a high degree of repetitive actions on the part of the learner. Learning happens through repetition. These principles have been translated into the educational setting through the act of praise for correct answers and the immediate correcting of mistakes for wrong answers. When information technology was first introduced into education, behaviourism reared its head in the form of the "drill-the-skills" software that was typically used for learning factual content like times tables. The software, in the form of electronic flashcards, would show "4 x 4," and then the learner would enter the correct answer. If they got it right the computer would feedback a positive response, and if the learner got it wrong the computer would indicate this and show the learner the correct answer.

Radical behaviourist asserted that the study of observable behaviour, an overt external process, should be a natural science (e.g., physics). One of the fundamental tenets of behaviourism is that psychology should only concern itself with observable behaviour, rather than unobservable events that cannot be measured. Behaviourists make no acknowledgement to the inner cognitive processes that occur during the learning process. The influence of the traditional sciences is clear in this approach, and many criticise behaviourism for being a one-dimensional approach that takes no account of the multiple influences that impact learning and human behaviour in the real world.

Cognitivism is the psychological theory that argues that knowledge is generated "sequentially" by learners as they engage in mental processing (e.g., analysing, applying, evaluating). These processes develop and strengthen the synapses in the brain. From the cognitivist perspective, the purpose of education is to develop conceptual knowledge, and the learner adopts knowledge from their interactions with other learners and their environment. The teacher's role in this process is to assist learners in developing their knowledge by providing and managing appropriate learning activities to assist the learner through their development, which for the most part is a linear and predictable pathway.

Constructivism is the theory of learning that emphasises the importance of learners' interaction with their environment and how they "construct" their own personal meaning through their engagement with that environment.

Learners must engage with their environment to "test" and "construct" their own theories about the environment in which they are situated. They are active participants in these environments, and they influence their environment as the environment influences them.

However, as Mayer (2001) argues, not all constructivist approaches are effective, or efficient, for learners. Constructivism relies on higher cognitive processes (e.g., critical thinking, problem solving), but active learning and engagement with information does not necessarily produce knowledge. Therefore, if the cognitive requirements needed to process the information and construct meaning exceed the learner's available processing capabilities or working memory capacity, the information will not be learned. Further, if a learner cannot remember the basic facts and information, it is not possible to engage in critical thinking using the information available.

Cognitive Load Theory and Effective Learning

This phenomenon can be explained by Sweller (1988), who developed cognitive load theory (CLT) while studying problem solving. Cognitive load is a term used to describe the executive control of working memory in the brain. Because working memory has a limited capacity, complex tasks that involve a high degree of processing power can overload working memory (Paas, Tuovinen, Tabbers, & van Gerven, 2003). The idea that humans are only capable of holding seven (plus or minus two) pieces of information in short-term memory came from classic experimental work (Miller, 1956) on memory that was later built on by Simon and Chase (1973), who subsequently coined the term "chunk" to describe the organisation of information in short-term memory. The idea of chunking information is synonymous with Gagné's (1965) theory of instructional design. Learners cluster semantically related data and information together to enhance memory recall. These ideas were elaborated further, and the term "schema" was used to describe how patterns of thought or behaviour are organised in the mind. Schemata are mental structures and frameworks humans use to represent the world around them. These mental structures represent the way we organise and perceive the world around us – an idea not too far from constructivist theory. They affect the way we learn new information, as people are more likely to attend to things that fit into their own personal schemas, or things that can be "assimilated" into their personal schemas of understanding.

Sweller (1988) argues that instructional designers should limit the cognitive load on learners by designing learning activities like worked examples (step-by-step demonstrations of how to perform a task or solve a problem). Van Merriënboer (1997) argues that worked examples are effective learning tools because they provide expert mental models to teach complex problem-solving skills to novices. However, problem solving is a procedural task, and a learner needs to have a grasp of the lower-level conceptual knowledge and information to be able to make the appropriate decisions at each stage of the problem-solving process, which is a principle well argued for by constructivists and cognitivists alike. Therefore, even with guidance and assistance, complex problem-solving tasks would not assist learners who do not have a basic conceptual understanding of the target domain. Biggs (2007) argues that learners move through phases of understanding – from a quantitative phase (knowing lots of stuff) to a qualitative phase (understanding how information is related and linked together). Therefore, a lower-level grasp of basic concepts (being able to name, identify, list and describe) is needed before a learner can work at a higher level with that information (e.g., problem solving or critical thinking).

What is important to note is that in laboratory experiments as noted by Muller, Lee, and Sharma (2008), learning materials are prepackaged and presented to participants in a controlled linear environment. Whereas in real learning situations, learners do not engage with material in such a controlled, linear, Gagné-style fashion. Most often, learners will reread information and will jump from the top of the page to the bottom and look for connections between what they read earlier and what they are reading now. They will look to the table of contents in an attempt to understand the structure within the knowledge domain. This nonlinear behaviour is fundamental to effective learning as it adds both repetition and reinforcement to the learning process.

Contemporary Educational Theory

Student learning research has investigated a combination of attributes of learning environments (e.g., teaching approach, assessment, learning resources) in relation to learning outcomes. Some of the key concepts that have come from this research include students' approaches to studying – "deep and surface" (Marton & Säljö, 1976, 1997) – which have been investigated in a number of studies (Biggs, 1989; Entwistle & Ramsden, 1983; Entwistle, McCune, & Hounsell, 2002). While deep approaches are characterised by student-centred strategies in which students are critical of ideas and link what they are learning to previous knowledge and examples in the real world, a surface approach is characterised by the tacit acceptance of information and "unreflective" rote memorisation strategies that focus on reproduction (Marton & Säljö, 1976, 1997; Thomas & Bain, 1984). Therefore, a deep approach leads to understanding while a surface approach does not. What is important to note is that while students may have a potential preference for a certain approach, these approaches are not attributes of a student, and students choose a strategy in reaction to the learning environment itself. The goal of the instructional designer and online teacher is to design the learning environment (e.g., learning activities, assessment processes) to encourage students to take a deep approach to their learning and studying.

Biggs (2003) outlines the SOLO taxonomy (the structure of the observed learning outcomes) and describes how a learner's understanding of a domain increases in complexity over time – from a simple quantitative understanding (multistructural) to a more complex qualitative understanding (extended abstract). The SOLO taxonomy is used not only to classify learning outcomes and identify the level at which a learner is currently working, but it also provides a framework for learning architects to design learning environments that move a student from a simple to a complex understanding of a domain of knowledge. Figure 7.1 (omits the prestructural level) outlines a graphical representation of the SOLO taxonomy and a list of verbs that are used when writing learning outcomes that indicate the level to which a student is expected to achieve. At the unistructural level a student is able to concentrate on single items (e.g., information and knowledge) and is expected to be able to achieve simple tasks, but

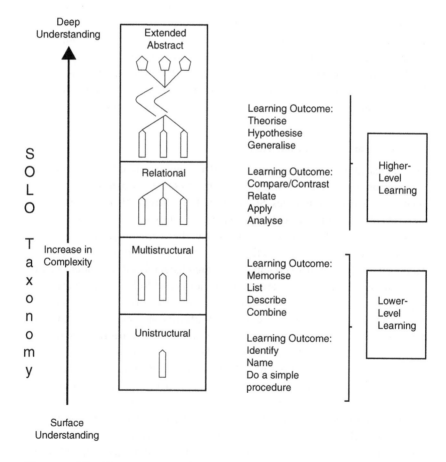

Figure 7.1 The SOLO Taxonomy (Biggs, 2003)

understanding is fragmented and limited. At the multistructural level, a number of facts and information are retained but the connections between these items are not clear. Students are expected to be able to complete a number of tasks at this level, but how all these tasks relate to completion of the overall goal is not clear. At these stages students have a surface-level understanding of the target domain. When students reach a relational understanding, they start to see the connections between the facts and information they remember and are able to foresee how lower-level tasks achieve a higher goal. At this level, they are considered to have a deep understanding characterised by a more coherent and richer understanding of the domain. At a relational level they understand how the facts and knowledge within a target domain are integrated and connected while at an extended abstract level, this understanding is looked at in a completely novel way and can be applied to "new" domains and used for prediction, generalisation and hypothesis building.

Biggs (1999) adds to these learning principles another core strategy for designing effective learning environments. Using the principle of "constructive alignment," we identify the expected outcome of learning we intend the student to achieve (e.g., describe, compare and contrast), and we align the learning environment activities and assessment to that outcome. The SOLO taxonomy assists learning architects in doing this as it contains an example list (although not exhaustive) of active verbs that indicate the type of activity appropriate to meet that learning outcome.

Therefore, the robustness of the SOLO taxonomy using the principle of constructivist alignment allows instructional designers to build learning activities that are matched to course learning outcomes and identify appropriate assessment methods to assess these outcomes. This is crucial because it allows students to first engage with course content at a lower level (focusing on retention of the core concepts) prior to moving to higher-level tasks that encourage students to apply their knowledge and understanding within a target domain – for example, "Compare and contrast the five principles of . . ." Knowledge is "constructed" through the learning activity the student carries out. Further, this must also link appropriately to an assessment task that provides a valid measurement of learning that is expected of a student (e.g., a critical essay) working at that level.

It therefore becomes clear to the learning architect that when you design a learning environment, lower-level learning outcomes need to engage students in behavioural tasks that focus on information recall (e.g., repetition and reinforcement) while higher-level tasks need to engage students in higher-level cognitive processing (e.g., critical thinking, problem solving). The misalignment of the learning tasks and assessment with the learning outcomes causes both confusion and fragmented knowledge in a student's developing understanding.

One way to design a learning environment that ensures a coherent and aligned learning experience for students (from lower- to higher-level understanding) is to build a course curriculum around the target domain's "threshold concepts" (Meyer & Land, 2003). Threshold concepts are the concepts that are fundamental to the mastery of a target domain. A tendency of many designers is to "stuff" the course with as many topics as possible that compose the specific target domain. However, this leads to fragmented understanding within the target domain because the learner is not able to assimilate and encode all the knowledge and information. A threshold concept allows the learner to see the interrelatedness of the information and knowledge within the target domain. Further, while it is often counterintuitive, it is also irreversible, in that once learned it is rarely forgotten.

Arguably, since these concepts are fundamental to achieving a higher level of learning within a target domain, it would make sense, from a learning design perspective, to focus strongly on threshold concepts when designing activities and assessments. Further, because these concepts are interrelated to other concepts and ideas, it is practical to design a course so that the threshold concepts are continually "revisited" multiple times and from multiple perspectives. This allows the learner to construct a much more complex understanding of the target domain.

Instructional Design Versus Learning Design
Gagné (1965) popularised the nine events of instruction and defined the curriculum as a sequence of content arranged sequentially into manageable chunks for the learner by the teacher. Learning depends on mastering each unit of content in order. This theory has been at the basis of instructional design approaches for decades. It is most often touted as a behaviourist approach as it provides an easy-to-follow structure that begins with gaining a learner's attention and outlining the learning outcomes for the session, stimulating the recall of previous sessions, presenting the content, providing feedback and assessing learning. This approach is also fundamental to classical ideas of effective classroom teaching. However, it also employs cognitive strategies when the learning outcomes require higher-level thinking (e.g., critical thinking). The basic idea is that learning events or lessons can be broken down into component parts and linked together to provide the kind of linear pathway through a subject or domain of knowledge. However, arguably, knowledge structures do not exist as hierarchical constructs, and engaging with knowledge in a cyclical fashion is sometimes more effective than learning content in a structured sequence.

Conole and Fill (2005) point out that the concept of "learning design" was first introduced to educational technology in the early 2000s. Carr-Chellman and Duchastel (2000) suggest that learning architects need to choose a mix of behaviourist and constructivist learning activities that are the most appropriate to meet the outcomes of online courses. However, Koper (2006) argues the concept has always been around and simply puts the focus on the "learning" that occurs during a learning event. Therefore, while instructional design is teacher focused and centres on approaches to designing effective instruction, learning design is student focused and centres on how to design effective environments that encourage learning.

Wild and Quinn (1997) argue that learning activities in virtual learning environments are fundamental to supporting learning outcomes. They facilitate the approach learners will take when engaging with the course content and ultimately how they will construct their own knowledge and understanding. They must be built into a learning environment that sets the purpose (i.e., based on the learning outcomes of the course) and the context (i.e., the environment in which the learning is situated) to allow learners to engage successfully with the course material (Duffy & Cunningham, 1996). The activities must provide the purpose and the context for learners to deal with the content and information. Collaboration on online environments is now a crucial element of effective learning environments. It allows learning architects to create engaging and interactive environments (e.g., Savery & Duffy, 1995) that allow learners to work in teams and engage in the kind of higher-order thinking (e.g., problem solving, critical thinking) that enhances understanding.

Expert Versus Novice Learners in Online Environments

Kalyuga (2007) argues that learning environments that are effective for "low prior knowledge" (i.e., novice learners) learners are not necessarily effective for "high prior knowledge" learners (e.g., experts). This effect relates to how "prior" knowledge affects the consolidation of "new" knowledge. This idea, derived within the cognitive load theory model, assumes that learners' current knowledge structures can affect how they learn new information. If the goal of learning is to assimilate new information into current knowledge structures, the complexity, or lack of complexity, can have an impact on how that new knowledge is assimilated. This suggests that learning environments need to be adapted as learners build their knowledge within a specific domain. Kalyuga, Ayres, Chandler, and Sweller (2003) argues that while detailed guidance can enhance the learning experience for novice learners, too much instructional guidance may have a negative impact on more experienced learners.

Low-level learners, who are characterised by a lack of a conceptual understanding of a topic, can "accommodate" new information into their knowledge structures with supporting information that leads them through the learning process in a new domain. Their low-level understanding is based on a process of memory consolidation, and the focus of learning is more related to rote processes. However, learners with experience in the target domain already have complex knowledge structures developed, and too much information can disrupt the assimilation process as the increase in information, and the capacity of working memory to link all the new information to the already well-developed cognitive structures of the experienced learner, causes information overload and interferes with memory consolidation.

Kalyuga (2007) argues low knowledge learners lack a sufficient knowledge base in the target domain so support and guidance assists them to problem solve and engage with novel tasks in the target domain. If guidance is not given, learners' cognitive capacities can be overwhelmed (i.e., information overload), which results in inefficient learning strategies (e.g., problem solving) and difficulties in navigating the target domain. There have been some criticisms of cognitive load theory because the research has been based on subjective measures of cognitive load (Ayres, 2006; Paas et al., 2003); these criticisms question the reliability and validity of such measures and greatly affect the determination as to whether an overload of working memory has occurred. Further, expertise reversal effects may also be seen to be caused by motivation factors (Paas et al., 2005; Schnotz, 2010).

Experts have complex mental schemas that have developed over time during their engagement with their target domains. The complexity of these mental schemas allows them to see the patterns and relationships that exist within information and data from within their domain. Whether they are experts in biology, physics, psychology, or geography, their complex schemata representing their area of expertise allows them to easily assimilate new information into their existing knowledge structures – essentially, they can more effectively and efficiently relate new information to what they already know. Therefore, they have the ability to sort through large amounts of data and information and assess what is important and not important, what is credible or not and how the information from multiple sources all relate to each other.

A novice, by contrast, has a simple schema and a much simpler understanding of a new target domain. Novices struggle to prioritise and are not able to categorise or arrange what information is the most pertinent. Knowing "how" important the information is and where it should be arranged hierarchically is crucial to the learning process when learners are presented with a high degree of information at a point close to their "information threshold." Further, they are not able to see the kinds of patterns that exist within the information, which means that new information has a high probability of becoming fragmented. Their ability to encode information is enhanced by strategies that encourage repetition and reenforcement between the schemas that make up a more complex concept. Such techniques can include examples, stories, metaphors and other techniques that assist the learner in relating new information to already learned information and to things that exist in the real world (i.e., deep learning). Novices need well-structured and guided support that assists them in encoding the new information more effectively into long-term memory.

Dynamical Systems Theory as a Basis for Learning Design

Effective learning is a dynamic and flexible process in which learners are able to control their engagement with the domain of knowledge. Learning design needs to move away from the premises of traditional reductionist science that have permeated popular pedagogical theories for decades and start to look at learning as a dynamic learner-controlled event. This does not mean a complete disregard for decades of research that has demonstrated some very effective elements of pedagogical design. It simply means looking at domains of knowledge and how they develop from a variety of perspectives and accepting the dynamic way that effective learning happens in these domains under real learning situations.

Systems theory, first proposed in the 1940s by the biologist Ludwig von Bertalanffy (1968), was an attempt to point out the limitations of reductionism in science. Von Bertalanffy argued that within real systems qualitatively new properties emerge which represent the system's continual evolution while the system interacts with its environment. Rather than reducing an entity to the properties of its parts or elements, systems theory focuses on the arrangement of and relations between the parts. The founders of systems theory believed the same concepts and principles of organisation underlie the many scientific disciplines (physics, biology, technology, sociology, etc.) and could provide a basis for their unification as well as an explanation of the rapid and dynamic expansion of knowledge in these disciplines.

A recent increase in dynamical theorising has led to one of the most influential developments within the cognitive sciences – connectionism. Connectionism models cognition (i.e., learning) as a dynamical system (Smolensky, 1988) and seeks to understand the brain from a dynamical perspective (Gelder, 1998). Dynamics forms the general framework for growing amounts of work in artificial intelligence, psychophysics, social psychology and autonomous agents research. While the dynamical hypothesis (DH; Gelder, 1998) is the unifying essence of dynamical approaches to cognition, it raises important questions of how general systems thinking could change the way we interpret and understand the world around us. Arguably, it provides us with a set of standard terminology and principles that can be adapted into a general framework to understand and model knowledge and learning in a dynamic way.

Connectionist thinking, from a cognitive neuroscience perspective, views the neurons as objects that exist in many different forms that integrate and pass information about their interactions to other neurons. The structure of the brain system is layered. Neurons interact with other neurons, and as information is output its transformed signal becomes input to the next layer. The influence of one neuron or object on another depends on the strength of the connection between them. Learning is considered to have taken place when the system develops and changes the strengths of the connections between neurons (McLeod, Plunkett, & Rolls, 1998). Connectionist models try to model how a set of experiences can lead an unstructured system to a more complex system with acquiesced knowledge (McLeod et al., 1998).

Most complex systems have multiple variables that coexist within a dynamic environment (Combs & Winkler, 1995, p. 51). A dependence on the principle of reductionism has led scientists to simplify systems to an unrealistic degree because they feel if they can understand the simple system they can extrapolate to the actual complex system. Arguably, this has also occurred through the misapplication of pedagogical approaches in education, and at the forefront of this has been the dependence on the Gagné notion of compartmentalised education. However, it is possible that systems thinking and classical science do not necessarily exist as opposing forces within a dichotomic relationship as Gleick (1998) argues but may exist on a continuum that ranges from discrete and static systems at one end to complex and dynamic systems at the other. These system states may represent a continuum of overlapping system properties, which many scientists may encounter depending on which aspects of a system they are measuring. Within pedagogy, this can be interpreted to mean that during learning there are instances when learners need structure and guidance while in other situations they need the freedom to control their own learning (as demonstrated by expertise reversal effect).

Dooley (1997) argues that there are three fundamental principles of complex systems:

- Order is emergent as opposed to predetermined.
- The system's history is irreversible.
- The system's future is often unpredictable.

The patterns and occurrences of new and unexpected elements (e.g., elements that emerge from the interaction of other elements) within the system are regarded as the emergent properties of the system. It is this emergent behaviour that is a defining feature of a complex system and is an influential property closely tied to the future evolution of a system and is highly dependent upon the system's initial conditions. Other important characteristics of a complex system are the strong interdependence of the parts; the nonlinear interaction of the parts or elements of the system, which is foundational to the intrinsic chaotic ingredient of a complex system; and the existence of fractal dimensionality represented by a rich structure over several scales of the system. The intrinsic order of a complex system is dynamic rather than static while some form or process of self-organisation is evident in the system's ability to maintain a dynamic equilibrium, in contrast to an ideal non-chaotic world.

Design Principles for an Effective Dynamic Online Learning Environment

Based upon the ideas set out earlier we can now propose that to be most effective a learning environment should do the following:

- Encourage the development of increasingly complex knowledge networks

- Be reactive to the developing conceptual representations of the learner (from novice to expert) characterised by decreasing guidance as the complexity of the knowledge structures increases
- Allow the learner to engage with the external knowledge systems from different perspectives
- Allow the learner to construct internal schemas that are partial representations of the external network of knowledge (i.e., universe of knowledge)
- Contain a universe of knowledge (i.e., curriculum) that is constructed by a subject expert from the beginning so that a learner can flip back and forth between the target and personal knowledge network (i.e., knowledge encapsulation)
- Have a flexible approach to modularity – low-level knowledge should be designed in a modular framework while higher-level knowledge should be non-modular
- Be a mix of behaviourist and constructivist learning activities that are constructively aligned to meet the intended learning outcomes of the course

Practical Application of the Model

This chapter suggests that an online learning environment should be dynamic and support student-generated content through learning activities that focus on both low-level learning and higher-level knowledge construction. While lower-level activities focus on engagement with modular learning objects, higher-level engagement needs to engage students to interact with multiple learning objects using higher-level cognitive processes.

A course curriculum is a network of data, information and knowledge that are all interconnected. A course (or network of data information and knowledge) can be considered synonymous with a universe of knowledge (i.e., a network of data, information and knowledge). Our personal universe of knowledge is intrinsic and personal – however, we all share an "understanding" of certain concepts within a shared universe (e.g., a course curriculum), although that understanding will not be *exactly* the same for everyone.

Information can exist as modular learning objects while knowledge is distributed and cannot exist as separate modular entities. Knowledge is emergent – new knowledge emerges from the interaction of the learner with new information and knowledge and other learners within the course. The interpretation and understanding of knowledge is context sensitive – knowledge is constructed from the perspective within which the learner is situated.

Low-level learning should be focused on repetition and reinforcement – learners should engage with course topics more than once and threshold concepts constantly throughout the learning process.

124 • Mark Weyers

High-level learning is about building more complexity within the learner's knowledge structures.

Learners can be tested at a lower level to assess their understanding of core course information. However, they must engage at a higher level with the information using higher-level learning strategies to understanding deeper conceptual knowledge.

One of the reasons why students in higher education have difficulty engaging with course content at a higher level is because they lack the basic understanding of the information at a lower level. This does not suggest that all learning and assessment in higher education should focus on lower-level understanding. However, it does suggest that a grasp of the basic concepts should be part of the learning process and a prerequisite of learning at a higher level. The verbs you use in constructing your learning activities and assessments can indicate the level of engagement you are requiring of your students.

Example: In the course learning outcomes of a cognitive psychology course the focus on higher-order verbs – such as apply, generate (develop) and contrast – indicate that there is a focus on developing a relational understanding, which is

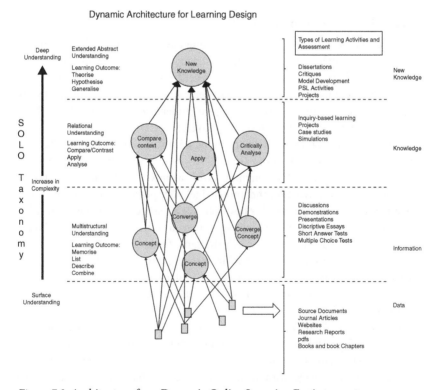

Figure 7.2 Architecture for a Dynamic Online Learning Environment

appropriate for a second- or third-year psychology course. Student achievement in such a course can be assessed by evaluating the level of complexity demonstrated in their assessment work and how well that aligns to the course learning outcomes.

Using a dynamic approach, learning designers can identify and assess the learning outcomes from a course module and constructively align the online activities and assessment with the expected learning outcomes. As Figure 7.2 demonstrates, reusable learning objects can be constructed around basic core concepts. Reusable learning objects (RLOs) can incorporate text, video and interactive Flash or HTML5 interactions. In addition, following the principles of constructive alignment, learning activities that would be suitable at this level to engage learners with the core concepts are online activities such as online discussion groups, multiple choice questions and short answers to online questions. The behavioural approach to learning design is prominent at the information level (Biggs's multistructural level) of the model, and the learning activities should focus on lower-level learning activities and methods of assessment (e.g., multiple choice). So for example we have a learning objective such as: "By the end of this module students are expected to be able to: state and describe the five theories of . . ."

When reusable learning objects have been designed for the lower-level and threshold concepts covered in the course, the designer will assess how these lower-level concepts can be combined into higher-level RLOs that focus on higher-level engagement, activities that allow the learner to construct his or her own knowledge and understanding of the target domain. While these RLOs may be designed by the learning architect and comprise text, video and interactive elements (e.g., Flash, HTML5 interactions) the fundamental difference is that at the knowledge level (Biggs's relational level) of this model these RLOs must also contain space for learners to collaborate and interact with other learners. It must also allow the learner to draw on new information contained in the source documents (and not built into the RLO). These spaces can take the form of wikis or blogs or other interactive forums that allow learners to engage in problem-based or inquiry-based learning activities, case studies, or online simulations that focus on higher-level learning outcomes (i.e., analyse, apply, compare and contrast). So for example the learning objective may take this form: "By the end of this module students are expected to be able to: compare and contrast the five theories of X . . ."

At the new knowledge level (Biggs's extended abstract level), learners must engage in learning activities that allow them to construct new knowledge within the target domain. At this level, learners will draw on the knowledge they have learnt during engagement at the previous level, but at this stage RLOs are often constructed by the learner (i.e., learner-generated content) based on the lower-level core concepts they have engaged with in earlier learning events. They should again be required to draw on the source documents and assimilate new information from these documents when engaging with appropriate learning activities at this level. Within an online environment, blogs and wikis and other online mediums can be used to support learning activities such as research projects, theory or model generation tasks, or some other form of project work. At this level, students are focusing on achieving higher-level learning outcomes (e.g., theorise, hypothesise). We see that at this level the learning objective is more likely to be of this form: "By the end of this module students are expected to be able to: construct their own unique theory of Y . . . based on the five theories of X . . ."

This kind of approach to design allows students to engage in lower-level activities when they need to engage with basic course concepts and information. However, when they have developed an appropriate level of understanding, they use this understanding to construct a more complex conceptualisation of the knowledge domain. Lower-level or multistructural RLOs are designed by the learning architect while relational RLOs are pre-designed for the learner but allow the learner to adapt or alter them during the learning activities. Extended abstract RLOs are completely student generated but allow the students to engage with lower-level RLOs and the course's source documents to generate content.

Conclusion

Traditionally, these systems have begun with static content (i.e., books, lecture notes, videos) that has been compartmentalised into a structure that designers feel best supports effective learning. Then when the learner begins to interact with the static content (i.e., knowledge domain) his or her behaviour (e.g., login times, click rates) as well as assessment data (i.e., number of correct test answers) is analysed by the use of "learning analytics" to establish a demographic profile. This profile is used to recommend future static content. However, the problem with this approach is that it still infuses into the learning environment a teacher-controlled, linear, Gagné-style learning experience that takes control of the learning from the students. In this environment students are getting answers to questions they have not asked.

However, with the introduction of "intelligent" systems a more flexible student-controlled learning environment is possible; in such systems, knowledge is constructed by the learner. Thus, the system can adapt in real time to the learner. Environments can be created with problems of varying complexity that allow the pedagogy to be adaptable. Learners ask their own questions, and it is these questions that drive their learning and subsequently their construction of knowledge within the target domain.

References

Ayres, P. (2006). Using subjective measures to detect variations of intrinsic cognitive load within problems. *Learning and Instruction, 16,* 389–400.
Barnett, R. (2000). *Realizing the university in an age of supercomplexity.* Buckingham: Society for Research into Higher Education/Open University Press.

Bertalanffy, L. (1968). General system theory: Foundations, development, applications. New York: George Braziller.
Biggs, J. B. (1989). Approaches to the enhancement of tertiary teaching, *Higher Education Research and Development, 8*, 7-25.
Biggs, J. B. (1999). *What the student does: teaching for quality learning at university*. Buckingham: Open University Press.
Biggs, J. B. (2003). *Teaching for quality learning at university* (2nd ed.). Buckingham: Open University Press/Society for Research into Higher Education.
Biggs, J. B., & Tang, C. (2007). Teaching for quality learning at university. Open University Press/McGraw-Hill Education.
Carr-Chellman, A., & Duchastel P. (2000). The ideal online course. *British Journal of Educational Technology, 31*(3), 229–241.
Combs, A. & Winkler, M., (1995). The nostril cycle: A study in the methodology of chaos science. In Robertson, R. & Combs, A. (Eds.) Chaos theory in psychology and the life sciences. Mahwah, New Jersey: Erlbaum.
Conole G., & Fill K. (2005). A learning design toolkit to create pedagogically effective learning activities. *Journal of Interactive Media in Education, 8*.
Dooley, K. (1997). A complex adaptive systems model of organization change. *Nonlinear Dynamics, Psychology, & Life Science, 1*, (1), 69–97.
Duffy, T., & Cunningham, D. (1996). Constructivism: implications for the design and delivery of instruction. In *Handbook of research for educational telecommunications and technology* (170–198). New York: MacMillan.
Entwistle, N., McCune, V., & Hounsell, J. (2002). *Approaches to studying and perceptions of university teaching-learning environments: concepts, measures and preliminary findings*. Occasional Report 1. Teaching and Learning Research Program, University of Edinburgh.
Entwistle, N. J., & Ramsden, P. (1983). *Understanding student learning*. London: Croom Helm.
Gagné R. M. (1965). *The conditions of learning*. New York: Holt, Rinehart & Winston.
Gelder, T. (1998). The dynamical hypothesis in cognitive science. *Behavioral and Brain Sciences, 21*, 1–14.
Gleick, J. (1998). Chaos: The amazing science of the unpredictable. London: Vintage.
Gonzalez, C. (2004). The role of blended learning in the world of technology. In G. Seimens, *Connectivism: a learning theory for the digital age*. Retrieved from http://www.elearnspace.org/Articles/connectivism.htm
Jenkins, A., Healey, M., & Zetter, R. (2007). *Linking teaching and research in disciplines and departments*. Higher Education Academy. Retrieved from http://www.heacademy.ac.uk/assets/documents/research/LinkingTeachingAndResearch_April07.pdf
Kalyuga, S. (2007). Expertise reversal effect and its implications for learner-tailored instruction. *Educational Psychology Review, 19*, 509–539.
Kalyuga, S., Ayres, P., Chandler, P., & Sweller, J. (2003). The expertise reversal effect. *Educational Psychologist, 38*, 23–31.
Koper R. (2006). Current research in learning design. *Educational Technology & Society, 9*(1), 13–22.
Marton, F., & Säljö, R. (1976). Symposium: learning processes and strategies. On qualitative differences in learning. 2: Outcome as a function of the learner's conception of the task. *British Journal of Educational Psychology, 46*, 115–127.
Marton, F., & Säljö, R. (1997). Approaches to learning. In F. Marton, D. J. Hounsell, & N. J. Entwistle (eds.), *The experience of learning* (2nd ed., 39–58). Edinburgh: Scottish Academic Press.
Mayer, R. E. (2001). *Multimedia learning*. New York: Cambridge University Press.
McLeod, Plunkett, & Rolls (1998). Introduction to connectionist modeling of cognitive processes. Oxford University Press, New York, NY.
Meyer J. H. F., & Land, R. (2003). Threshold concepts and troublesome knowledge – linkages to ways of thinking and practising. In C. Rust (ed.), *Improving student learning – ten years on*. Oxford: OCSLD.
Miller, G. A. (1956). The magic number seven plus or minus two: some limits on our capacity to process information. *Psychological Review, 63*(2), 81–97.
Muller, D. A., Lee, K. J., & Sharma, M. D. (2008). Coherence or interest: which is most important in online multimedia learning? *Australasian Journal of Educational Technology, 24*(2), 211–221.
Paas, F., Tuovinen, J. E., Tabbers, H., & van Gerven, P. (2003). Cognitive load measurement as a means to advance cognitive load theory. *Educational Psychologist, 38*, 63–71.
Paas, F., Tuovinen, J. E., van Merrienboer, J. J. G., & Darabi, A. A. (2005). A motivational perspective on the relation between mental effort and performance: optimizing learner involvement in instruction. *Educational Technology Research and Development, 58*, 193–198.

Savery, J., & Duffy, T. (1995). Problem-based learning: an instructional model and its constructivist framework. *Educational Technology, 35*(5), 31–38.
Schnotz, W. (2010). Reanalyzing the expertise reversal effect. *Instructional Science, 38*, 315–323.
Simon, H. A., & Chase, W. G. (1973). Skill in chess. *American Scientist, 61*, 394–403.
Smolensky, P. (1988) On the proper treatment of connectionism. *Behavioural and Brain Sciences,* 11, 1–74.
Sweller, J. (1988). Cognitive load during problem solving: effects on learning. *Cognitive Science,* 12(2), 257–285.
Thomas, P. R., & Bain, J. D. (1984). Contextual dependence of learning approaches: the effects of assessments. *Human Learning, 3*, 227–240.
van Merriënboer, J. G. (1997). *Training complex cognitive skills: a four-component instructional design model for technical training.* Englewood Cliffs, NJ: Educational Technology Publications.
Wild, M., & Quinn, C. (1997). Implications of educational theory for the design of instructional multimedia. *British Journal of Educational Technology, 29*(1), 73–82.

Part 4
Practitioners

The four contributions in part 4 span national boundaries and deal with all levels of education from adolescents who have been excluded from formal education through graduate and postgraduate education for in-service teachers and on to the continuing professional development of health care professionals in developing economies. What the contributions share is that they all address ways in which practitioner knowledge can be accessed and shared by communities that exist outside the bricks and mortar of traditional academia. Cunningham shows us how a learner-centric approach always starts with the "P" mode – a real problem of pressing interest to the learner – as opposed to the "S" mode, which delivers up preordained content the wise and the good have determined you need to know. He illustrates his message with a range of compelling case studies. Heller reports on his initiative, Peoples-uni, aimed at developing professional competence at postgraduate level amongst health care practitioners. The need was to provide scalable and cost-effective education, and he looks at how this can be achieved by deploying open educational resources within a social enterprise business model. Terrell and Zoubir also look at continuing professional development (CPD), but this time with full-time working primary (elementary) and secondary (high school) level teachers and faculty managers. They too look towards the efficacy of self-managed learning and collaborative education. In the final chapter in this section Howarth calls for the university lecturer to become the hands-on craftsman who understands how metaphorical language and kinaesthetic teaching can be unleashed within an online learning environment.

8
Explorations in Self-Managed Online Learning

IAN CUNNINGHAM

Strategic Developments International Ltd., UK

Editors' Introduction

Cunningham draws on years of experience to demonstrate the effectiveness of self-directed learning strategies across a wide range of abilities and academic levels. He draws a valuable distinction between static and dynamic modes of learning and points out that both have a role in learner-centred approaches. He introduces us to four roles mapped to capabilities he considers to be critical for those engaged in the design of learning programmes, namely theory, design, manage and interact. He expands the interact role into two modes which he terms "P" and "S." His premise is that too much of our online learning starts in the "S" (teacher-centric) mode and that the effective self-directed learner generally starts in the "P" mode. The chapter concludes with some compelling case studies that show how these ideas can be and are applied in practice, offering some great insights for all who strive to create and support a more learner-centred approach at all levels of education.

Introduction

I had thought I might call this chapter "Explorations in the South East" – but that would have been, perhaps, too elliptical and mystifying. My thought about the title was influenced by the model from Coomey and Stephenson (2001) as shown in Figure 8.1.

Put simply, they postulate two dimensions in relation to learning – one about who decides the process (shown as the horizontal axis) and one about who decides the content and tasks (shown as the vertical ax-is). The juxtaposition is of teacher controlled versus learner controlled. There is more to their work than my simplified version here, but what I want to do is get into the practicalities of what it looks like to work in the South East quadrant. As the authors identified, most online learning has been in the North West quadrant. It is still

131

132 • Ian Cunningham

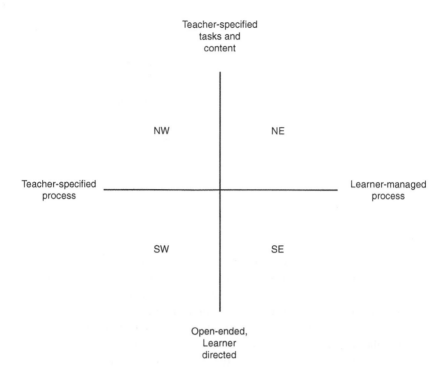

Figure 8.1 The online paradigm grid (Coomey & Stephenson, 2001)

about teachers (or others in authority) deciding both what to learn and how to learn it. Just changing the process from classroom-controlled learning to online instructor controlled misses the point about the potential shift when we think differently about the liberating potential of online learning and the use of technology.

In this chapter I will offer models that underpin practice, but my aim is mostly to show that working in the South East quadrant is perfectly feasible. I will do this by introducing some real examples of practice. Why we should work in this way is explored more fully in many other texts. The work my colleagues and I undertook in developing self-managed learning as a specific approach is covered in, for example, Cunningham (1999) and Cunningham, Bennett, and Dawes (2000). These texts provide both theoretical justifications for the approach as well as research evidence of practice in organisations.

In what follows I will go through examples of experiences along the journey I have taken in exploring a more self-managed approach to online learning. I have organised this chronologically to make some sense of how things have changed over time. In various cases I will show how the experience links to theory.

Explorations in Self-Managed Online Learning • 133

In summary the chapter follows the following path:

- A brief critique of other modes of e-learning and of the misuse of technology
- An outline of an early experience of computer conferencing
- The distinction between dynamic and static e-learning
- A practical example of an online master's degree using a self-managed mode
- A model identifying what is needed to create an effective e-learning programme – using the master's degree as an exemplar
- Self Managed Learning College as an example of e-learning practice with young people
- Digital Education Brighton as a collaborative project
- A brief conclusion

A Brief Critique of Other Modes of Online Learning and of the Misuse of Technology

Through to the mid-1980s I had been somewhat disillusioned with the use of technology to support learning. The translation of rigid teaching material from the teacher-controlled classroom into rigid material in machines – initially devices such as teaching machines and then computers – did not seem to herald much progress. Other technology uses such as film and overhead projectors were still teacher-led modes of instruction. They had their uses but were no breakthrough in learning methodology.

This strand of the use of technology has continued in the shape of Power-Point, highly standardised e-learning material and so on. When I am told that we all know this and that the world has moved on I am inclined to disagree. I am not "flogging a dead horse" – I am with Koestler (1964), who posited the notion of a society for the preservation of dead horses. Most e-learning and educational technology in general continues in the same vein as the past, and it is not flogging a dead horse to continue its critique.

We also need to address the continuing problem of teacher control of resources. For instance, I was told that when interactive whiteboards were created the idea was for a horizontal surface which learners could use for their learning – with a group gathered around the surface. What happened was that teachers made certain that the device was hung vertically behind them in a traditional classroom layout and that students accessed it via permission from the teacher. This way of thinking needs to change.

An Outline of an Early Experience of Computer Conferencing

In the mid-1980s I was keen to cooperate with other researchers in different parts of the UK. This was before the age of the Web and e-mail so we either had to meet up or write to each other or phone. There were no other choices available. The phone mode was very one-to-one, and meeting up was difficult, time-consuming and costly. Sending written work to each other was time-consuming and did not allow for interaction.

One of the group, David O'Connell (O'Connell, 1994), introduced the rest of us to computer conferencing. We did this via JANET (the Joint Academic Network that linked various UK universities via a server in Lancaster University). Given that this was before the Web, the software was somewhat clunky, but the fact that we could share ideas and collaborate via the computer was an eye-opener. We were able to manage our own learning. We were in control via a process that allowed us to do what we wanted with it.

This facility is now commonplace via the Web, but at the time it showed possibilities for empowered learning that was not controlled by the teacher or by a curriculum. The distinction in learning modes that I want to draw is between the following:

- Dynamic modes

    and

- Static modes

Computer conferencing is an example of a dynamic mode. It allows for interaction and flow that goes where the users want to take it. Learning is more social and more open, and it is managed by the learners. Static modes are characterised by the provision of unalterable material or material controlled by another (for example, a teacher). Such material may also be sequenced in a way that cannot be altered, as in many e-learning programmes. Indeed, a textbook you can dip into and flick through can be less static than sequenced e-learning materials that control the way you have to progress through the material.

Rose Luckin's (2010) book entitled *Re-Designing Learning Contexts – Technology-Rich, Learner-Centred Ecologies* is one I will return to later, as her stance is linked to a relevant case study she researched. Here I will quote from her introduction (Luckin, 2010, p. 3):

> I worked alongside Lydia Plowman who drew my attention to the concept of "Lines of Desire", a term borrowed from architecture and planning that refers to the routes that people take through open or semi-open spaces, in preference to those marked out as paths by planners . . . I found this concept offered an appealing metaphor as I considered how learners might be able to look around them and find out enough information about people, buildings, books, pens, technologies and other artefacts within their landscape to chart a learning trajectory that would meet their needs.

In this context the opportunity for learners to use static modes for their own learning trajectories makes sense. Another way of putting this is to say that if learners are in charge of their learning strategy, the fact that they use static tactics to support this does not run counter to a self-managed mode. In our research group working at a distance, the computer conferencing strategy (dynamic) did not preclude the use of static tactics such as reading existing literature. The key was the overall strategic approach that made a big difference in how we could work together and share our ongoing research work. And the ongoing research each of us was conducting was enhanced by the strategic learning collaboration.

A Practical Example of an Online Master's Degree Using a Self-Managed Mode

The story now leaps to the mid-1990s when the Internet became much more available. I was involved in the early days of an MA in organisation design and effectiveness at what was then the Fielding Institute in Santa Barbara, California. Part of the basis of the degree was for participants to learn to do the following:

- Work internationally (they were largely senior people in international companies)
- Use the technology

The way participants would learn both these would not be through overt teaching but through the process of the programme.

This is an example of using the power of the process curriculum – the actual way of learning – as opposed to the content curriculum of traditional education. In the traditional classroom it gave rise to the notion of the "hidden curriculum." Writers identified that the hidden curriculum either encouraged dependency on the teacher or counter-dependent rebellion. The process of a teacher-controlled learning environment has these effects on many learners, which undermines the ability of young people to grow up as fully autonomous human beings.

The notion of a hidden curriculum was originally articulated by Jackson (1968) and then explicitly developed by writers such as Snyder (1970) who saw the socialisation of the classroom as reducing autonomous action and having longer-term negative effects. Vallance (1983) makes the case for considering the strong role of the hidden curriculum in her statement that it includes "the inculcation of values, political socialization, training in obedience and docility, the perpetuation of traditional class structure-functions that may be characterized generally as social control" (pp. 136–137).

These, and many other writers, only saw the process of learning in educational institutions as a negative factor. However, I have suggested that we can take a positive position on how, for instance, the teacher/professor works with learners and how the design of programmes can actually assist learner autonomy. If we want to develop autonomous learners then the process needs to match the aim – means and ends need to be harmonised.

In the MA programme the idea was to use the process curriculum to good effect. The process was made overt and did not therefore constitute a hidden curriculum. We were designing and implementing a process to liberate learners from the constraints of classroom learning.

We, the faculty, made it abundantly clear that we were encouraging cross-cultural learning and learning about technology as part of the process curriculum. We judged that these abilities would become crucial in an increasingly globalised world. This judgement was made on the basis of the trends occurring in the global economy and the way technology was becoming more central to people's lives. The judgements we made at the time have been justified by developments since. For instance, at the time many managers in organisations did not have their own e-mail addresses – something unthinkable now. Similarly, the work of researchers such as Hofstede (2001) and Trompenaars and Hampden-Turner (1997) has spawned a massive literature in cross-cultural working.

In order to implement the process curriculum, participants were recruited from around the world and were linked via the Internet using what is now defunct software – Alta Vista Forum. The participants met face-to-face for three days at the start of the programme to learn about each other and to learn how to use the software. Remember, this was in the early days of the Internet, and it was strange and new for many of the participants. After the opening induction they did not meet – all communication was via the Forum software. This was also true of the international faculty – I worked from my home office in Brighton, England, and others worked from where they were.

I had a number of groups to work with on a course on leadership. Students in each group (of around six students) had to log on at least twice a week – so that at the very least you knew they were still alive and well even if they did little. All communication was asynchronous and had to be via the Forum – no phone calls, no chat. Given the objective of cross-cultural learning via e-learning I made one rule for passing the course and that was that people should log on regularly (twice a week); if they did this they would pass. The grade would be a separate issue.

Other faculty members used the online environment to create a content curriculum that participants went through over the period the course ran. I worked differently. At the start I sent out a piece about the nature of knowledge, identifying three distinct modes based on the use of personal pronouns.

- First-person knowledge: This is what I know – what the individual knows.
- Second-person knowledge: This is what you know – it could be an individual or a group (i.e., it could be singular or plural).

- Third-person knowledge: This is the world of the textbook and the disconnected knowledge domain. What do they know? What does he know? What does she know? It is also "it" oriented – detached and often labelled as being "objective."

The formulation of this typology started with my PhD research (Cunningham, 1984) and is something I have developed and tested extensively since.

I offered a reading list to cover third-person knowledge and suggested that part of the process of the course would be how they could integrate these three knowledge domains. They each came with individual experiences of leadership – the first-person area. They could explore the second-person area via the Forum – and they could use the Forum to work on an integrative model. This integration of knowledge was carried out by each person so there was not one model. Rather, the interaction in the forum provided a basis for each person to test the way he or she was bringing together the different knowledge domains.

Traditional university education in this area has been based on the faculty presenting the abstract models of theorists and then expecting learners to absorb and implement these. However, where the learner has his or her own model, one not in keeping with the professor's, the personal one tends to be the one implemented by the learner rather than the one that was taught in the lecture hall. Argyris (1976) has researched and written extensively on this problem in relation to organisations and specifically how leadership learning can be ineffective because leaders may have an "espoused theory" that does not match their "theory in use."

Prior to going online I had, in the face-to-face meeting, introduced them to the self-managed learning methodology – and two specific features of it. First there was the use of a learning group where individuals could work together to support each other's learning. Second was the use of a learning contract whereby the individuals negotiated their own learning goals with their group and agreed, with the group, what they would do to carry them out.

When it came to the online work I was then able to ask students to start by negotiating with the group via the Forum what they wanted to learn and how that would be assessed. This had to be in the area of leadership but could otherwise be anything they wanted. Some senior managers worked on their own leadership and used theory and research to explore how they could understand how they led. Some used 360 degree feedback as a good example of taking criteria from theory (third-person knowledge) and then providing their perspective on themselves (first person) and the perspectives of others at work (second person). They shared this online, getting other second- and third-person perspectives. It also created interesting cross-cultural dimensions as groups had participants from the US, Australia, Japan, Europe and Africa. And all this was done online through regular posts in the Forum group.

One example of the cross-cultural dimension was the challenge to the US-centric participants who often started with an assumption of the universal value of theories developed through purely US research. A trainer working with African managers was articulate about the demands of the African context, and even there he identified cultural differences as he was asked to run workshops in a variety of countries.

The dynamic Forum software gave participants the chance to discuss their own work and develop a rigour in their thinking through the interactions with others. Their learning was also much more coherent and integrated than if there had been an imposed curriculum that provided purely detached (third-person) knowledge. For participants, their original personal theories were developed and made more sophisticated through the integration of the three knowledge modes.

One participant was involved in a choir and decided to draft a book on how to lead a choir (she had not found a book on this subject in her searches). Although others in the group had no experience of singing in a formal choir they were able to engage with her on what she was writing. This generated much mutual learning; others had to ponder on the applicability of many supposedly universal leadership theories by considering and commenting on her work.

A Model Identifying What Is Needed to Create an Effective Online Learning Programme – Using the Master's Degree as an Exemplar

The MA programme exemplifies what I have discovered in other developmental programmes. I will apply the following model to online learning using this example. The model comes from extensive research, summarised in Cunningham (1999). The initial basis for the model was from my PhD research (Cunningham, 1984), and the model was then tested in the ensuing years. The evidence from this research is that there are four basic roles that development professionals need to carry out – see Figure 8.2. Ideally a person should be highly capable in all the domains indicated, but often a professional team can be created that combines different capabilities so that all angles are covered.

The Four Roles in More Detail

Theory Effective practitioners are able to articulate the theory that is the basis of their professional activities. In the context of the MA we were clear about specific learning theories underpinning what we set out to do. Some have been indicated earlier, such as the role of a process curriculum. Our theory about the future nature of business also had an impact. In my course I was working from a theory of self-managed learning and why that should be the basis of the course.

- A factor in the theory area is the extent to which a professional person might create totally new theory (rare), modify existing theory, or articulate theoretical propositions and models. At the very least we would expect an articulation of theory as a way of being open with

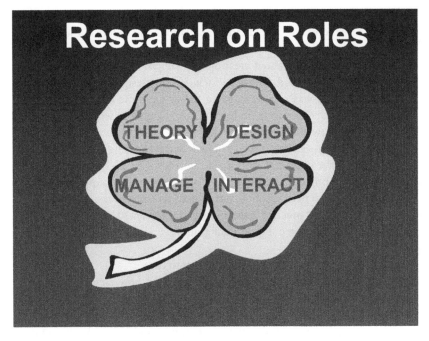

Figure 8.2 Four key roles in online learning development

colleagues and learners. In teams the discussion and clarification of theory is an important factor that can be omitted as people in the team may just assume others have the same theoretical basis as themselves.
- In the aforementioned I have not indicated how theory arrives and the interplay of theory and practice. Clearly professionals may modify theoretical assumptions as they experience new information from practice, and the three-factor typology of knowledge arenas (outlined earlier) has a role to play here.

Design There are two parts to designing:
- Macro designing is about having the strategic capability to design total processes. The requirements here are to think strategically and to implement theory in practical ways. In the MA there was a clear basis to the macro design of how to use the Internet and the associated software. We had to consider the whole programme and the interplay of the various factors in the design. This included the decision to have a three-day start-up event followed by solely asynchronous online contact. The choice of Alta Vista was similarly part of the macro design. The decision to use international faculty was an important design choice along with the way the faculty would work together. As

with all design decisions there are constraints to be accommodated. In this case there were accreditation regulations and California state laws to be followed.
- Micro designing is about creating specific processes such as the way the Forum was used. This also included the design of the three-day start-up as it was crucial to begin the programme in the right way. Aspects of the process were the ways the logging in would be organised and how participants would access material to assist in their learning. Constraints in this area included resourcing factors (annual budgets have to be met) and, again, state laws. In the latter case I was not able to implement my preferred option for each group to work out the grade each person should have, based on consensus decision making. My normal practice to do this was circumvented by California law that prohibited the publication of grades.

Manage Here again the role can be divided into two:
- Leading the programme was important, and how faculty provided this leadership function was vital. This also linked to aspects such as marketing and recruitment – the need to get an international mix was considered to be critical as the programme could not work without it. The capabilities required in the team were at one level similar to any other team. However, the dimension of the academic environment added a layer of complexity. An example was the division in roles between academics and administrators.
- Administering a programme is also crucial. Budgets have to be managed, systems created and managed, e-mails answered and so on. The librarian was crucial in signposting material via the online environment. Also those with the role of administrator for the groups had to be prepared at all times to make it work. Efficient administration of the online environment was crucial as we were working with busy senior managers as participants. The occasional crashes were a problem, when mutual contact was impossible. When the system was working it was essential for each faculty member to be highly organised in responding to what people posted.

Interact Interacting with learners is often the most visible part of developmental activity. I will comment more in the following as this dimension raises some specific issues for educational professionals.

Note that the four leaves, or segments, interact and overlap. Also they need to be brought together in a harmonious whole. It's no use getting three out of the four right – all four have to work together. All are necessary and sufficient to make an online learning programme work.

The Interactive Role of Online Learning

Ideally learning needs to start with what I have called the "P" mode, where "P" stands for the following:

- PERSONS – We need to understand the person if we are to assist their learning. Each person is different and have different needs.
- PATTERNS – Each person will have patterns of behaviour and of thinking.
- PROCESSES – Each person has their own processes of working and living.
- PROBLEMS – One way of thinking of learning is as a solution to a problem. For example if you can't speak French and you need to then you have a problem, and the solution is to learn French. Or if you need to write well to progress in life and work then the solution is to learn to write well. And so on.

Note that in the latter example, problems come before solutions. In our approach, the "P" mode comes before the "S" mode.

The "S" mode stands for the following:

- SOLUTIONS – To respond to a person and their problems there may be a need to look for solutions.
- SUBJECTS – Subject knowledge may help to meet the "P" needs.
- SKILLS – Skills may be needed to progress.
- SPECIALISATIONS – These may contribute.
- SYSTEMS – Systems, such as IT systems, may also have an impact.

Online learning too often starts with "S" – people have imposed on them Subject knowledge and Solutions to Problems they have not yet formulated. Or the Solution distorts the way the Problem is tackled. In the MA it was important to have the three-day induction event so I could understand the students with whom I was working. Then when we were online I was in the best place to offer help – whether through Subject knowledge, possible Solutions to the Problems they were dealing with, ideas about Skill development and so on.

In thinking of the role of staff, we find that we start in the "P" mode. Once learners are clearer about what they want to learn and how they want to learn it they may need to draw on expertise in the "S" mode. It is here that more static online learning comes to the fore. In the past teachers were seen as the main source of "S" learning. Now we have a vast array of material available on the Internet, and teachers have a different role. However, we find that learners often welcome support, especially where they can get help to avoid wasting time on irrelevant Web sites.

Self-Managed Learning College as an Example of Online Learning Practice With Young People

It is now time to come up to date and skip from the mid-1990s to the present day. Also here I want to shift the focus from adult learning to work with young people. The case I will mention is of Self Managed Learning College. The college works with 11- to 16-year-olds who have rejected or been rejected by school. Students decide the following for themselves:

- What they learn
- When they learn
- Where they learn
- How they learn
- Why they learn

The college is located in the centre of Brighton on the south coast of England and rents a floor of Brighton Youth Centre. Students attend Monday to Friday from 9 a.m. to 1 p.m. When they newly arrive they are helped to plan an overall strategy for learning (see www.college.selfmanagedlearning.org for more on this and other aspects of the programme not covered here). They are assisted in writing their own individual timetables at the start of each week, and they review their progress against their learning objectives at the end of each week.

The programme clearly fits in the SE corner of the Coomey and Stephenson (2001) model. Students choose the extent that they use computers, smartphones and other technology. Unlike local schools there are no controls on what students can access online – apart from a control on the use of chat rooms. There is a rule (agreed by students) that a maximum of 30 minutes per morning ought to be for computer games and Facebook. This is not followed strictly, but the students are challenged by their peers if they abuse computer or smartphone use.

We are able to demonstrate how we can integrate digital technology with other learning modes – and we make a self-managed learning mode work. We return here to the distinction between dynamic and static approaches. Dynamic approaches are where students create their own material via Facebook, self-created games, creative designs via Photoshop and so forth. Dynamic approaches are driven by the process rather than the content. Students create their own content.

Static approaches are where students access pre-created content such as the use of the Kahn Academy for learning mathematics. For students to use a static approach they will first determine what they want to learn and how best to do it. They are then in the position to get assistance from staff (if needed) to access an appropriate Web site or other resource. Hence the static approach is not used as a result of a prescribed curriculum (there is no content-based curriculum) but rather as part of a more dynamic learning process.

Some commentators might describe this approach as "blended learning" as it is not based solely on online learning. We would not use such terminology.

For one thing, much blended learning is generally about using e-learning with classroom learning – and is clearly teacher controlled. We have no classrooms. Students use a wide range of learning approaches that suit their needs. A better formulation is within Luckin (2010). She uses the term "ecology of resources." In the research Rose Luckin and Wilma Clarke (of the Institute of Education, University of London) conducted with our students they initially worked to identify the range of learning modes available to students and then studied how these were used. The case explored in Luckin (2010) is of a trip to the Royal Observatory at Greenwich. The researchers showed how a range of learning modes could be integrated based on the "ecology of resources" model – explored more fully in Luckin's book.

Mentioning trips is a good example of how students would use the online environment. In the college we meet every morning at 9 a.m. to sort out any issues and to plan ahead. Students might come up with the idea of a visit, say to a museum or art gallery. Those students who are most keen on the trip take on the task of organising it. The first stage tends to be doing an online search to assess the feasibility of a trip. After that the Web site of a selected museum would be searched to find the best time to go, how to maximise the time at the museum and so on. Note that this is all student driven and that they learn a whole range of skills in doing this planning – not just effective searching (they are usually already good at this) but how to cost, how to get agreement in the learning community about what to do, how to schedule, how to organise transport and so forth.

While in this example students would typically use a laptop, increasingly much learning is via smartphone. Ofcom (2012) report that, in the UK, 4 in 10 smartphone users say their phone is more important than any other device for accessing the Internet. As the Ofcom report shows, smartphones are essentially handheld computers that just happen to be able to make voice calls. This is what we observe. Unlike most local schools, which ban the use of smartphones in the classroom, we encourage students to use them.

> Clive is a fifteen year old who is keen to run his own business at some time in the future. He is using various modes to further his possible career including formal learning about business. Another student, David, had identified an app on his phone that allows you to pretend to have £25,000 to invest in the stock market. You can then make pretend investments and see, in real time, how they are doing on the stock market. Having shared this with Clive, the two of them started a competition to see how well their investments were working out using this app. I challenged Clive as to how much he knew about the companies in which he was investing. As I suspected he was largely guessing. I then showed him that he could do more effective online searches about companies including going onto the Companies House site and downloading company reports. This led him

into having to be more knowledgeable about how to analyse company accounts (an area he had started to cover in his formal learning).

Margaret Mead was once challenged about her support for more child-friendly modes. Her adult critics commented along the lines of, "We were young once so we know what children need." Reputedly, her response was, "Yes you were young once but you have never been young in the world that young people now are young in." This response is even more relevant today. While there is controversy as to the extent that children's brains are being rewired due to technology there is no doubt that the availability of advanced technology and of the Internet creates a whole new world for young people. Our students have grown up in this world, and learning modes need to respond to it.

Through collaboration with the University of Sussex two groups of master's degree students in the Informatics Department have worked with two of our 11-year-olds. Each of the 11-year-olds has come up with an idea of something they would like to develop, and they have been prepared to learn computer programming in order to achieve what they want to do. For instance, an 11-year-old boy is interested in aircraft and has already developed his knowledge and skills in this area. He had used a simulator and wanted to develop something along those lines. One of the master's degree groups worked with him to understand what he wanted and then went away to produce material so that he could program a game featuring aircraft. This is an example of how our students can drive the learning process.

The existence of the online environment is now part of everyday life. Whether schools and universities like it or not, young people are increasingly managing their own learning via the Internet. Unfortunately the tendency in educational institutions is to try to continue with control mechanisms they are used to. For example, no local schools where I live allow access to YouTube, yet our students use it all the time – to learn guitar chords or how to tune the drum kit. One student (a good singer) has recorded numerous songs that are out on YouTube and has gained great feedback. Her confidence has grown enormously in being able to access a worldwide audience for her music. In school she would not be allowed to do this.

Of course there are undesirable materials out there on the Internet. By keeping our college small and working as a community to monitor usage we generally have no problems. Many young people with computers in their own bedrooms can, in any case, access quite appalling material without their parents' or teachers' knowing. The main issue for adults to face is that the Internet exists, it has its downsides, but it is here to stay. We have to help young people learn how to use it sensibly, not try to keep it under control, because the controls will not work anyway.

Our approach has been to operate as a learning community which we keep small and where the community as a whole polices any rule breaking. The community meets every morning to address any issues that may have arisen. The only time we had an issue with computer use was three years ago when a new student went on a dubious chat site. After that incident the community agreed to block chat sites. This incident is the only one we have had in 12 years, so we know that creating a trusting environment with simple rules and collective policing works. However, I have seen students in a local school accessing appallingly violent images, even though the school has ferocious controls that block many sites.

A development, which we have responded to, is BYOD (bring your own device) (Dunnett, 2012). This is growing in the business world. In our context it means that students bring in their own laptops (smartphones have been mentioned already). Clearly we have to trust that parents will put in any controls they want. So far we have had no problems, and students are able to work on and take away work on their own kit – to their advantage.

Digital Education Brighton as a Collaborative Project

Digital Education Brighton is another example of a current development. It was set up in the summer of 2011 to bring together local digital companies and schools and others (such as ourselves) involved in education. The group works on the basis of real projects delivered via self-selected project groups. An example of a project is one that came about through contact with a group from the Cherokee Nation in North America. Their young people wanted to interact online with school students in Brighton. This was set up involving history and geography teachers in schools. The interactive mode has allowed for mutual learning between young people in the Cherokee Nation and Brighton young people. Note that it is not being run in school IT/computing departments but rather through teachers in relevant subject areas and allows for live learning.

A formal launch of the project occurred on 19 September 2012 in Brighton, although work between the two Cherokee schools and the two Brighton schools had already started. More is on the Digital Education Brighton site (at digital-educationbrighton.org.uk/?p = 276). However, here is the flavour of one person's response to the launch.

> Just to give you a quick update on last night's launch event. I thought it was great. There were about 60 school students from Blatchington Mill and Cardinal Newman [the Brighton schools] creating a visual and verbal mash up of Cherokee culture and their own. I loved the audio mix of Cherokee Nation lullabies and the Brighton kids talking (quite prosaically) about what they would take to the afterlife ("I'd Take One Direction" was my favourite). The school students creating the cleansing

flames of the afterlife through dance and that then being superimposed on Cherokee iconography was also really cool.

It was also great to hear the heads of the two schools talking afterwards to us all about how excited they were to be part of the project. And the welcome video from Cherokee people and teachers was also strangely moving. As one of the Cherokee schools described it, a digital pow-wow.

A Brief Conclusion

What I have wanted to do is to show examples of how a real learner-centred approach can work. I have tried to show that there can be a different way of thinking. The chapter contains well-researched models that can inform practice as well as examples of practical applications. None of this is complex – it just requires the mind-set to go with the approach.

I suggested an important distinction between dynamic and static approaches to online learning. Later in the chapter I showed how we need to have a basis in the dynamic so that static modes can be used effectively. I showed how a master's degree can work using self-managed learning as a basic methodology, and I used the experience of this programme to flesh out a model for professional practice. I outlined how a programme for young people can utilise an integrated self-managing approach to the application of the opportunities inherent in online learning. The final example was of a cross-cultural project involving young school students in England and in the Cherokee nation.

My aim in providing a variety of examples linked to some general models is to show that the theoretical and empirical basis of the models makes application viable and practical. I have produced what I label process models which are content free. The use of process models allows practitioners to insert their own factors and variables into the models. For instance, the four roles model of professional practice was exemplified in this chapter by reference to experience in the MA programme. However, in creating any online learning experience the factors involved in that can be inserted into the model, and it can be used, for instance, to assess the capabilities in a development team. Are all aspects covered within the team? And are there coherence and integration of the factors? For instance, if the programme is based on a particular theoretical framework, is the design consonant with that? And will the interactions with learners exemplify the application of the theory?

References

Argyris, C. (1976). *Increasing leadership effectiveness*. New York: Wiley-Interscience.
Coomey, M., & Stephenson, J. (2001). It's all about dialogue, involvement, support and control. In J. Stephenson (ed.), *Teaching and learning online*. London: Kogan Page.
Cunningham, I. (1984). Teaching styles in learner-centred management development. PhD thesis, Lancaster University.
Cunningham, I. (1999). *The wisdom of strategic learning* (2nd ed.). Aldershot, Hants: Gower.

Cunningham, I., Bennett, B., & Dawes, G. (eds.) (2000). *Self managed learning in action*. Aldershot, Hants: Gower.
Dunnett, R. (2012, May). Bring your own device. *The Director*, 55–59.
Hofstede, G. (2001). *Culture's consequences: comparing values, behaviours, institutions and organizations across nations* (2nd ed.). Thousand Oaks, CA: Sage Publications.
Jackson, P. W. (1968). *Life in classrooms*. New York: Holt, Rinehart and Winston.
Koestler, A. (1964). *The act of creation*. London: Hutchinson.
Luckin, R. (2010). *Re-designing learning contexts – technology-rich, learner-centred ecologies*. London: Routledge.
O'Connell, D. (1994). *Implementing computer supported cooperative learning*. London: Kogan Page.
Ofcom (2012). *The communications market report*. London: Ofcom.
Snyder, B. R. (1970). *The hidden curriculum*. New York: Alfred A. Knopf.
Trompenaars, F., & Hampden-Turner, C. (1997). *Riding the waves of culture: understanding diversity in global business*. New York: McGraw-Hill.
Vallance, E. (1983). Hiding the hidden curriculum: an interpretation of the language of justification in nineteenth-century educational reform. In H. Giroux & D. Purpel (eds.), *The hidden curriculum and moral education*. Berkeley, CA: McCutcheon.

9
People's Open Access Education Initiative: Peoples-uni

RICHARD F. HELLER

Peoples-uni

Editors' Introduction

In this chapter Heller looks at the potential contribution of online learning to the continuing professional development of health care professionals in emerging economies. The solution described offers postgraduate-level, accredited education delivered in a scalable and cost-effective manner by employing open educational resources linked to a social enterprise model and volunteer practitioner tutors. Despite adopting a design that places a strong emphasis on learner control and collaborative knowledge creation, experience has shown that many students at this level expect to be taught, want to hear expert advice rather than that of their peers and value a direct relationship with a trusted mentor. The need for recognised accreditation also created conflict with the quality assurance processes common in the traditional awarding bodies for higher education. Despite these challenges the programme is making a difference on the ground, and Heller rounds out the chapter with a discussion of potential future developments to increase the breadth of collaboration and knowledge creation.

The Idea

The idea is to utilise open educational resources (Atkins & Seely Brown, 2007), an open source e-learning platform and a volunteer workforce to provide low-cost but high-quality education to assist with public health capacity building in developing countries. This builds on my personal experience in two universities – first a paper-based distance learning programme established in 1991 which morphed to include some e-learning (Treloar, 1998), followed by a fully online master's programme which started in 2002 (Heller, 2003; Gemmell, Sandars, Taylor, & Reed, 2011).

While traditional institutions have provided a means of achieving accredited learning, they are failing many people in developing countries for reasons including availability, scalability, access, available tutoring, cost, situation and so on. Online learning techniques represent a way to create a whole new infrastructure to support these incredibly important capacity-building needs. However, as we structure these new online learning mechanisms we will need to think whether the traditional university model will be able to cope in a low-cost open access setting. We probably need new ideas of what is possible, what can be accredited, and what represents an effective business model for delivery. The developments in open access resources on the Internet, including an educational e-learning delivery platform, provide the opportunity to explore a new way of education provision to those in developing countries wanting the skills to improve the health of their populations. Could a not-for-profit social enterprise (Wikipedia, 2012) be the business model to make this happen?

Why It Is Important to the Community

There are massive public health needs in developing countries; as identified by McMichael, Waters, & Volmink (2005), "The global burden of disease and illness is primarily situated in developing countries. As developing countries have limited resources, it is particularly important to invest in public health and health promotion strategies that are effective."

The demonstration of effectiveness requires evidence to be collected – so an evidence-based approach is required to identify and help solve the problems and improve the health of these populations. This approach requires human capacity building via education – which should be at a high enough level to cover the ability to take a critical approach to information. An important way of meeting the education needs is through higher degrees, aimed at "training the trainers" so that the knowledge and skills can be applied to improving the health of the population, as well as transmitting these skills to others. Higher degrees are in theory available either in the developing countries themselves or in developed countries. There is, however, insufficient local education capacity within developing countries, and the costs of higher degrees in developed countries are greater than can be met by most; if these degrees require the student to travel they also have the effect of depleting the in-country workforce. Preliminary situation analyses in five developing countries, conducted for Peoples-uni (Heller et al., 2007), revealed a lack of local resources in each of these countries to train public health professionals in adequate numbers.

A wide variety of health professionals may contribute to the public health workforce – ranging from medical practitioners in clinical or public health services, nurses and those with other health-related qualifications in similar situations and others such as those working for nongovernment organisations (NGOs) or various parts of local, regional, or national governments. Peoples-uni has decided to focus on "training the trainers" so that the education can snowball to others in need of skills development. Thus we have pitched the education at the master's level. Students will require a prior degree, or considerable professional experience, to be able to cope at this postgraduate-level work.

Examples of the work planned by two of those who have found themselves studying with Peoples-uni are given in the following. Jerome and John, both students of the Peoples-uni, have been planning their dissertations as part of their Master of Public Health programme. The background to their ideas gives a good indication of the problems facing communities such as theirs and how the skills they may gain from the education may help tackle the real community issues.

Two Stories

Jerome: "Nigeria is losing an estimated 54,000 women a year to maternal and childbirth-related causes. An additional 1.2–1.8 million women suffer short- and long-term disability that put their lives in danger during subsequent pregnancies. Improving access to health care on three levels – improving prenatal care, improving intranatal care and improving postnatal care – should help reduce this problem. Hitherto Nigeria has not been able to optimally operationalize these sorts of initiatives." He is proposing a study which would "contribute to the knowledge base of anti-maternal mortality programming and public policy with regards the public sector response."

John: "Zambia is one of the countries in the world most affected by the HIV/AIDS pandemic, with a measured adult prevalence of 14.3% and an estimated 82,681 new infections each year, translating into an average of 226 new HIV infections in the country every day. For every two people who initiate antiretroviral therapy, an estimated five more become newly infected with the virus. The Zambian Ministry of Health has therefore sought to incorporate effective, evidence-based prevention initiatives, including couples' voluntary counselling and testing (CVCT), male circumcision (MC) and increased uptake of the adolescent sexual reproductive health. My plans focus on carrying out programs that increase the uptake of sexual reproductive health services among the adolescents in five districts of Zambia. This project will be undertaken by an organisation called ZCCP under the auspice of the National Council. As a programme officer in charge of social and community mobilization, I'm directly linked to this project in terms of facilitation of design, implementation, and evaluation. The reason I like this plan is that it tends to target the adolescents, a group which has mainly been overlooked in many health interventions which have targeted the adults and children at the expense of the adolescents. Adolescents form the largest population of Zambia, and overlooking this group amounts to committing suicide, and deliberate steps need to be made to address the many sexual, health, social, and economical challenges faced by the adolescents."

It is by giving skills to people like Jerome and John, who work in developing countries, that Peoples-uni aims to help build the capacity to tackle important public health problems and improve the health of their communities.

Peoples-uni was conceptualised to offer a high level of education in public health for practitioners in developing countries at low cost. An Internet-based course, using open educational resources and delivery mechanisms and staffed by volunteers, had the potential to meet these needs. The same factors allowed the power of collaboration to be unleashed to develop and deliver an appropriate programme. Figure 9.1 is taken from the Peoples-uni Web site.

How This Approach Builds on or Advances Our Current Understanding

This approach has the potential to reach new, nontraditional audiences. The development of the Internet has facilitated an explosion of access to information and in the education sector has followed through the development of open educational resources where educational resources are posted on the Internet

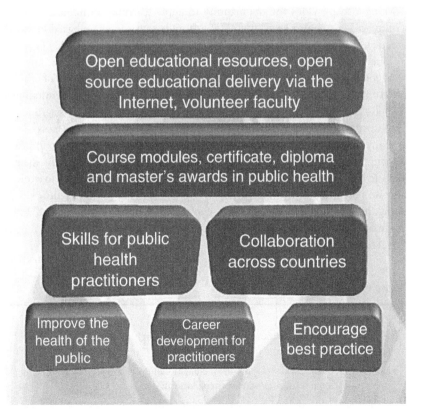

Figure 9.1 Conceptual diagram for Peoples-uni from http://peoples-uni.org

under a licence which allows others to use them in their own teaching. While information about public health issues is readily available through the Internet (in fact the resources used in the Peoples-uni educational programme are mostly open source – hence freely available), there is no way for people to gain educational credit recognised by potential employers from accessing and learning from these sources. While online learning platforms and open educational resources exist, the usual way for these to be offered to the intended target student audience (in our case, health professionals in developing countries) in an educational context is through a traditional university. As we have discussed, capacity is limited within developing countries, and those outside these countries are more expensive (in money and time) than can be afforded.

Peoples-uni was established to offer a solution – provide an educational context for educational materials available through the Internet – and to do this outside the traditional university setting, at a cost seen as affordable.

Learning at a distance allows those who cannot travel to access educational opportunities – opening this to women, those with disabilities and those whose work or family responsibilities do not allow travel. The ability to study while working also provides the opportunity to apply learning immediately in the workplace – as is also seen in emerging trends towards work-based learning practice such as at Middlesex University (Middlesex University, 2012).

Due to the size of the health problems facing developing nations, and the need for capacity to help tackle them, we need to explore methods of scaling up to enrol large numbers of students. There are some educational limitations, such as the need to facilitate online discussions and set and mark assignments. The use of the Internet allows for scalability since the materials are accessible by as many people as wish to do so – for the discussions all we need is to increase the number of groups and find more online facilitators. The assignments are likely to be the major stumbling block to scaling up – and we do need to explore how we can automate the assignment process, keeping in mind the difficulty of doing this at the master's level. As we explore these options, we will have to be pragmatic about how to assess its success – in the absence of setting this up as a trial or educational experiment.

Table 9.1 The problem and solution

Peoples-uni

The problem: Lack of educational offerings at low enough cost/accessible without need to leave employment

Facilitating factors: New developments in educational provision – e-learning using open educational resources/open source platform

Our solution: Use new developments to provide credentials using volunteers in an e-learning social enterprise model

Adopting a Nonacademic Approach to Development

Practitioner input to both the content of education and the delivery is very important to make sure the education is fit for the purpose of meeting real needs. We have had input to the development of Peoples-uni from practitioners in the form of professional bodies, and, more importantly, a large proportion of the tutors are practitioners themselves.

While there are key academic issues of methodology to learn about at the master's level, the application of knowledge to practice is critical – there is no point understanding theory if it cannot be applied. Our decision to use practitioners who do not usually work in academic settings as teachers not only gives them the opportunity to pass on their knowledge, but also ensures that the practical application of knowledge will be included in the course and emphasised in the teaching.

Adopting a Social Enterprise Model

The main rationale for the creation of Peoples-uni was to make public health education available to those who cannot access it through other sources. Keeping costs low enough to be afforded by the target audience in developing countries is key to this. While the use of open source delivery methods (the Moodle educational platform), open educational resources and, most importantly, a volunteer workforce are all part of the low-cost approach; there are some infrastructure costs to cover. A secure IT server and support are vital to an online course, and this does involve cost. A secure administrative infrastructure, beyond that which can be covered by volunteers, is also important. For these reasons, we have a need to generate some limited funds. Seeking grants and donations is not a fully sustainable method for long-term existence. There is a literature about the suitability of the social enterprise business model in education, where social outcomes rather than profit are the goal (Scofield, 2011).

The social enterprise model has provided a basis for us to generate funds. Initially, we have charged a low fee (£30 per module) to all students who can afford it (with a bursary scheme for those who cannot). As a main plank of our efforts to be able to offer a credible academic award to our students to allow them to develop their careers (in addition to improving the health of their population), we negotiated a partnership arrangement with Manchester Metropolitan University in the UK. This allows students to enrol in a Master of Public Health programme and gain a highly credible degree. We ask students for an extra fee for this enrolment, which is a little beyond the charge made to us for the student enrolment and quality assurance offered by the university. Again we have a bursary scheme for those who cannot afford the fee. This extra charge allows us to fund some infrastructure. Our current goal (as of 2012) is to identify short-term funding for an executive officer whose goal would be to identify further ways of generating funds through the social enterprise approach so that we can become fully self-sustaining into the future.

Peoples-uni breaks new ground, both in the way this type of education can be provided and in the way of supporting it through a social enterprise model (Heller, 2009).

Ways to Enhance the Learning Process

The educational context we have developed comprises a standard format by which each module (unit) contains five topics, each run over two weeks. Each module starts by listing the competences and learning outcomes to be gained; these were developed though a literature search (Reynolds & Heller, 2008). Each topic contains a set of resources, with hyperlinks to the resource itself and metadata to help the student navigate these resources (we provide .pdf versions in .zip files for those with poor Internet connectivity, see Figure 9.2). In addition, there is a discussion forum in each topic, a self-test quiz and one or two assignments for credit in the module as a whole.

In developing our programme, we took great heed of the work of Salmon (2000) and others. However, there is a notion that moderating e-learning (or online facilitation) has slipped after a number of semesters: "in e-moderating there is very little teaching in the conventional sense of instruction or 'telling'. Online learning offers the participants opportunities to explore information rather than accept what the teacher determines

---

2   **Topic 2**

(April 10th to April 22nd)

Title. Values, Principles and Determinants of Health
Headline Competence (Learning Outcome): Develop a systematic understanding of the values and principles underlying the way in which health promotion might influence the determinants of health.
Assessment criteria:
Evaluate the key health promotion values of empowerment, social justice, inclusion and respect.
Develop an understanding of the way in which the determinants of health may be influenced positively by health promotion.

- Resources Topic 2: Values, principles and determinants
- Discussion forum Topic 2: Values, principles and determinants
- ZipFile Resources health promotion for Topic 2

Figure 9.2 Example of what the student sees when going to one of five topics in a module (taken from the Health Promotion module)

should be learnt" (Salmon, 2000). Consistent feedback from students indicates that expert feedback from the online facilitators who respond to individual student posts in discussion forums is greatly appreciated by students. This may reflect cultural differences among our students who are from developing countries.

Higher-level skills required for master's-level learning, such as critical thinking, synthesis and evaluation, are also assessed through the posts to discussion forums, and feedback is given to the students about these issues as a formative assessment by education coordinators (who do not act as facilitators of the discussion, but rather provide feedback as to whether the student has reflected on the resources presented in the module rather than just offering an opinion). The discussion forum has thus developed a different role from that envisaged by Salmon. While the sharing of experiences between students and responses to each other are encouraged, there is more direct expert "teaching" and use of the forum as a formative assessment with feedback. To what extent this reflects our particular situation or the cultural environment in which our developing-country students work is unclear, but by evolution we have deviated from standard educational practice.

Resources

The resources used are also not those that might have been expected by the creators of the OER movement. Most of the resources have not been created by educational institutions, but rather are journal articles, documents prepared by NGOs and other open access sources. Using materials directly created for educational purposes may actually reduce their ability to be used in a variety of settings where the context, software requirements and level of education may all differ. The model developed by Peoples-uni, where we work on the context and search for and use a wide variety of open source materials – a focus on the context rather than the materials themselves – may be worth considering by others in the OER movement.

Discussions

Although we are focused on individual learning, each part of the course includes a discussion forum facilitated by an expert tutor (an example of the introduction is seen in Figure 9.3). The group discussion process encourages students to compare their experiences with each other and share solutions. As part of the educational process, we provide feedback on whether the students have responded to others in their discussion postings. As time goes on, we are planning ways to explore the benefits of collaboration within the student body both for the learning process itself and also to help meet the population health needs of the students' populations after graduation – some of this is discussed in the following in relation to continuing professional development.

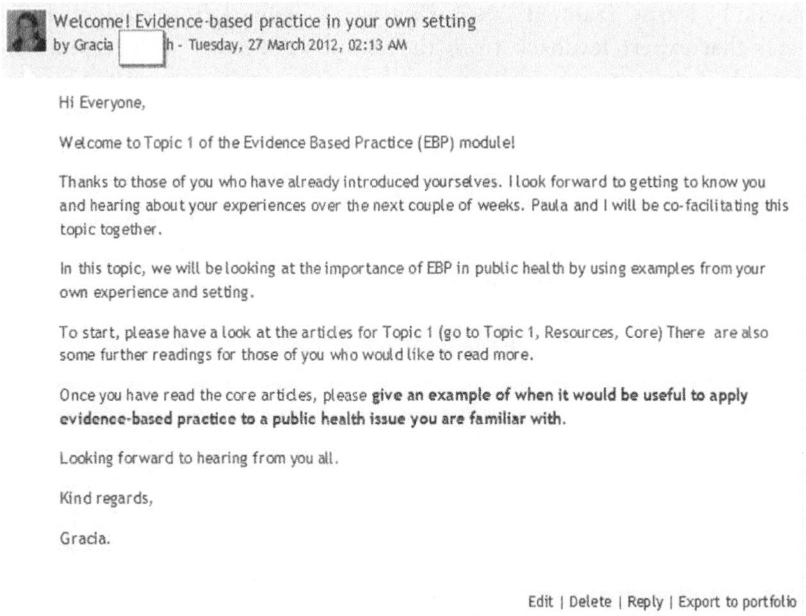

> **Welcome! Evidence-based practice in your own setting**
> by Gracia   h - Tuesday, 27 March 2012, 02:13 AM
>
> Hi Everyone,
>
> Welcome to Topic 1 of the Evidence Based Practice (EBP) module!
>
> Thanks to those of you who have already introduced yourselves. I look forward to getting to know you and hearing about your experiences over the next couple of weeks. Paula and I will be co-facilitating this topic together.
>
> In this topic, we will be looking at the importance of EBP in public health by using examples from your own experience and setting.
>
> To start, please have a look at the articles for Topic 1 (go to Topic 1, Resources, Core) There are also some further readings for those of you who would like to read more.
>
> Once you have read the core articles, please **give an example of when it would be useful to apply evidence-based practice to a public health issue you are familiar with.**
>
> Looking forward to hearing from you all.
>
> Kind regards,
>
> Gracia.
>
> Edit | Delete | Reply | Export to portfolio

Figure 9.3 Example of the tutor's introduction to the discussion forum in one topic in a module (taken from the Evidence Based Practice module)

Factors That Predict Success

Philip and Lee explored the dataset in two separate semesters and found that the main predictor of success, defined as passing the final assignment in the module, to be engagement with the programme (Philip & Lee, 2011). Engagement included contributing to the discussion forums, as well as having uploaded details to a personal profile. A pass in a previous module was also a predictor of success; however, there were no personal characteristics that predicted a pass (including highest level of previous education). At this early stage of our development, it is too early to identify predictors of outcomes such as graduation and our main goal of career development and use of the skills to improve the health of populations.

Student Perceptions

Student feedback has been important in the modification of the programme. Feedback has been generally positive; however, we have learned a number of lessons leading to changes in the programme. The most important was that academic credit is strongly desired – of 48 students polled in the early days of the programme, 39 wished to receive academic credit rather than continuing professional development credits (Philip & Awofeso, in press). This has led us to develop a partnership with Manchester Metropolitan University so that students can gain an accredited award from a highly credible university on the basis of their study with us. The quality assurance (QA) requirements of the university have meant that we have had to tailor our course in a more structured way than originally proposed. We did plan a much more fluid process as identified by Keats and Schmidt (2007) who said: "Education 1.0 is mainly a one-way process; Education 2.0 uses the technologies of Web 2.0 to create more interactive education but largely within the constraints of Education 1.0. Education 2.0 is laying the groundwork for Education 3.0, which we believe will see a breakdown of most of the boundaries, imposed or otherwise within education, to create a much freer and open system focused on learning." However, the feedback from students and tutors, as well as the requirements of meeting university regulations, has sent us back towards a more traditional mode, even if we have been able to utilise many of the benefits of online learning. Whether others have had similar experiences or not will be of interest. As Table 9.2 attempts to demonstrate, the constraints of adapting to the quality assurance processes have reduced the flexibility for experimentation such as student-to-student and learner-generated content approaches.

Students also wanted more interaction with their tutors – as discussed earlier – and we have developed more structured instructions for online facilitation and a guide for facilitators.

Continuous Professional Development in the Field Post Graduation

The first group of students are now enrolled in the dissertation and will expect to complete the Master of Public Health soon. We see this as only the first part of our stated goal: "To contribute to improvements in the health of populations in low- to middle-income countries by building Public Health capacity via online learning." We are planning an active alumni association that may utilise the Mahara e-portfolio system with which we are experimenting and which includes a social networking facility. The goal of this will be to provide support to encourage putting into practice the skills learned during the course.

Table 9.2 Constraints of requirement for academic credit from traditional universities

		\multicolumn{2}{c}{*Academic credit from traditional university with stringent QA processes*}
		Rigid, process dominated	Flexible, outcome based
Flexibility to experiment with new educational approaches	Low flexibility	Current situation for Peoples-uni	
	High flexibility		Preferred option for Peoples-uni

This could develop into a kind of mentoring exercise, but we would prefer that the leadership come from the graduates, with support only from Peoples-uni. Having "escaped" the rigid requirements of a traditional educational institution, we will be free to experiment and unleash the power of collaboration.

We are considering two areas. The first is collaborative research or policy development between students and tutors. This is to attempt to unleash the power of collaboration based on the experience we have had as tutors and students communicating online in the educational programme. The relationships were forged online across cultures and geography, with the common goal of building capacity to improve population health, and thus should be able to continue once the formal education ceases. The dissertation requires students to plan a project, so developing collaborations afterwards to see these projects through and developing collaborations around them seems an obvious place to start. We have had previous experience with an educational programme leading to collaborative research amongst tutors and students and will build on that experience.

The second area is to cascade the education. One way will be to engage some of the graduates as tutors in our programme. We already have a few examples of students who have enrolled with us joining the educational tutor group (and vice versa!). We will also attempt to establish collaborations between Peoples-uni and the institutions in which our graduates work, so that not only can the skills be shared, but also the material used in Peoples-uni education.

Evidence From the Field

We have a number of publications and presentations to date about our experience (Peoples-uni, 2012), and information from some of them has been quoted in previous sections of this chapter. We have plenty of student applications (240 students from 40 countries are enrolled in semester one of 2012), with word of mouth being the most common way for new students to make contact. We have had our programme validated by a major UK university, and while this has necessitated a "regression to the mean" effect to meet the more traditional university QA requirements, it does provide considerable credibility for our educational processes and reassurance to our students.

The first of our modules was run in 2009, following a pilot in 2008. In 2011, we started our partnership with Manchester Metropolitan University, and the first students are only now (in 2012) enrolled in the dissertation and so will graduate at the end of 2012. It is too early in our evolution to explore real outcomes in terms of impact on the population or career development of our students. However, what we can say is that we have shown that such an educational initiative is feasible, sustainable in the short-term, appreciated by students and found to be of high quality by a credible higher education institution in the UK.

To Summarise

While this has been an innovative approach to solve the problem of a need for low-cost education for public health capacity building in developing countries, the methods would be highly applicable elsewhere. I would encourage those who might be tempted to develop in a similar way for a different specialty to do so. An educational programme targeted at real needs, the identification of the competences to meet these needs and the use of open educational resources and a volunteer workforce has led to a viable initiative, at least in the short-term. Long-term sustainability is a definite possibility.

If we reflect back on the examples quoted at the start of this chapter, we can identify various sets of skills students might obtain from this education: How to describe the size of a health problem in the population, understand its causes, and develop and evaluate interventions designed to improve care or prevent the onset of the health problem by the development of evidence-based health policies. Both maternal mortality and HIV are major problems in developing country populations, and creating the capacity to tackle them is of major potential importance.

It is perhaps fitting to finish with the thoughts of Olawumi, one of our students from Nigeria. He summarises his experience in this way:

> The modules and courses made available to me at the peoples university will go a long way in adding to my knowledge and improving my skills in the areas I would like to specialise in public health. I stand a chance of having a good grasp of what statistics and evidence-based practice entails. I would have a good understanding of the causative factors of maternal mortality and how it can be abated. The prevention of childhood morbidity and mortality would be within my grasps. It would be of great advantage to me and my community, this knowledge acquired, and to the nation as a whole.

References

Atkins, D. E., & Seely Brown, J. H. A. (2007). *A review of the open educational resources (OER) movement: achievements, challenges, and new opportunities.* Retrieved from http://hewlettprod.acesfconsulting.com/uploads/files/Hewlett_OER_report.pdf

Gemmell, I., Sandars, J., Taylor, S., & Reed, K. (2011). Teaching science and technology via online distance learning: the experience of teaching biostatistics in an online Master of Public Health programme. *Open Learning: The Journal of Open, Distance and e-Learning, 26*(2), 165–171. doi:10.1080/02680513.2011.567756

Heller, R. F. (2003). Developing an e-based postgraduate programme in public health and health promotion: Masters in Population Health Evidence, MPHe. *Health Education Journal, 62*(2), 153–155. doi:10.1177/001789690306200207

Heller R. F. (2009). Experience with a "social model" of capacity building: the Peoples-uni. *Human Resources for Health, 7*(43). doi:10.1186/1478-4491-7-43

Heller, R. F., Chongsuvivatwong, V., Hailegeorgios, S., Dada, J., Torun, P., Madhok, R., & Sandars, J. (2007). Capacity-building for public health: http://peoples-uni.org. *Bulletin of the World Health Organization, 85*(12), 930–934. Retrieved from http://www.pubmedcentral.nih.gov/articlerender.fcgi?artid = 2636296&tool = pmcentrez&rendertype = abstract

Keats, D., & Schmidt, J. (2007). The genesis and emergence of Education 3.0 in higher education and its potential for Africa. *First Monday, 12*(3). Retrieved from http://firstmonday.org/htbin/cgiwrap/bin/ojs/index.php/fm/article/view/1625/1540

McMichael, C., Waters, E., & Volmink, J. (2005). Evidence-based public health: what does it offer developing countries? *Journal of Public Health, 27*, 215–221.

Middlesex University (2012). Retrieved from http://www.mdx.ac.uk/aboutus/Schools/index.aspx

Peoples-uni. (2012). *Publications and presentations.* Retrieved from http://www.peoples-uni.org/content/publications-and-presentations-about-peoples-uni

Philip, K. E. J., & Awofeso, N. (in press). *Internet based public health e-learning student perceptions – evaluation from People's Open Access Education Initiative (Peoples-uni).* Open Learning.

Philip, K. E. J., & Lee, A. (2011). Online public health education for low and middle-income countries: factors influencing successful student outcomes of emerging technologies in learning. *International Journal of Emerging Technologies in Learning (iJET), 6*(4), 65–69. Retrieved from http://online-journals.org/i-jet/article/viewArticle/1797

Reynolds, F., & Heller R. F. (2008). Peoples-uni: developing public health competences – Lessons from a pilot course module. *International Journal of Emerging Technologies in Learning (iJET), 3.* Retrieved from http://online-journals.org/i-jet/article/view/548/0

Salmon, G. (2000). *E-moderating. The key to teaching and learning online.* Routledge. Retrieved from http://books.google.com.au/books/about/E_Moderating

Scofield, M. R. (2011). *The social entrepreneur's handbook: how to start, build, and run a business that improves the world.* New York: McGraw-Hill.

Treloar, C. J. (1998). Evaluation of a national and international distance education program in clinical epidemiology (691). *Medical Education, 32*(1), 70–75. Retrieved http://www.ncbi.nlm.nih.gov/pubmed/9624403

Wikipedia. (2012). *Social enterprise.* Retrieved http://en.wikipedia.org/wiki/Social_enterprise

10
A Case Study of the Tensions and Triumphs in Building an Online Learning Community

TAREK ZOUBIR AND IAN TERRELL

Middlesex University, UK

Editors' Introduction

Increasingly the higher education establishment seeks to support continuing professional development by offering postgraduate qualifications that recognise the contribution of work-based practice. This case study, presented by Terrell and Zoubir, reports on the successes of one such programme over an 8-year period. Central to the design of the programme is an approach to learner-designed and learner-controlled research projects conducted in the participants' workplace that are reliant on technology-mediated remote tuition supported by rich online collaboration. But for all the richness of design the programme has revealed tensions between the needs of the individual and the needs of the establishment. The case employs a mix of quantitative and qualitative data in presenting the experiences of the tutors and the participants on the programme. Readers engaged in building or delivering accredited work-based programmes will find the chapter full of practical advice that points to the challenges of online collaborative professional development and points to key enablers of success.

Background

The Middlesex Partnership for Professional Development is based at Middlesex University and its major work is the organisation and delivery of MA Education and MA Inclusive Education programmes for teachers. The partnership is diverse and includes local authorities, schools and other agencies such as Real Training and Attainment Partnership.

A typical programme might be Dissertation, preceded by Action Enquiry preceded by Developing Professional Practice. The latter might be substituted by a specialist Developing Teaching and Learning module or Leadership and Management module.

161

Modules are designed to identify a professional need or problem and justify it with reference to practice documents, national and local policies, and data. Modules then entail planning a project that involves implementing practice suggested by literature and research, for which we might use the contentious term "best known practice." Participants are expected to use their new knowledge in implementing potential improvements to their practice and then to collect data on the effects and impact.

School-based groups, including consortia and local authority groups, make up over 90% of the cohort and are led by appointed associate staff or by appropriate staff in the schools themselves. This diverse and distant group was a major reason for the programme director's decision to keep centralized (university) control and quality by establishing a strong connection to the online community where essential documents and communications are made available to all participants, school based or otherwise.

Modules guided by module handbooks or instruction manuals are based around online conversations, which prepare candidates for each part of their assignment and the conduct of their project. In addition, scholarship and research skills are developed by face-to-face workshops that are also offered live online as webinars and recorded for asynchronous viewing.

In addition, there are Hotseats arranged for specific content areas. The Hotseats are online asynchronous conversations offered by selected guests acting as facilitators. These conversations are not module specific and span across MA Education and MA Inclusive Education programmes. Hotseat facilitators are invited to open a dialogue between students on a variety of education-related topics. Before a Hotseat is open to student participation, facilitators are required to produce content-focused stimulus material to engage with the students. Facilitators are also encouraged to share a photo and short biography of themselves. Examples of stimulus materials include video, PowerPoint presentations and links to Web sites. Students can also upload copyright-free material directly to the conversation or point peers and facilitator to online resources.

Almost 500 practitioners (around 20% of whom are non-UK based), mostly teachers, are on the programme at any one time working as postgraduate practitioner researchers. Participants are "learning while working," and therefore for them time is at a premium. This underpins the programme director's decision to focus on creating an engaging online learning community where learning can be maximized and shared across modules and institutions.

Key Elements of the Programme Design

The Middlesex Partnership for Professional Development has adopted many of the characteristics of a learning community through, for example, having open discussion, providing action learning sets, and exchanging ideas and materials across modules and schools (Lave & Wenger, 1996; Wenger, 1998). In this respect the partnership's work is based on and encourages the adoption of the three characteristics of a community of practice suggested by Wenger (1998):

- Mutual engagement
- Joint enterprise
- Shared repertoire

These characteristics are displayed by student engagement in group conversations (module based and Hotseats), peer review of assignments prior to submission and other activities where meaningful participation requires mutual engagement in the completion of activities to build the social ties required for further work and the negotiation and interpretation (joint enterprise) of what constitutes "high"-quality work. The end product of this negotiation process contributes to the shared repertoire of the community and influences such things as students' suggestions for future module conversations, Hotseats, or other activities.

Learning on the programme is open-ended in two ways. First, the assignments are projects that are negotiated. Most of the lead is by students in conjunction with their stakeholders. Participants are required to appoint an "institutional advocate" to assist in this contextualization of the project. Second, learning is open-ended in the sense that participants are free to browse through all the activities, Hotseats and module materials. Researchers are encouraged to share their research with each other through a variety of means, such as the following:

- Study buddies or learning sets
- Executive summaries of previous work
- Published examples of whole works or sections

Students are encouraged to share emerging and finished work both within and across modules. However, the team have felt this to be a difficult aspect with many barriers to overcome, including these:

- Timescales for completion
- Relevance of individualized projects to a wider audience focusing on different projects
- Delays in production of work by researcher
- Tension between collaboration and assignment completion for the individual (given time constraints)
- Coordination and organisation at a distance by staff and students
- Confidence of researchers
- Teacher-specified process and learner-managed process

The programme and learning have a high level of "teacher-specified process." This is for two main reasons. First, passing the award is dependent upon clear instruction based upon experience that it is safer to constrain choice by offering clear specifications of both final product and stages to achieve that product. This helps reduce failure rate and noncompletions. The process is easy to monitor and to take action on if projects appear to be going off track. Second, since there is often no content as such, process issues fill the vacuum.

Typically in the "teacher-specified process," directing staff focus on questions such as these:

- Has section 1 been completed?
- Have needs been identified and justified?
- Is learning planned for?
- Are the learning activities appropriate?
- Is there implementation?
- Will data be collected well?

The focus of feedback and tutorials then become the process and not the content of the learning. The wide variety of project topics adds to this emphasis, and perhaps relatively little attention is paid to content questions about the topics, be it leadership, change, learning theory, questioning technique, or other. However, activities including face-to-face workshops, online conversations and peer review are set in place for students and tutors to consider and negotiate the relationship between project topics and the process of completing the assignment. For example, students are asked to present "practitioner research presentations" to introduce their topic in the context of the requirements of the master's qualification. In this way students across modules "tutor" each other on how different topics can be explored to meet the same criteria.

Despite teacher-specified tasks and processes, students are able to define their own responses to the structure and make many choices about the selection and design of projects, the timeline and the structuring of their findings.

The Research Methodology and Methods

The research team calls the methodology adopted in this programme "practitioner research," as based upon notions of "action research" and the work of Stenhouse (1975), as well as notions of experiential learning (Kolb, 1984) and communities of practice (Lave & Wenger, 1996; Wenger, 1998).

These works all refer to the work of Dewey, Piaget, and Vygotsky and others referencing constructivist forms of learning (Kolb, 1984). That is, experience, observation and data collection are used to make professional judgements of worth and value and to plan further action. Schon (1987) and Eraut's later revisions (Eraut, 1994, 1995, 2000) all emphasize "reflection" on experience and data. Work by Lave and Wenger (1996) outlines the community of practitioners creating knowledge about practice. This methodology is the basis of the research, and it is worthy to note the philosophy behind the online community being researched.

The MA student's work is not value neutral. The project is fired by a belief in the value of the notion of the online learning community and struggles to achieve it, even though it recognises there are relatively few existing models.

In reviewing the programme to date we have collected data and experiences from a variety of sources, including the following:

- Practitioner accounts presented here as "voices"
- Questionnaire surveys of students (both online and paper)
- Formal and informal meetings with students and staff
- The construction and editing of the research narrative with participants

Voices

The Director's Voice

I am Dr Ian Terrell, director of professional development in education programmes at Middlesex University. The aims and direction of my online work differ significantly from institutionally driven e-learning programmes because of the specialised and bespoke nature of partnership work.

Learning is a holistic experience including the module activities, discussions through workshops (which are live broadcast), online Hotseats on specialist subjects, research and scholarship skills, exchanges between participants and examples of students' work.

The online environment is both open across different modules and aspects of the programmes and open to the public. Materials and content are accessible and freely available. In the institutional online system, registration (usually on individual modules) allows access. This appears to ensure content remains private until the payment of fees. Then content is released module by module.

My belief is that content is ever changing and improving and is already available from many sources online. What must be paid for are the assessment and qualifications and the individual support of students. This latter has to be high quality to ensure successful completion of the award.

The content management system platform I chose requires virtually no training. I believe the platform should be intuitive enough for people to start with simple instructions, and they should then improve their use by trial and error and exchanging technique within the community. Participants are not training to be online technicians and do not want to spend time learning the technology. This does place limitations, however, on the achievement of other goals such as the ability to create and publish materials and therefore share.

The Academic Assistant's Voice

I am Tarek Zoubir, and as an academic assistant at Middlesex University, I have been responsible for maintaining the online community under the direction of the director and staff who lead modules.

There is, in the view of the majority of staff with whom I have come in contact, a clear need for an online learning portal that stitches together different activities of the programme and presents them in a coherent manner to interested parties, tutors and students. Such a platform is seen to create opportunities for education professionals who are enrolled in the programme or otherwise to keep up to date with programme information, share ideas and create new knowledge.

In my role, creating material for and updating the online area, I have found the coherent presentation of online information to be most problematic. This is somewhat exacerbated by the number of tutors who are responsible for maintaining different areas of the site.

For example, this past year I have organised the online Hotseat calendar, uploaded related material and created several asynchronous conversation pages to be accessed by the online learning community. A mixture of university staff and external field experts facilitate the Hotseat conversations. The team agrees to supply a set of materials that would help the partnership present these conversations in a clear and consistent fashion: a photo, a short bio and stimulus material to engage users.

This stands in contrast to module conversations, which I assist in moderating, where there may be a lack of material, a lack of consistency in presentation, or out-of-date information (or indeed better examples than the adopted Hotseat approach). Rather, I have come to learn that the disparity of the material presented is representative of the demands on staff of whom the majority are part-time and work away from the university. Similarly, the majority of students are full-time employed and find little time to log on to the online community and put pressures on their tutors to respond to their queries via e-mail rather than resorting to the online area.

In this case, teaching and learning online appear to be dependent on the tutors and their individual, not institutional, relationship with the student and vice versa. The tasks and processes are adjusted according to need, affected by time constraints and other factors, rather than a pure theory of learning.

The Students' Voice

> Continue uploading the videos and archiving the past videos with relevant materials, i.e. readings list, tasks to complete – I find these significant in developing my learning in the MA. The online materials (PowerPoint slides, Hotseats, videos) are superb, I feel the tutors work hard to provide quality material to support your learning.

As part of the effort to "blend their own observations with the self-reports provided by subjects [students]" (Denzin & Lincoln, 2001, p. 29), regular attempts are made to capture the students' voice, and they are quoted throughout the narrative of this chapter. This helps us gain a better understanding of the student experience, compile reports, review the programme and improve the student experience. Above all it assists tutors and students in negotiating teaching and learning as they happen in the programme.

Examples of such data, presented in the following, include these:

- End-of-module evaluation
- Online activity/engagement survey
- Qualitative comments offered by students (from the aforementioned and other online comments/written feedback at the end of sessions)

The end-of-module evaluation gives a general understanding of the impact of the programmes without specific focus on the online work. To compensate for this, an activity/engagement survey was made available online for students to complete. The results of this highlight certain tensions to online engagement.

Online Activity/Engagement Survey

In an additional data collection exercise, a hyperlink to an online questionnaire was placed within the online learning community Web site (www.mdxpartnership.org.uk) to evaluate engagement with online activities. Some of the results are presented in Table 10.1.

The maximum activity and usefulness scores were for instructional activities and inputs by tutors (live broadcast = 57% [ranging from 3–5]). This is reflective of the need for guidance from experts that cannot be achieved solely through mutual engagement and the development of a shared repertoire. This suggests that such activities should be taken advantage of to encourage further engagement. For example, a live broadcast can have a follow-up page to disseminate materials from the face-to-face workshop, such as PowerPoint, handouts and recordings, but should also be linked to a module conversation, Hotseats, or peer activity.

The interrelationship between online activities provides one such explanation as to the lower level of engagement with Hotseats (46%). It is true that Hotseats are more content focused and themed according to recurrent project themes, but their alignment with module-specific stages and conversations is unclear.

Some typical reasons for participants failing to engage with the online activities are as follows (comments taken from three separate students):

I do not learn well in an online environment. I prefer taught courses.

Could not access any of the conversations or Hotseats, etc. Despite raising this as an issue more than once, it was ignored and suggested that the fault

Table 10.1 Student online involvement/engagement

Please grade your personal involvement/engagement with the following activities:					
	1	2	3	4	5
Live broadcast (research and core programme)	21%	21%	18%	18%	21%
Hotseats (asynchronous discussion)	27%	27%	19%	15%	12%
Module conversations	33%	11%	22%	19%	15%
Study groups	42%	8%	19%	15%	15%

5 - Very frequent, regular and active involvement
4 - Frequent, regular and active involvement
3 - Sound, reasonable or expected levels of engagement and activity
2 - Some involvement/engagement and activity
1 - Virtually no involvement/engagement and not active

was at our end. I have given up trying to access the online work and will proceed without it.

Mostly busy and not too sure of what to say. Not too confident with some concepts.

These issues can be addressed with better guidance and clear instruction on the requirement for online participation, a known problem (Russell, n.d.; Salmon, 2000). In our programme we face the further complication of a large number of members in the partnership and school-based participants who often belong to at least one other programme-related learning community outside of the university. Differing guidance to school-based and individual participants may be the solution for articulating the required level of online participation.

Less clearly evidenced and more difficult to measure was participant-to-participant sharing and support. How participants perceive this is difficult to record; 42% said they had no involvement in study groups, which were not features of online activity, but had been stimulated by some discussion threads in the online media. As such this activity was relatively new, and defining a "study group" when many participants were working in their own schools with and alongside colleagues who may have been performing similar functions was problematic. One student's comment captures this:

I had a problem with the study group as work seemed to be put in random folders. Also not sure how to let people know I have looked at their work or ask for comments on mine.

However, it does happen through discussion points in online workshops, through participant-led presentations (which are live broadcast) and through formal study groups and informal discussions.

The community continues to encourage this aspect of learning while seeking to capture its impact on research and practice. At regular intervals data is collected on how students' work contributes to their institutional aims and everyday practice. "Practitioner Research Presentations," a title for a series of presentations by MA students, are arranged on campus for reflexive accounts on participants' research. These are also live broadcast and video recorded when possible.

Participants were also asked to rate the usefulness and value of the online activity; 70% valued the live broadcasts as useful, with 40% being very positive. Similar figures were returned for both the Hotseats and online module conversations, although in these cases only 30% provided the higher ratings.

In the "blended" environment of this online community, where many participants are meeting colleagues and co-researchers, and their tutors, at face-to-face sessions, the expected "norm" for online participation and engagement is difficult to set. As such, participation and engagement in online learning is a known problem for those working in the field (Russell, n.d.; Salmon, 2000).

There is also a time factor in the growth of participation in the community. Team meetings observed that over the 8 years of the community being online there is now less resistance from participants. In the early days it was not uncommon for people to say, "I cannot go online because I have no computer" (field notes). Indeed, the MA staff felt it is now rare for "technical" problems to be reported as a reason for lack of engagement or contribution. On the other hand, the team had been much clearer and forceful in explaining to participants that work was online and sharing would be expected. This is likely to have meant the community had become more accepting of online community work, even if only through self-selection.

Additional data is found in correspondence; a typical comment from one participant stated, "I must thank you for your interesting and helpful on-line tutorials and comments during my three years of study at Middlesex."

Participants were asked for suggestions for increasing their involvement/engagement in online work in the future, and several interesting comments, which emphasized an extension to current practice, were collected. Notable examples (three separate students) included these:

Being able to access the broadcasts at a later date, rather than just the power points etc.

I have been accessing the videos of the lectures at a more suitable time and this has allowed me to keep up with the work. I can then e-mail any questions or concerns to the lecturer concerned.

> I enjoy the variety of Hotseats available, and learning about others views and experience, but it would be great increasing the time a Hotseat is available.

One participant valued the way in which information was archived for a much later date, saying as such:

> I really appreciate the recordings of the sessions; they are extremely useful referring back to past videos to support my research.

Another candidate complained about the lack of other participants in the community:

> I've really enjoyed the broadcasts I've seen, and found it easy to access the sessions. I've found the hot seats and discussions useful, but it seemed that many people weren't taking part, which meant that the momentum was hard to sustain. Overall though I found this method of learning to be useful and enjoyable.

Future guidance on online participation should stitch together different activities and issue appropriate guidance to all cohorts so as to increase engagement. This can be done in negotiation with students, school-based advocates and other interested parties.

Dimensions and Tensions

The data and experiences of staff have been analysed and debated over the 8 years of the online communities' existence. Emerging from these discussions is the following account of dimensions and tensions within the community as they relate to the Coomey and Stephenson (2001) model of online learning. This has been verified by staff discussion prior to release of this account. A reflective analysis of these resulting dimensions and tensions is provided here. These we have called:

- Differing experiences
- Need to pass versus creativity
- Pressure for content
- Linear processes – Nonlinear learning
- Individualized learning versus collaborative learning

Differing Experiences

The team and especially the director see the notion of online learning being developed over a period of time. An example here is the ever-changing nature of online learning platforms which are developed by communities of practitioners and lifelong learners in parallel to their use of such platforms for teaching and learning. This development runs alongside other Web 2.0 developments which directly affect online learning. Platforms, which include the Plone Content Management System used within the MA directorate, and other popular open source applications like Moodle, aim to improve the user experience. However, fast-paced developments often make it difficult to assess the type and level of engagement at any stage of development and more difficult to attribute this to specific programme activity.

There are some signs that the longer staff and students have contact with the online community the more likely they conceive a "team" vision of this approach to teaching and learning. This is evident to a degree in the account, or "voice," of the learning assistant. As a relatively new member of staff (1–2 years) it was of little surprise to the director and other staff members that he found the coherent presentation of materials problematic. Other staff members expressed similar feelings, but when they came to understand the developing and dynamic nature of blended learning that affected participants' experiences they were better equipped to employ flexible approaches to meet differing needs. Such flexible approaches take advantage of developments in online learning, including open educational resources and other Web 2.0 applications such as Slideshare and YouTube. Many of these applications are already in use by students, and incorporating them into the programme in the form of activities helps ensure a similar experience for different participants who may be less willing/able to search for them.

A step forward would be to encourage students to create their own program/module support pages consisting of Creative Commons licence materials. This could be a mini project for students or a summary of their online searches when working on particular assignments. This would help address a tendency by staff to see the learning process as directed by them, rather than students (practitioner researchers), who often see their projects as being student-directed and open.

A programme tutor reported that students often expressed such things as:

> My Tutor was helpful, but my study partner really understood my working situation as she also was a primary school teacher. Her feedback on my draft work made a real difference to my thinking.

Although there is evidence of growing activity in the area of learner-generated content by participants, some of the following tensions and dilemmas affect the degree to which desired outcomes of sharing, mutual support and the creation of new knowledge by participants for participants can be achieved.

Need to Pass Versus Creativity

Tutors often describe situations where they encourage creative responses to activities/assignments but advise on the dangers of them. For example, they say,

"A dissertation normally has a certain structure, but you can have any structure as long as the assessment criteria for the award are met."

However, it is known that certain structures work well and that any new original structure may be suboptimal. There is therefore an in-built conservative perspective that grows with weaker candidates and draft submissions. One tutor stated as such:

> I want the MA student to be creative in their writing and style of presentation, but when it is late at night and I have already assessed many reports, it is much easier to follow the narrative of the project report when it follows the suggested chapter headings and structure. You don't mean to, but you will give a better mark to a student that has a structured document than a more creative display that is harder to follow.

Already available online for our students are example assignment structures designed by tutors. Examples of "creative" structures by students which have been successful are now required. Indeed, a table of the different elements of possible structures with a column of suggested resources would be of great benefit. This would be similar to a reading list, but contributed by students and more like a Web 2.0 resource list from which many readings, videos and activities can be found. Alongside providing a traditional reading list, tutors are also encouraged to do this, which would help address some of the pressures for content by students on tutors.

Pressure for Content

There are several pressures that mean that content is important. A case example would be the online live broadcasted workshop session on "The Ethics of Practitioner Research." The learning outcome of this webinar is that students need to complete an ethical checklist form and demonstrate appropriate reflection on the ethical issues of their research project.

There are chances for participants to reflect on their knowledge or air their views from the perspective of their workplace context. During the webinar a situation is analysed concerning a case study involving ethical procedures in a practitioner enquiry.

However, most of the hour-and-a-half session is spent in outlining the various ethical concepts, dilemmas and issues that face them. The content is critical as there are legal and ethical implications of not knowing or not applying the correct ethical protocols concerning research with children.

Feedback from students identify that they like content delivery in both face-to-face and online sessions. They feel money has been well spent and like to hear the wisdom of the experts. As well as at face-to-face sessions, there are also interactive slots for response activities during webinars, and there are opportunities for discussion. Content is used in asynchronous Hotseats, the text discussion groups from expert presenters and module discussions as a stimulus for debates. Some staff are better than others at generating learning through students due to their blended learning tutor capability. Some are better live lecturers and often consider those who are not physically present first, as once this is done those present can be catered to more easily. A possible solution to this issue is the staff development of tutors to master the media and tools used in the programme.

Linear Processes – Nonlinear Learning

The tension between outlining a process and series of activities to complete an individualized project and the nonlinear way in which learning takes place has already been alluded to.

This is to the fore over the question of timelines. Clearly, you cannot have a student-led discussion about the analysis of professional autobiographies, or alternative mechanisms of data collection, unless all participants have completed that task. Although learning on the programme as structured is scaffolded and linear, online learning is less so. A simple Google search leads to many links and searches in a random order where one individual's "linear" path differs from that of another individual.

This argument has no simple resolution. Structure of the report is needed to ensure all the assessment criteria are met, yet one of the goals of this MA programme is to promote innovation in learning. Flexibility is needed to promote the transdisciplinary nature of this work-based practitioner researcher design. One direction forward is a focus on the role of staff development to help the tutors provide academic advice to the learners so all the assessed outcomes are met.

Individualized Learning Versus Collaborative Learning

The example of the degree of structure compared to creative flexibility is also one of the tensions between the individualized project and the collaborative learning of the online community. Individuals are essentially in the programme to gain the award. They are required to undertake their own selected project. Yet we wish to encourage partnership, collaboration and shared learning. Clearly, some interpret flexibility as being based on doing their work on their own, more than any need to share or discuss with others.

The tutor needs to carefully plan appropriate opportunities for sharing learning and collaboration. Some ways this is done are the following:

- School-based cohorts already within communities of practice
- Study groups (face-to-face and online)
- Executive summaries
- Other open materials created by participants for participants

The advantage for MA students in a group at one school is the opportunity to collaborate in person at the school. But this can lead to a narrow perspective on the issues examined in the project, which are often bigger than the confines of the school walls. It is important in these workplace practitioner researcher studies to look at ethical issues and school policy from a larger perspective that includes the learning authority (e.g., the borough or county), national-level concerns and regulations and, at times, European or international agencies and regulations.

Study groups add value to the learner's experience as supported by one student's view:

> Last term I did a module on my own, but did not understand all of the steps involved in conducting a [workplace] project. I felt alone. Now, by working with my study partner, I have a sounding board – someone I can share and compare my thoughts, experiences and samples of work. What a difference it has made.

Executive summaries, like abstracts for research publications, provide an at-a-glance summary of the workplace practitioner research dissertation. A way forward for this resource is to place them online so the keywords are searchable. Future MA students could then easily find prior work done in their areas of interest from over a decade of studies done through the university. The executive summaries could then be linked to digital copies of the full dissertations for review. One student said about reading the hard copies of the reports:

> It was very useful to see the structure and writing styles of past [dissertation] work. Although some of the [Ofsted] regulations have changed since it was written, many of the theories and teaching principles are still relevant.

Learner-generated content is the way forward for an online learning community. Web 2.0 tools (e.g., wikis, blogs, etc.) can be integrated more into the MA programme design to promote more opportunities for the MA students to collaborate with the Education Doctorate programme. This is also a helpful feeder for the students to progress their professional development and career paths.

Conclusions

A new dimension of collaborative learning across the community is being developed by mdx Partnership for Professional Development, and this recognises the professional community of practitioners as a major source of knowledge creation and exchange.

This case study illustrates the nature of a blended experience rather than simply a process to facilitate online delivery of content; here, technology is used for appropriate tasks and processes by the community.

Yet this technology has to be learned, developed and practiced, and the community needs to build participation to receive the benefits in learning. A way in which this can be tackled is by offering non-credit-bearing or, better still, credit-bearing staff development short courses that employ university- or programme-endorsed technologies. This would help in aligning the efforts of staff at on-site and at a distance and encourage coherence in the different activities offered online and thus increase levels of participation. It is anticipated that this would improve the student experience and provide a richer engagement with the tutors. Such a short course could be adapted for students to complete prior to embarking on the main programme content.

References

Coomey, M., & Stephenson, J. (2001). Online learning: it's all about dialogue, involvement, support and control – according to the research. In J. Stephenson (ed.) (2001). *Teaching and learning online: pedagogies for new technologies* (ch. 4). London: Kogan Page.

Denzin, N. K., & Lincoln, Y. S. (2001). *Handbook of qualitative research*. London: Sage.

Eraut, M. (1994). *Developing professional knowledge and competence*. Lewes, UK: Falmer Press.

Eraut, M. (1995). Schön shock: a case for reframing reflection-in-action. *Teachers and Teaching: Theory and Practice*, 9–22.

Eraut, M. (2000). Non-formal learning and tacit knowledge in professional work. *British Journal of Educational Psychology*, 70, 113–136.

Kolb, D. A. (1984). *Experiential learning: experience as the source of learning and development*. Englewood Cliffs, NJ: Prentice Hall.

Lave, J., & Wenger, E. (1996). *Situated learning: legitimate, peripheral participation*. Cambridge: Cambridge University Press.

Russell, A. (n.d.). *An analysis of a successful online community within Talking Heads*. Retrieved from http://www.naec.org.uk/ultralab/ww3/publications/challenges.pdf

Salmon, G. (2000). *E-moderating: the key to teaching and learning online*. London: Kogan Page.

Schon, A. D. (1987). *Educating the reflective practitioner: toward a new design for teaching and learning in the professions*. San Francisco: Jossey-Bass Publishers.

Stenhouse, L. (1975). *An introduction to curriculum research and development*. London: Heinemann Education Books.

Wenger, E. (1998). *Communities of practice: learning, meaning and identity*. Cambridge: Cambridge University Press.

11
Metaphor and Neuroscience: Implications for Online Learning

MIKE HOWARTH

Mike Howarth Associates, UK

Editors' Introduction

Metaphor is an integral part of communication and learning. Indeed, research suggests that when engaged in everyday conversation we can use as many as four metaphors per minute. This has led some researchers to use clean questioning to help students explore their own metaphor for learning and thereby seek clues as to their preferences for information access. Howarth has taken a different tack, drawing upon research about the way the brain processes metaphor to suggest that metaphor has a physical component and that metaphors that are embedded within the actions of the teacher and the learner play a role in sense making. He develops this theme by examining his own career in educational broadcasting and draws out a series of heuristic approaches that have guided his professional practice. He presents these approaches in a way that will resonate with education professionals who increasingly find themselves working to camera in the form of webinars, webcasts, YouTube video clips and broadcast lectures. His premise is that we are all increasingly using remote technologies and we can therefore all benefit from guidelines learned during a life in broadcasting.

A startling discovery made in neuroscience research literature is that metaphorical language and physical activity are linked inextricably in the physiology of the brain; metaphor is no longer just a figure of speech, but rather a way we learn. If this is the case then perhaps it is time for online practitioners to view metaphor differently and make use of these new ways of viewing the world in our teaching.

I first came across the physical aspects of metaphor through research degree enquiries into computer interfaces for children (Howarth, 2003). I proposed that navigation metaphor and screen interaction require the experience of hands-on motor activity in a pseudo-three-dimensional environment in order to be effective. The research drew upon the experiential aspects of metaphor

(Lakoff & Johnson, 1980), the role of eye scanning in navigation tasks and physiology in cognition (Hall, 1969) and physiological aspects of eye search in navigation through text (Chapman, 1987).

Recent researchers in the field now reject the traditional definition of metaphor as just "a figure of speech in which a word or phrase is applied to an object or action to which it is not literally applicable or . . . a thing regarded as representative or symbolic of something else" (*Oxford Dictionary*, 2013).

Lakoff and Johnson (1980) question the general popular assumption indicated in the definition. Kuntz (2009, p. 380) provides an example of their experiential metaphorical concept approach in an academic context:

> More specific to the study of higher education, faculty who articulate a need to "keep up" with research in their field and not "fall behind" in their tenure trajectory invoke embodied metaphors that are decidedly [spatial] *sic* (the field) and draw meaning from the embodied experience of keeping up and falling behind.

The move from a linguistic analysis of metaphor to a study of the way the brain works to produce metaphor has been rapid. Cognitivists studying embodied learning, driven by the prize that embodied experiences might lead to more effective learning, soon began to discover scientific evidence that nearly all of our experiences are in some way grounded in the body. Lakoff (2009) has also moved from an analysis of language – experiential metaphorical concepts to exploring embodied scientific realism:

> Since we are neural beings, our categories are formed through our embodiment . . . Categorization is thus not a purely intellectual matter, occurring after the fact of experience. Rather the formation and use of categories is the stuff of experience. It is part of what our bodies and brains are constantly engaged in. What that means is that the categories we form are part of our experience! (Lakoff, 2009, p. 19)

Early information from brain scanning technology and the use of probes drew simplistic evidence that left and right areas of the brain specialise in specific activities. However, Jarrett (2012) considers, "As well as having metaphorical appeal, the seductive idea of the right brain and its untapped creative potential also has a long history of being targeted by self help gurus peddling pseudo-psychology." Current neuroscience evidence suggests that functions are shared across both segments, but broadly act in the manner of right brain – wide perspective – and left brain – fine detail.

New scientific research provides significant insights about the role metaphor plays in learning. Ramachandran (2011) proposes that metaphor is an integral part of the structure and function of the brain as in Figure 11.1.

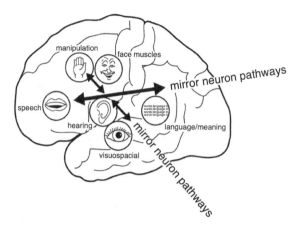

Figure 11.1 The left Inferior Parietal Lobule area of the brain showing the pathways that link body mapping and language to create metaphor.

In the left inferior parietal lobule (IPL) area of the brain the horizontal mirror neuron pathways and vertical motor message pathways physically cross each other. These "cross-modal" interactions link speech, hearing and visual/spatial areas with language, manipulation and face muscle centres. Cross-modal interaction occurs in ordinary healthy humans and is demonstrated in the "bouba kiki" experiment that relates sound to shape. The question – "Which shape is "bouba" and which shape is "kiki"? – provides consistent results even in different cultures. Sharp inflection of the tongue mimics the jagged visual shape of the word "kiki" (Figure 11.2).

Another exercise devised by Ramachandran shows how mirror neurons fire both when you make and observe facial expressions. Biting on a pencil makes it difficult to detect another person's smile (Figure 11.3).

The process of biting on the pencil activates muscles which are also responsible for smiling. The flood of messages by the mirror neuron system, between action and perception, results in confusion. Try it and experience this bizarre sensation! Here is a demonstration that may suggest empathy, which our culture considers to be purely abstract thought, may actually have a physical component.

If, as the research suggests, the brain uses both the linguistic and the physical (spatial) components of metaphor when processing experiences to make meaning, then what are the implications for those of us engaged in education and online learning?

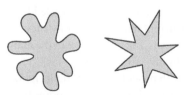

Figure 11.2 The Bouba/Kiki Effect. (Ramachandran, V. R 2011, p. 109)

Metaphor and Neuroscience: Implications for Online Learning • 179

Figure 11.3 Example of the Empathy test. From Ramachandran (2011, p. 109)

Perhaps we need to think of online teaching materials as artefacts and the making of them as central to learning and to understanding and therefore essential in any teaching experience.

Reflection on My "Analogue Online" Practice

I suggest that there is nothing new in the problem of creating an engaging online learning experience. In the past the same issue of engagement faced educational broadcasters. Taking the long view and looking back at my time as a BBC education radio producer, I am reminded of my colleagues' advice at BBC Education when I arrived in 1972. "It is not the technology, but the quality of the thought that goes into a teaching resource, that we expect from our producers."

The advice was "sound." I quickly learnt that new technology was not enough; rather, one had to use every opportunity to stimulate the imagination with language and fill the broadcasts with movement and action. Also needed were integrated publications to provide teachers with resources to carry out activities "offline" in the classroom: interpreting images, playing games, making objects and making experiments – learning by activity – stimulated by the media. Broadcasts and publications, including the Radiovision filmstrips, formed a coherent resource. BBC Education producers now use a Web site to deliver all the resources online. These resources continue to work because of the quality of engagement.

The quality of engagement was due to two active processes: first, the activity of making, and second, thinking and acting like a teacher. These were my particular experiences of grounding the design of quality teaching resources. An education producer had to organise and make the teaching resources: hands-on meant still camera work, editing, publication and artwork briefing;

all this was part of the job specification. The creative process of planning and making becomes second nature and still drives my current work in higher education (HE) and in the design of online learning resources.

Increasingly HE staff find that they are required to deliver to remote audiences using webcasts or other movie-type media. In the next section I offer practical professional advice for teachers and education professionals who find themselves operating out of their comfort zone and wishing to take advantage of metaphor as a trigger for active learning.

Guidelines for Effective Online Teaching

My general view is that using metaphorical language and activity in teaching, as well as making teaching resources, is an integral part of the teaching process. Whether the role of teacher is presenter of information, moderator of feedback, or personal tutor, neuroscience discoveries light up all kinds of new possibilities when there is pressure to perform for teaching, learning and understanding. The following ideas may help the lecturer think confidently like a teacher, get hands-on, get active and manage the demands on his or her professional performance.

Metaphor and Video

Increasingly your online learning situations may include delivering content via large lecture, YouTube videos, mini lectures and lecture flipping. I have been exploring ways to facilitate "the media-savvy academic," revisiting video techniques and thinking about the medium from a *different angle*. Of all the new developments a HE lecture faces, the general videoing of lectures and requirement for routine online webcam interaction with students frames and focuses the teacher to very public, very close-up and enduring scrutiny. The academic may have no choice but to get caught in the public gaze, resulting in permanent trial by YouTube. Many universities now have automatic video recording of lectures. Neuroscience may interest a camera-shy academic in intellectual reasons for reassessing the value of video, paying more attention to the implications of metaphor and activity in media often seen as superficial to learning, reassessing their performance and moving forward with confidence in light of these ideas.

Lecturers who embrace their creative side and pay attention to the academic argument for doing so can craft the making of video teaching resources and possibly enhance their career. To make video resources in particular may no longer be a chore, but rather a way to explore, feel and experience how production metaphors "contain" visual, audio and activity memory in the mind as "understanding" and can bring clarity to concepts and theories. For example, I am intrigued that the media might work because of the way neuroscience powers the metaphors of "depth," "headroom," "thinking space" – the visual syntax of the cameraman who "frames" the speaker. The results may enhance the quality of engagement with the viewer and add educational value to the finished product if the lecturer can see these tried-and-tested methods work because of the new scientific discoveries of the way metaphor works.

Large Lecture Video

Automatic video recording technology varies in quality. At its worst the lecturer is in semidarkness and appears as a small dot next to a large image of a PowerPoint slide whilst others technologies allow the viewer to alternate between the slide and the presenter. Often the audio is of very poor echoing quality, despite the use of a radio microphone.

To make the best of the situation is to understand how to "work" both a live audience as well as the camera. It is likely the speaker personally experiences the presentation as a projection to a large room yet is somewhat taken aback when confronted with him- or herself on a recorded framed medium close-up – head and shoulders – either staring at the computer or looking away at the audience, checking the projector screen, or moving out of the picture altogether, or even not moving at all. This experience is to understand the concept of *performance level*. The camera has the power to exaggerate the ordinary. Experienced practitioners use the following range of techniques:

- *Only speak when you face the audience.* Lecturers usually introduce an idea while facing the screen or walking to the computer to click to the next slide. Pause, and check the slide if you have to, before you start. The live audience will be happy because you are talking to them – recognising their existence. The online viewer will experience a person talking to them – not a talking top of the head.
- *Glance in the direction of the camera, not at it.* Do this once in a while, but not all the time. This technique can create the startling impression on the online viewer that you are talking directly to them.
- *Introduce each section of the lecture.* How often are new stages introduced just with a "so" or "now"? This is the result of using the computer slide as the prop that carries the "change" message, but often this is just a new slide without a caption, such as "part 2," or the use of a correct title slide with large text in the middle. Deal with this situation by standing still, pausing and then clearly state the subject aim and objective of the session while looking right at the audience.
- *Don't use "so" or "yes" or "next" at all.* So much of lecturing uses the storyteller's method of "and then" – a continuous link of events and consequences. The viewer needs clearly identified and segmented information in short "chunks," each with a beginning, a middle and an end. They also need to see the connectivity between the chunks. Many times the links remain in the lecturer's head. Be ruthless with yourself; spell out clearly what you want to say.

- *Think props.* Any ideas are fair game to illustrate a point, add to the story and focus attention on a key aspect.

I help the lecturer to develop ideas and interactive activities, segment the lecture and help with screen text and layout. I record mid close-up, ignoring the PowerPoint show. In the editing, the long lecture is segmented into sections, and in each section the slides are superimposed over the video, and judicious timing makes sure key points are given emphasis as the slide either appears or a previous theme slide disappears.

I also try asking academics to summarise their lecture directly to camera – usually after the event when all is fresh to mind – to use as an introduction to the segmented videos on the Web page. If there is time, further editing of highlights link the summary to the key elements of the lecture.

Webcam

Performance level may be even more important with an online webcam. Actors are taught that every small movement is exaggerated by the camera. When the camera is close to you, that slightest movement has a much greater impact on the viewer, just because that very closeness heightens the performance level. A little flicker of the eyes, a slight twitch of the mouth, is all an actor – and you – need. Any more and the viewer is overwhelmed or worried something might be happening. The worst aspect to avoid is quick head movement looking away from the screen and/or downwards. These are visual codes for "something probably worrying and unpleasant is going on" and certainly convey a sense that "my tutor is not really paying attention to me." These points draw attention to a range of generic presentation media methods that seem to be largely ignored by the webcam medium, which prides itself on not being the same as conventional media (Collins, 2012).

My checklist for online teaching helps me prepare for a session by thinking about the following:

- *Be aware of the camera position.* Mostly we accept the camera sitting on the top of the screen. The result is the viewer watching someone looking down all the time.
- *Think about the angle of the screen or the camera.* This can affect the angle of the webcam. I suggest putting the camera on a homemade stand right in front of the centre of the screen. I now have eye contact with the student. This has the added advantage that the microphone is close to you and does not pick up so much background noise.
- *Check the view behind you.* Make sure the ceiling light does not stick out of the top of your head. Blank white walls suggest an atmosphere of bleakness. A mess of books suggests chaos.

- *Lighting is essential.* Experiment with a small light on your face, which focuses visual attention on yourself rather than a brightly lit background object, which may also shade your face and makes expressions difficult to interpret.
- *Warn others with a notice on the door.* Unexpected interruptions stop the flow of the session.
- *Prepare your active content.* Have with you a list of items that illustrate your teaching point. Pick up an item and hold it to the camera. Demonstrate with objects on- or off-screen. Use your hands to demonstrate points, but keep them in the camera view.
- *Prepare your core script.* Make a few notes of opening comments positive and encouraging, three or four key messages, and a closing statement.
- *Think "presence."* Smile. Lean forward. Do not slouch. Be aware of the impact you give by looking all over the place. This is a human activity, and the online viewer deserves your attention.

YouTube, Mini Lectures and Lecture Flipping

You can apply the design principles already suggested to create quality YouTube videos and mini lectures before you work face-to-face with students. The advantage is that you can do all the hard work in peace and quiet, where you can practice and retake and apply the ideas of quality engagement. The rule is to keep what you say short and to the point. Enjoy taking complex ideas and practice ways to simplify and use fewer words – "recraft" them on paper – before giving the information clearly and succinctly to the camera, saying only what you need to say. Structure a series of short videos, perhaps an introduction to the scope of the field in the first video, and then subsequent bite-sized sections, each with extra sources of information. There are many screen-grab software applications such as IShowU HD that allow the lecturer to show both slides and images of the lecture. Adobe Connect's Web video–conference platform records all interactions (e.g., Web video, PowerPoint slides, text discussion, voting polls, participant list, etc.) as a downloadable Flash file (Adobe, 2012).

Students should receive your pre-planned online lectures before the lecture event, the essence of lecture flipping. Students can fulfil the requirement to come to the lecture well prepared. The lecturer's task is no longer to waste time putting across essential information, but rather to engage in a learning conversation. PowerPoint may not be used at all. The lecturer can focus entirely on the audience. He or she engages in conversation. The lecturer is seen talking to the audience beforehand. He or she greets them with a handshake and questions. The lecturer walks the floor, slowly, uses his or her hands to emphasise key words, gives clear signposts for new themes and subjects, paints pictures with words, uses emotional language and metaphor. But the pressure is now on to be a teacher, and the following ideas suggest a range of methods for a lecturer to embrace the new role.

Effective Preparation

It is my experience that the academic mind is particularly inefficient in lecture planning, which carries over to the structuring of webcasts. One particular pattern of lecture structure is common – the development of an argument with a key message at the end. I reflected on my BBC experience as I filmed recent academic lectures, and long-forgotten instinctive writer's tricks and tips suddenly reappeared in my mind. I knew I had been here before. Why not apply them as ways to structure webcasts and remote lectures to greater impact? Here are a few fast-track professional tricks that may help you.

- Use five sheets of paper to plan your Web lecture. On each sheet clearly state one idea, using as few words as possible. This is to ensure that your webcast has a central punchy core running through it.
- Reshuffle and reorder for impact.
- Build on the core by speaking out aloud the key idea per page, and only use the spoken English to bring the textual concept to life.
- Draw sketches of the idea. Dream about yourself making the presentation and collect these visual images (originally these illustrations would form the accompanying broadcast publications – now they become your PowerPoint slides).
- Always think about ways to break free of the usual lecture structure; one method is to use attention-grabbing examples before analysis of academic implications.
- Finally, bind the elements with a thread of chained keyword language with links, bridges and signposts so the listener can navigate easily from beginning to end.

Writing a long, wordy, linear PowerPoint structure from start to end can be very time-consuming, and reediting of a completed first draft lecture can cause dangerous errors and omissions and introduce an imbalance. Adherence to the design principles I have set out will ensure that your core lecture material is sound and that the pause points linking the key ideas – the bridges – will be in place. The recorded session video can then be split into meaningful sections for easy streaming on the Internet and digestible segments of resources for study.

The media-savvy lecturer melds together the best of the two worlds of the public lecture and the private video performance. Most lecturers already plan presentations using PowerPoint; the next stage is for the media-savvy academic to use the aforementioned paper exercise and PowerPoint merely as a storyboard. Others might then feel confident enough to forget about a computer presentation and just perform live!

Metaphor and Neuroscience: Implications for Online Learning • 185

Test Yourself!

See what you can observe in the following figures (shown in Figure 11.4 and Figure 11.5) as a quiz of the application of some ideas in this chapter: the process of hands-on activity that improves engagement driven by the value of metaphor as informed by neuroscience.

Which of these images has the most impact on the viewer? Who would you like to view first? There is no right answer. Find your own personal style, but make sure it measures up to what you prefer in conventional media images.

The example shows the impact of metaphors that embody foreground and background presence and lighting depth to a subject. Ask yourself which of these two presenters you would prefer to hear speak and what might be the value of their statements.

Figure 11.4 Think about your body language in your online presentation. Consider the value of conversation. Prepare your event as a professional broadcast.

186 • Mike Howarth

Figure 11.5 Move position to make a point. Use your hands, make "depth" of the content in the manner of your presentation. These are familiar media skills but driven by metaphor. (Howarth, M. S. 2010b)

In Figure 11.6, I show a very common method of presenting to camera as an opportunity to provide an illustration for an alternative structuring for a typical logical academic presentation: introducing a subject by segmenting information – "the three bites of the cherry" method – with pauses for digesting the information to avoid a long single narrative, which can lose the attention of the audience. Notice how a similar method is used in newspaper writing in the first three paragraphs of any article where the information is released in manageable amounts. The example also attempts to illustrate how the physical qualities of reflection, depth, perspective and distance metaphors are not just a media method. They are an embodied concept and are of value to the learning process.

Consider a new reward for your well-prepared and well-filmed videos; you can now have students using your material before the lecture. They can come to the lecture prepared. There can be no excuse! Of even more significance is that your focus in the lecture can move to quality teaching time, both face-to-face

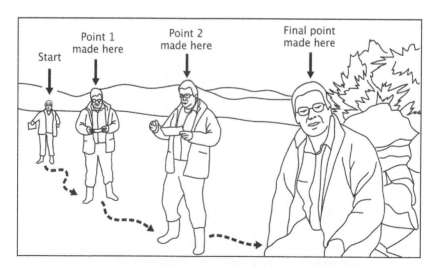

Figure 11.6 An example of a frequently used style of video presentation

and engaging in online conversation and discussion instead of the transfer of information.

In the next section I suggest ways to use metaphor to greater impact in your conversations and discussions with students.

Metaphor and Activity Within Live and Online Conversation

Learning conversations that consciously use metaphor can help illustrate key teaching points. Practitioners who already find learning journeys and heroes (Campbell, 1988) valuable in their teaching are explicitly applying the principles of the experiential metaphorical concept proposed by Lakoff and Johnson (1980). Conversation and story are strong themes in learning and business development: see the *Cluetrain Manifesto* (Locke, Searls, & Weinberger, 2000) for an early example. Laurillard (2004), Stephenson & Critten (2003), and Gibbs (2011) are also practiced theoretical exponents of these techniques.

The Art of Rhetoric

Metaphor always was a tool in the art of discourse, but it is traditionally defined and confined to "the use of an image to stand for an idea" – functional and useful. But, as I argue that metaphor has extra teaching value as informed by neuroscience, what about applying other "tricks of the rhetoric trade" that are already familiar to teaching? For example, a radio producer knows that to deviate from the standard "three-ring" sound effect for a phone can have significant dramatic implications. I have always called this "the rule of three." I also hear it when politicians always repeat phrases three times. Check whether you clap your hands three times, or repeat instructions three times to gain attention, or *ram home a point* three times for effect. I discovered that the rhetoric term for this method is called tricolon – the familiar rule of three (Collins, 2012).

As I watch lecturers in front of an audience and observe their patterns of behaviour through the camera lens, I note that some "walk the talk" in their presentations. There appears to be a pleasing connection between walking and discourse. I have developed the self-editor, a suite of ideas to help students with their academic writing:

- Take a break and walk while reading aloud. Explore the concept of writing as a physical activity (Howarth, 2010). Writers frequently mention going for a walk clears the mind and provides thinking time for ideas. I always walked up and down reading scripts out aloud as essential to "rhythm" and "pace."
- Physically "walk away" from a problem and watch your mind work automatically to come up with a solution; amazing how getting up from the computer to make a cup of coffee gives you a new perspective when you come back.
- Sleeping on it is such a very good natural, practical tool for solving problems.

Most people do these actions instinctively, but now we have good scientific reasons for them, and I would encourage you to make the methods explicit as learning tools for your students.

These observations on rhetoric arise from an audio or aural world, or a world where performance is already accepted as an academic skill. What if the powers of rhetoric discourse tools still have value during online conversations? The online lecturer has an audience, so why not explore other rhetoric methods? Why not use the old tried-and-tested methods with the new technology? Enhance your effectiveness online armed with these principles.

In any field of study you can engage in deeper learning. Identify in your mind when academic argument is required and when the metaphorical language of "understanding" is appropriate. Consciously apply metaphors to your academic point in feedback. For example, the classic, "You need to be less descriptive and more critical" elicits the usual note, "Try and identify key positive and negative aspects you can comment upon." Add a metaphor reference to your feedback – perhaps a suggestion to "weigh up the two sides of the argument." Then add a quick sketch of some scales. Finally, even on your webcam, pick up a few books and do a balancing act.

Other examples further illustrate my points:

- *Structuring an argument*: The metaphor "shifting boxes" or "lining up the team" might also become embodied during a standard webcam link using objects in front of you, such as small boxes with issues, problems, or stages written on them that can be moved around. Hold them up to the webcam.
- *Ethnography*: Students will find a deep understanding and a greater engagement if they draw, video, or practice exploring their physical presence in their investigation workspace.
- *Ontology*: A concept often used to encourage discussion of an aspect of a subject or issue; it can come to life and be understood for the student quickly through the manipulation, movement and grouping of objects in a three-dimensional space. One good ice-breaker is to have an online poll that identifies where the audience is geographically located. This gives them some context to possible cultural perspectives.

Conclusion

The lecturer who embraces the need to be a teacher, who understands the creative process of resource production and the online learning designer, can now see that his or her new understanding of metaphor has several practical implications. A deeper understanding of metaphor naturally informs the quality of conversations. A good teacher will combine metaphor activity and language in the teaching process and aim to use media – graphics, photography, video and activity – as an essential part of online learning. The online learning designer can move swiftly away from learning theory to learning practice and make products that have spirit and humanity. Together we can shift the cultural attitude that separates science from experience, theory from practice, and in doing so we can reach for a more coherent teaching experience.

In the future, I see these ideas of particular value to help meet new challenges to improve standards of HE teaching through deeper understanding, research-led learning and student-centred approaches.

References

Adobe (2012). *Adobe Connect 9 for schools and universities.* Retrieved from http://www.adobe.com/education/products/adobeconnect.edu.html?showEduReq = no

Campbell, J. (1988). *The hero with a thousand faces.* London: Paladin.

Chapman, L. J. (1987). *Reading: from 5–11 years.* Milton Keynes: Open University Press.

Collins, P. (2012). *The art of speeches and presentations.* Chichester, UK: John Wiley.

Gibbs, P. (2011). Finding quality in "being good enough" conversations. *Quality in Higher Education, 17,* 139–150.

Hall, E. T. (1969). *The hidden dimension: man's use of space in public and private.* Garden City, NY: Bodley Head.

Howarth, M. S. (2003). *Children and computers: the development of graphical interfaces to improve the quality of interaction.* PhD, Middlesex University. Retrieved from http://www.mhmvr.co.uk/site/phd.html

Howarth, M. S. (2010). *The self-editor: a strategy for improving reflective writing.* Middlesex Annual Learning and Teaching Conference. Engaging the Digital Generation in Academic Literacy. Retrieved from http://altcmu.blogspot.com/ and http://www.mhmvr.co.uk/site/write/writing1.html

Jarrett, C. (2012, June 27). Why the left-brain right-brain myth will probably never die. *Psychology Today.* Retrieved from http://www.psychologytoday.com/blog/brain-myths/201206/why-the-left-brain-right-brain-myth-will-probably-never-die

Kuntz, A. M. (2009). Turning from time to space. *Conceptualizing Faculty Work.* doi: 10.1007/978-1-4020-9628-0_9

Lakoff, G. (2009). *The neural theory of metaphor.* Retrieved from http://ssrn.com/abstract = 1437794

Lakoff, G., & Johnson, M. (1980). *Metaphors we live by.* Chicago: University of Chicago Press.

Laurillard, D. (1993). *Rethinking university education: A framework for the effective use of educational technology.* London: Routledge.

Locke, C., Searls, D., & Weinberger, D. (2000). *The cluetrain manifesto.* Cambridge, MA: Perseus.

Metaphor. Oxford Dictionary (2013). Retrieved from http://oxforddictionaries.com

Ramachandran, V. R. (2011). *The tell-tale brain: unlocking the mystery of human nature.* London: Heinemann.

Stephenson, J., & Critten, P. (2003). *Maximising benefit from researching learning through work.* Symposium paper presented at the 2003 American Education Research Association.

Part 5
Transition

These two chapters have been grouped together because they deal with two sides of the same coin: namely, the challenges faced by traditional institutions and learning cultures when confronted with the potentially disruptive introduction of online learning. Narend Baijnath and Pamela Ryan report on the intertwined fates of a nation, South Africa, and its major university in transition. For these authors, online learning in not just a convenient tool but also a metaphor for the changing face of the way the university engages its student body. Built upon the premise of learning with and through others (heutagogy) and an international partnership approach to the development of six "Signature Courses," this institution is trying to redefine the role of the university as an enabler of social change. Interestingly, the second contribution in part 5 is also set largely in Africa, but here Pamela McLean sets out her vision for an "alternative academia." She describes what it is to be a "free-range" learner and gives inspiring examples of how people can use the Internet to come together and collaborate to learn and resolve real and present issues. What binds these authors and these chapters together is a recognition that teaching and learning online is about so much more than just a new way for existing institutions to deliver content to a captive audience. It is about connecting people together within a shared context to leverage collective experience to generate new insight and, in so doing, to release the potential of individuals, groups and, indeed, whole nations.

12

Virtual and Virtuous: Creating New Pedagogies for a New South Africa

NAREND BAIJNATH AND PAMELA RYAN

University of South Africa

Editors' Introduction

The authors report on a bold programme set to transform the way students engage with the university and each other as they commence their journey through higher education. They set out the challenges inherent in moving from a traditional distance education model to a style of engagement and a learning paradigm (heutagogy) whose focus is to engage students in learning through and with each other. At the centre of the initiative is a set of new "signature" courses that have been developed in partnership with US-based institutions which will, when fully implemented, signify a creative shift from a traditional paper-based teaching approach to an e-tutor facilitated, self-directed, online learning approach. What follows is the story of an institution and a nation in transition; the hope is that these disruptive educational innovations will cascade through all levels of learning professionals and produce a new generation of learners – learners who are better equipped to release the potential of a nation.

Synopsis

Unisa is a unique institution with a unique role in Africa – to be the African university in the service of humanity. If we are to fulfil this role, we have to change our thinking, our practices and our pedagogy. This chapter focuses on one way in which we can envisage a pathway to the kinds of changes we have to undergo – through Unisa's newly and collaboratively designed Signature Courses and the impact they are having on people and processes at the institution. The design and delivery of the courses are premised on a heutagogical or peeragogical approach that is at this stage largely experimental. The idea is to enhance self-directed or self-determined learning by (mainly) first-year students in the hope that through interactive and frequent interventions with each other and with their tutors, the university will improve its teaching practice and thereby its retention rate. Signature Courses are aimed at enabling students to imbibe university values as set out in its Graduateness Statement, to acquire important skills needed in the world of work, and to function in society as socially responsible citizens.

Introduction

Before we begin, it may be useful to explain the two key terms in the title, "virtual" and "virtuous," which are used in more than an alliterative and metaphorical sense and which inform the underlying ethos of the chapter. They are drawn from and are in line with South Africa's recently launched National Development Plan for 2030, which uses the term "virtuous cycle" in the economic sense of "a complex chain of events that reinforces itself through a feedback loop" and in which each iteration of the cycle reinforces the previous one, thus creating the effect of a positive feedback. We hope to demonstrate in this chapter that the idea of a feedback loop and positive reinforcement are not only economic terms but also point to a pedagogic ideal in which self-organising learners reinforce their own learning and that of others through connectedness to the Internet and to each other. The word "virtual" is in such common parlance that we perhaps need reminding that it means "almost or nearly the thing described but not completely." This points to the tentative nature of what we are doing in our new pedagogies. The "thing described" here is our hope – that through engaging students in a new kind of learning experience, virtual or digitized teaching, they will not only survive the course but go on to become successful lifelong learners and teachers of others. Self-organisation also needs some reflection at this stage. In our case, it refers to self-directed or self-determined learning where students are organised into groups overseen by a teaching assistant but in which they are expected to interact and assist each other. The idea of self-organisation derives from the theory of heutagogy but also uses ideas from Sugata Mitra and colleagues' (2005) "hole in the wall" experiments to show how it is possible for self-organised learning to transform ideas about how students acquire knowledge.

Unisa's Signature Courses, which are to roll out in 2013, a few months from the time of writing, are based on a theory of learning called heutagogy which has been variously defined as a means whereby (mostly) adult learners take responsibility for their own learning and in so doing develop a series of skills including communication and teamwork, creativity and innovation, and positive values. For this to happen, students work in groups that are kept fairly small (the ideal is in the region of 20 per group) and are encouraged to bring knowledge to the group from their own life experiences. Beginning with what they know and reaching towards what they do not yet know, learners become co-creators of learning as they bring into the learning process not only their cognition, but also their meta-cognition and epistemic cognition, which is in turn shaped by the learners' diverse life worlds (Blaschke, 2012; Hase & Kenyon, 2000). There is a sense of play in heutagogy, where "play" is not simply or only a childish pursuit but is generative, productive and, above all, creative. Heutagogy (or peeragogy or heteragogy) is learning through and with others. How is this to be achieved through distance online learning with masses of students? That is our challenge.

Unisa's premise is that heutagogy is not only wholly consistent with Unisa's vision of community engagement and social responsibility but is also eminently suitable for implementation in online course delivery, which is the chosen delivery mode for the Unisa Signature Courses. "Techno-heutagogy" adds online learning (Web 2.0) to the equation and, in the Unisa context, fulfils part of our social mandate to ensure that all our students graduate as digitally literate people equipped to function in a 21st-century working environment. If we fail in this mandate, we do not deserve our place in society, nor do we have the right to trumpet our major goal to be the African university, so it is vital that we succeed. The premise of this chapter is to match our grand aspirations for Unisa with the reality of our students' circumstances. If we are to change a nation, and a nation's future, we must begin with our Signature Courses. It's a bold and ambitious aim, but it is also nonnegotiable.

Unisa: A Brief History

While Unisa has a proud history of being one of the oldest universities in South Africa and amongst the oldest of the world's open and distance learning institutions, its recent history parallels the reforms undertaken by the national Department of Education shortly after South Africa was formed as a newly democratic nation. In 2004, the new Unisa was established after a merger of three distinct institutions, the old University of South Africa, Technikon Southern Africa and Vista University Distance Education Campus, thus becoming South Africa's largest comprehensive university with a dedicated distance education focus. After 2006 Unisa adopted its Strategic Plan, which established a strongly African liberatory agenda with an even stronger social mandate to offer cost-effective, high-quality education opportunities to students across South Africa and into the African continent. Various levels of responsibility accompanied Unisa's mission and vision: responsibility to meet national objectives; responsibility to social transformation in helping create a society committed to social justice, fairness and sustainability; and most of all, responsibility to produce graduates who will be able to contribute to the nation's needs by being socially responsive citizens and, in the words of the National Plan, "active champions of their own development." Unisa has seven colleges, so-called because they are larger than most faculties; indeed, some of them are larger than entire universities. The only college not offering Signature Courses is the College of Graduate Studies because the Signature Courses are aimed, where possible, at entry-level students.

Unisa's Signature Courses: An Even Briefer History

In a global (and specifically US) context, Signature Courses are intended to stamp the signature or brand of the university on its graduating students. Their origins are most obviously derived from the idea of a signature as a mark of proof or intent but are variously described as foundational courses on topics of sufficient breadth and depth to be deemed as universal ("sweeping") in scope and essential to a liberal arts education.

In a Unisa context, Signature Courses are defined as introductory-level courses that uniquely express Unisa's vision to be the African university in the service of humanity. This implies that Signature Courses should be relevant to South Africa as a nation on the continent of Africa, its communities and its people. But they should also exhibit the key characteristics of Unisa's curricular identity, and the university's ambitions for its students are expressed in the Unisa definition of graduateness. In this document, we highlight the key characteristics of relevance, community engagement, social responsibility and Africanness. Accompanying the Graduateness Statement, our Curriculum Policy (of 2010) commits Unisa to align its pedagogy (how we teach) to a strongly transformational agenda through the following:

- Promoting African thoughts, philosophies and interests to counter the legacy of Western intellectual hegemony
- Highlighting the importance of learner centredness as an agent of change
- Practising a critical scholarship focused on African perspectives towards society and knowledge production
- Foregrounding an awareness of market-related strengths and opportunities

With this in mind, Unisa embarked on the design of six Signature Courses in close collaboration between a team of curriculum designers from Unisa and from various institutions in the US in the six fields of study: Environment and Ecology, Economics and Ethics, Computer Literacy, Language and Culture, and Teacher Education and Law. The teams functioned through virtual and contact discussions involving visits to the two host countries (South Africa and the US) each year, backed up by e-mail and site visits to the various platforms of the contributing universities.

The Partnership

The partnership arose four years ago with an exchange of views on Unisa's intended transformation from a distance teaching university to an open distance and comprehensive teaching and learning institution with a strongly focused vision to be the African university in the service of humanity. A series of engagements took place between the executive management of Unisa and Dr Sabine O'Hara, then head of the Council for the International Exchange of Students, which runs the Fulbright Programme. Dr O'Hara later founded her own educational company called Global Ecologies and is now dean of the College of Agriculture, Urban Sustainability and Environmental Sciences at the University of the District of Columbia.

Shortly after this exchange of views, Unisa signed a memorandum of agreement with Global Ecologies to enter into a formal partnership with the purpose of designing a series of Signature Courses at Unisa and to work closely with a carefully selected team of design and subject experts from the US, a team selected by Dr O'Hara. Over the three years since the signing of that agreement, the two teams have had several opportunities to work closely together, sharing views and knowledge through an engaged community of practice. Each team had much to learn from the vastly different contexts they operated in. For example, a visit to Johns Hopkins University had the South African team drooling with envy at the technological advantages of their colleagues, but conversely, the US team members were often in tears when exposed to the realities of the social conditions of many of Unisa's students and were sobered at the sheer size and scope of Unisa's student body. It is safe to say that the learning was mutual and the understanding gained profound.

This has been an extraordinarily productive partnership with the two teams learning through cross-border comparisons about student behaviour and staff competencies, differences in broadband delivery, social norms and the policy environment. The collaboration has brought huge benefits for both parties, enabling mutual wisdom to be shared and knowledge gained about our disparate environments. More specifically, the Unisa team had little experience in designing courses for full online delivery, so they benefited from careful coaching by their US counterparts, one of whom was accustomed to working with SAKAI, the open software used by Unisa for its virtual learning environment, MyUnisa. During the course of two hourly sessions, the team worked with two US designers in creating a fictional online course from scratch by following a simple set of guidelines. Similarly, the adoption of online rubrics for the assessment of courses, plus the use of a gradebook, was assimilated by the Unisa team over a series of days during a visit to the US. Although the teams were small, care was taken to ensure they were properly diversified to include teaching staff, professional staff and technical staff. The team's brief was to return to South Africa armed with relevant knowledge with the objective of passing this knowledge on to others in their different areas of concern, thus making this project effective and sustainable.

Unisa's Signature Courses as Disruptive Innovators

The term "disruptive innovation," first coined by Clayton Christensen (1997) to suggest an innovation that transforms an expensive and complex product into a simpler and cheaper one, thus creating a new market that disrupts the older version in unexpected ways, aptly fits Unisa's Signature Courses. As they move from a purely conceptual stage to a fully operational status, the Signature Courses are becoming the agents of disruptive change in the university environment. Departments such as Print Production, Dispatch, Registration and Assessment realise they have to reinvent themselves as digitized agents. Faculty are being persuaded to reimagine their role from being producers of knowledge to becoming custodians of a student's personal journey in a new environment where knowledge is everywhere and openly available. University structures, policies and procedures are in the process of being redesigned for a digital future. The extent and speed of this disruption has proved to be unsettling for support departments and faculty alike.

But there's more. When one adds their method of delivery to the equation, online Signature Courses signify a creative shift from the traditional paper-based teaching approach to an e-tutor facilitated, self-directed, online learning approach. Let's unpack the implications of this further:

- Whereas academic faculty under a print-and-paper mode and in an open distance learning environment have traditionally designed courses for print delivery with assignments ranging from multiple choice to short paragraphs or long essays, a techno-heutagogical approach entails the designing of fully interactive online courses by a lead lecturer working with a team consisting of a curriculum design practitioner, a multimedia expert, an academic specialist and an IT specialist.
- Whereas courses designed for print assume students work independently and at their own pace, heutagogical courses are designed for optimal interaction between students, peers and e-tutors. In the Unisa example, students are divided into groups of 30 with a teaching assistant taking on 10 groups of students who participate in focused, formative, weekly assessment tasks.
- Whereas under the old print model, the emphasis was on summative assessment with two or three formative assignments during the year, the Signature Courses operate on a switched-over model where formative assessment constitutes 80% of the final mark whilst summative assessment, which is non-venue based, constitutes 20%. This is, in itself, a considerable disruptive innovation for Unisa, and it is intended to improve the retention rate of our distance students on the grounds that more support, more practice, more discussion and more peer mentoring will give students a fair chance at succeeding since the work they do on a weekly basis will add to their store of knowledge, contribute to their year mark and provide a steady and cumulative acquisition of knowledge and skills.

The Implicit Disruptive Pedagogical Elements of Signature Courses

The Signature Courses are also rich in implicit pedagogical elements. By this we refer to the learning that takes place but which is not made explicit in the curriculum. Of course all modes of education contain some measure of implicit learning. The hidden curriculum where children unconsciously learn gender roles from their reading primers is one example of this.

No body of knowledge exists in a vacuum. There is more to being a chemist, economist, or psychologist, for example, than simply mastering the material and passing the exams. There are ways of thinking and being innate to professions such as these that paper-based distance education is or has been rather poor at. The Signature Courses allow students not only to interact with their lecturers and teaching assistants, but to also interact with one another. Discourse, debate and the thesis-antithesis cycle all hone the mental faculties of learners, and the isolation that goes hand in hand with traditional modes of distance education is mitigated by the design of the Signature Courses, which gives students and lecturers the freedom to decide what degree of synchronicity they need in order to optimally engage with the task at hand. When we compare this with the forced, asynchronous mode that distance learning has used in the past, it seems obvious that the heutagogical model is both flexible and empowering.

The work of Sugata Mitra (2005) and his colleagues on self-organised systems of learning suggests that we may observe unexpected (and unpredictable) augmentation to the facilitator-influenced learning built into the course design. Mitra installed ruggedized, Internet-connected computer kiosks in slum areas of India and allowed the local children access with no guidance, no teacher and no supervision. Emergent learning took place as a function of the interaction amongst the individual children as well as the children and the computer. Testing of the degree of self-organised learning that took place with the subjects revealed that they ranked near or at the level of their formally schooled peers for relevant tasks.

Similarly, we believe that the design of the Signature Courses allows for the occurrence of self-organised learning such as this. Although the Signature Courses are not designed to be without teachers, the modularity of the interaction channels could facilitate the formation of self-organised learning.

Unfortunately, Professor Mitra has admitted that once children are acculturated out of their natural desire to experiment with the unknown, they also lose the capacity to learn spontaneously. So what is the role of teachers in a self-organised learning environment where we must acknowledge that our students, who are mainly between the ages of 23 and 35 years old, may not necessarily adapt easily to self-organisation but must be nurtured and guided along the way?

Teachers in this new model must learn to stand back. They are no longer producers of content or custodians of knowledge. Content is everywhere, and knowledge is freely available. This alone is a shocking revelation for university teachers who are accustomed over long years of tradition to regard their role as one of purveyor and distiller of knowledge. Now that any student with access to the Internet can also access knowledge in diverse forms without the help of a university teacher, their role shifts accordingly. Their skills must be adjusted along with their self-image to incorporate design and curation. Let's look at that in a little more detail. Once a course has been suggested, say in economics, the academic teacher involved in that discipline will work in a team with various design practitioners, including multimedia designers, technology designers and pedagogical designers, to guide the course material into suitable teaching frameworks. Drawing on content that could be open source or licenced under Creative Commons shifts the attention of the teacher in the team to ensure that this content is suitably localized and contextualised for South African students. The readings or videos must be carefully chosen so that students can relate to them yet be stimulated into new ways of thinking about themselves and their environment; ample space must be given for interactivity, yet the exercises and tests must not exceed the time allocated to the "reading" hours of the student. Once the course design is complete, the teaching begins. Yet this is not teaching as it used to be. The university lecturer steps aside at this point, observing the work of the teaching assistant or tutor who is responsible for small groups of students. The university teacher becomes the custodian of the process, not directly engaging but ready to help or intervene when necessary. Through this observation, the teacher is not merely checking up on the teaching assistants and the students' progress but also recording the results of the process so the course can be adjusted if necessary to achieve more beneficial results. Through this self-reflexive process, course design and teaching are constantly improving in an interactive cycle of checks and balances. Teachers must realise the huge importance of their new role even though it may feel passive. They are, if you like, the hidden magicians of the learning process.

And What of the Students?

In shifting responsibility for learning to the learners themselves, heutagogy moves beyond andragogy in its assumption that students in an open distance environment in the 21st century are responsible adults, capable of self-organising, sharing and engaging each other in mutually constitutive learning activities. At the same time, as we suggested earlier, we recognise that students may be unfamiliar with the notion of self-organised learning since it is the opposite of rote learning, which the majority of them have become accustomed to in their schooling. Our greatest challenge then is to trust that students will want to self-organise, will be already used to sharing information through social media but may not necessarily link that social activity with formal learning. Our job therefore is to demonstrate the integrity of our belief in our students as capable learners. The Signature Courses are designed to build crucial capacities in students, viewing them as responsible citizens who will exit the university imbued with its values and equipped with sound skills. The ability to operate within a social context and in collaboration with others is key to arriving at solutions in day-to-day challenges. A carefully designed teaching and learning strategy is needed in order to impart the desired skills, knowledge and attitudes to learners – a strategy that acknowledges the surfeit of knowledge in present-day society and how Web 2.0 technologies enhance dissemination and acquisition of such knowledge. Through this technology, learners are proactive in learning – they search for pertinent information and use it to construct solutions to specific problems. Individually, and within a virtual social setting, they share ideas with peers and their mentors, in a productively interactive process allowing for iterative cycles of learning, reflection, communication and learning. Thus, learning is not only self-directed, it is also self-determined and self-empowering.

The Benefits of Disruptive Innovation?

The benefits of disruptive innovation at Unisa are twofold: the values inherent in the Signature Courses and the skills associated with the techno-heutagogical approach used to roll out the Signature Courses. The ramifications of these two benefits are illustrated in Figure 12.1.

At the time of writing this chapter, we cannot claim that our hopes for the Signature Courses will be realised. All we can do at this stage is itemise the intended and supposed benefits we hope will ensue for the two groups of key stakeholders, our students and our faculty. We hope we will have more capable teachers who are better prepared for the complexities of the learning environment and increased learner confidence in formulating ideas, critiquing ideas and sifting through layers of information and related perceptions. Our hope is that our students will relate to their peers, interact with their peer group and contribute to the teaching and learning journey by teaching each other and sharing diverse worldviews. We take comfort from the findings of research in other contexts, which confirms that the heutagogical approach supports students' control of their own and others' learning, collaborative reflection, learner's self-perception and professional development, and critical thinking and reflection (Canning & Callan, 2010).

In the short-term, the pedagogical advantages of online learning include interactivity, reflexivity and collaborative learning. The long-term benefits of online learning are explained by activity theory – that interaction with the technological tools transforms the mental state of the individual (Waite, 2005). Prominent social scholars like Giddens (1979) confirm that humans use tools to change the world and are in turn transformed through the use of tools. In Giddens's view, social systems are produced and reproduced through human agency. Human action is influenced by social systems, but human agency also transforms social systems. The downstream effects of student transformation at Unisa cannot be overemphasized, especially given that some of the students are

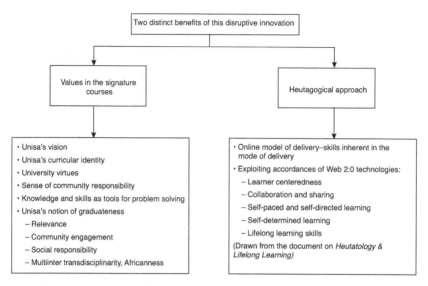

Figure 12.1 Two-fold benefits of signature courses at Unisa

educators in schools, who have direct influence on young people. The qualities imparted to such teachers during their studies at Unisa are likely to bear upon their teaching and therefore influence how learning in schools happens.

Thus, Unisa closely shadows the National Plan in its transformation agenda while retaining its autonomy and independence through critical thinking and scholarly engagement in innovative online learning practices. South Africa's National Plan of 2011 refers to a "virtuous cycle of expanding opportunities, building capabilities, reducing poverty, involving communities in their own development" (South African Government, 2011, p. 2). The Unisa Signature Courses are well placed to promote the ideals of the South African National Plan of 2011, especially with regards to building the capabilities and self-confidence of students. In this regard, the potential of the techno-heutagogical approach to engage learners in communities of practice during the learning process, to maximise learner scaffolding through peer support, and to improve the ability of learners to investigate ideas and construct solutions to problems cannot be overemphasised. The learning processes, which are fully determined by learners, lead to the production of responsible and disciplined graduates and, we hope, independent thinkers. Thus, the fundamental benefits of disruptive innovation brought about by Signature Courses are the production of self-organised, responsible, socially responsive and ethical graduates who are both the products and the progenitors of an educational virtuous cycle with its own feedback loop, one which is informed by Unisa's transformative agenda in producing virtuous citizens who act both as role models in their communities and as future leaders of South Africa.

The National Development Plan is unapologetic about breaking with the past and setting a new focus for its developmental agenda as the following quoted section clearly shows:

> The commission has drawn strongly from definitions of development that focus on creating the conditions, opportunities and capabilities that enable people to lead the lives that they desire. Development is the process of raising continuously the capabilities of all citizens, particularly those who were previously disadvantaged. National capabilities that enable competitiveness include human capital (built through education, health, skills and work experience), physical infrastructure (schools, clinics, ports and power lines) technologies, management skills and the social institutions needed to allow people to live decent lives. It requires shifting from a paradigm of entitlement to a development paradigm that promotes the development of capabilities, the creation of opportunities and the participation of all citizens. (South African Government, 2011, p. 5)

The Challenges That Lie Before Us

The delivery of online courses at Unisa is a giant step towards transforming the learning culture of our students and our faculty, and we are mindful of the need to keep the momentum for change whilst dealing sympathetically with the fears and anxieties that always accompany change of this magnitude. As an integral part of university preparations for introducing the Signature Courses curriculum, a survey was conducted at Unisa to determine how staff involved with the signature modules and with the learning platform, MyUnisa, felt about the possibility of offering courses fully online. Whilst there was general acceptance of online delivery in regard to Signature Courses, several challenges associated with going full out for online teaching are immediately obvious, and perhaps the most challenging of these is the long-standing tradition of reading hard text. Nor is this a local challenge. The world over, students seem to prefer to read books and lectures printed on paper despite being fully conversant with digital technologies, gaming, social media and so on. Somehow, studying means paper and print that can be underlined, highlighted, copied for the benefit of friends and so on.

Obviously, then, the Net-centric nature of the heutagogical approach for Signature Courses is a challenge, one the university will need to overcome by implementing effective mediation interventions that can excite and motivate students out of this old practice. Apart from equipping students with the basic technological skills, there is still the need to get students to appreciate that the online approach presents an ideal opportunity for them to enjoy the freedom of when and where to learn as well as determine and direct their learning in a way that gives them autonomy in the process of acquiring knowledge.

Unisa students learn at a distance, and we are fully aware of the loneliness of the long-distance student. In this respect, online learning is very different from print-based instruction, which is designed for reading alone. Through weekly assignments and tasks, students will have to participate in group discussions and significant connections in the process. Web 2.0 technologies present an ideal opportunity for our students to exploit the affordances of social media and interact with other learners on a regular basis. Students also keep in touch with the university through their tutor, hence bringing teacher presence into their learning process.

Our challenge, of course, is the hard sell we need to undertake to encourage staff and students to adopt online learning, become accustomed to technology and take control of their learning experience. But we hope that this shift of mind-set, once achieved, will create excitement and enthusiasm. As Tait (2000, p. 288) argues, learning often needs mediation of a sort in order to provide systematic support to help students manage the rules and systems of the institution so as to encourage persistence. In the absence of this kind of support, the accompanying change of mind-set will not happen and the student will remain stuck, becoming frustrated and eventually dropping out, something we want at all costs to avoid.

Effective introduction of our Signature Courses therefore entails change on the part of various categories of Unisa staff as well as on the part of students. To a very large extent, how this change is managed will determine the success of the Signature Courses and the new mode of delivery. Change management is therefore one of the biggest challenges associated with the roll-out of fully online Signature Courses at Unisa, and we are embarking on various ways of achieving this through a top-down as well as bottom-up approach. In time, we believe these conversations about going digital will diffuse throughout the echelons of the university and therefore break down the walls of doubt.

The Digital Divide

Changing the way people do things and think about things may be challenging, but there are more concrete impediments to the successful roll-out of the Signature Courses.

The "digital divide" in the present context refers to the gap between individuals, households, schools and geographic areas at different socioeconomic levels, with regard both to their opportunities to access information and communications technologies (ICTs) and to their use of the Internet for a wide variety of activities. The students registered for courses at Unisa represent a fair proportion of South Africa's young people in their language use, their cultural habits and their digital habitus (Czerniewicz & Brown, 2012). While the prevailing discourse is that many of our students, especially those from rural areas, are hugely disadvantaged, current statistics suggest that the majority of them manage to access the learning platform, MyUnisa. Clearly we need more, and more nuanced, social data on just how our students have access, whether from their place of employment, shared computers, Internet cafes, or smartphones. But until we do, we must assume that for a proportion of our students, being digitally interactive means having access to a computer for long-enough periods of time if they are to manage the Signature Courses demand for interactivity. To ensure that no student gets left behind in our Signature Courses, the team has designed a Flashdisk, based on the Flashtrack initiative started by Thomas Edison College in the US, which is attached to a colourful wristband and is to be posted to all students registered for a Signature Course. During the first phase of the software design, this Flashdisk, which we have called the Unisa Portable Online Offline Learning Environment (UNIPOOLE), will allow students to download the MyUnisa learning site to enable them to work on the course offline. The second phase goes further in mimicking the MyUnisa site to allow students to work online offline. It must be emphasized that we don't regard UNIPOOLE as a "solution" to the digital divide, rather as a necessary intermediary intervention until all our students have access to and can afford to go online for the time it takes to complete a course.

The other prevailing narrative, based very recently on real conditions in South Africa, is that of limited bandwidth and the instability of the online environment. Prior to the laying of several undersea cables linking South Africa to Europe, limited bandwidth caused slow download times and put pressure on Unisa's servers, causing crashing at peak periods. However, a new digital environment emerging with remarkably fast download speeds and marketed by the national parastatal Telkom suggests these problems will not continue. The second and prevailing limitation in South Africa has been the cost of connectivity with little meaningful competition around to force prices down. This too is changing, with conversations between Unisa and the major providers of bandwidth space in South Africa, and we are confident that we will be able to negotiate cheap bandwidth and 3G connectivity for our students. The final hurdle is that of devices. Unisa would like every student to have a device capable of connection to the Internet, one that allows for reasonable typing to take place – that is, not a phone, or at least, not a phone as currently designed. Discussions are taking place about the supply of tablets and netbooks for our students. Once this is achieved, the last barrier in the digital divide will fall away.

Final Thoughts

In designing our six Signature Courses, the team was acutely aware of the needs expressed in the National Plan: the need to invest time and resources in designing the courses, the need for pacing and frequent formative and interactive assessment, the need for decentralized student support, the need for a team-based approach and collaborative thinking and, finally, the need to go digital. Only time will tell if our careful planning has paid off. We have dared to dream – about ways in which we could imbue these courses with the values of our university; about nurturing our diverse student body through an exciting, dynamic learning process; and finally, about graduating a group of sharp and savvy thinkers who are distinctive and self-organising and who will change the face of this nation.

References

Blaschke, L. M. (2012). Heutagogy and lifelong learning: a review of heutagogical practice and self-determined learning. *The International Review of Research in Open and Distance Learning, 13*(1), 56–71.

Canning, N., & Callan, S. (2010). Heutagogy: spirals of reflection to empower learners in higher education. *Relective Practice: International and Multidisciplinary Perspectives 11*(1), 71–82.

Christensen, C. M. (1997). *The innovator's dilemma*. Boston: Harvard Business School Press.

Czerniewicz, L., & Brown, C. (January 2013). The habitus of digital strangers. *British Journal of Educational Technology.* 44 (1), 44–53.

Giddens, A. (1979). *Central problems in social theory: action, structure, and contradiction in social analysis*. Berkeley, CA: University of California Press.

Hase, S., & Kenyon, C. (2000, December), From andragogy to heutagogy. *Ulti-BASE In-Site.*

Mitra, S., Dangwal, R., Chatterjee, S., Jha, S., Bisht, R. S., & Kapur, P. (2005). Acquisition of computer literacy on shared public computers: children and the "hole in the wall." *Australasian Journal of Educational Technology, 21*(3), 407–426. Retrieved from http://www.ascilite.org.au/ajet/ajet21/mitra.html

South African Government. (2011). *National development plan 2030*. Retrieved from http://www.info.gov.za/issues/national-development-plan/index.html

Tait, A. (2000). Planning student support for open and distance learning. *Open Learning, 15*(3), 287–299.

Waite, T. (2005) *Activity theory*. Retrieved from http://www.slis.indiana.edu/faculty/yrogers/act_theory2/Wikipedia (2013). *Virtuous circle and vicious cycle*. Retrieved from http://en.wikipedia.org/wiki/Virtuous_cycle

13
Online Learning in Virtual Academia

PAMELA McLEAN

Dadamac, UK

Editors' Introduction
> Many developers of online learning environments aim for a learner-centric model where the learners have both the freedom to select what they learn and the flexibility to learn in a manner that best suits their individual preferences. But despite the lofty aims of the developers what often emerges is a framework with only token learner choice. In this chapter McLean paints an evocative picture not only of her own travels in self-directed learning but also her experiences of finding like-minded people who willingly commit to working virtually. She terms her learning world "virtual academia," and she explores the components of this world through a series of anecdotes that describe collaborative initiatives that touch every part of the globe. She points out that as collaborative networks expand to include diverse populations there emerges a very real need for a cultural mediator, and she provides a simple diagnostic planning tool to help scope the nature of this important role. This very human account provides a rich body of practical advice for anyone who aspires to be a part of this growing community of free-range learners.

Introduction

In this chapter I will develop ideas about online learning that have arisen through my work since 2000 as a researcher/participant in online programmes. These programmes started with people in UK and Nigeria who then connected with people in other countries. My work has interwoven threads related to education, development, learning and collaboration. The chapter draws on a mixture of individual-learning and group-learning experiences, outside of established academia. These occur in a informal online setting that I describe as "virtual academia."

My Work on the Internet

I came to the Internet not as a teacher, but as a learner. However, because I am also a teacher (and a systems thinker), two things happen when I learn. One – I think analytically about my learning experiences and related systems. Two – I can't resist sharing what I'm learning. I therefore moved on from simply being a learner who was using the Internet for personal learning to become someone who also enables others to learn in similar ways.

I arrived with an urgent need to learn. In December 2000 the tragic death of a friend, Peter Adetunji Oyawale (dadamac.net/network/peter-adetunji-oyawale), had put me on a steep learning curve. In my spare time I had been helping Peter and his wife, Agnita, in London, with the Oke-Ogun Community Development Agenda 2000 Plus (OOCD2000+, 2013), a visionary project he was launching "back home" in rural Nigeria. This meant I had a deep understanding of what Peter was trying to do, and I was committed to it because it touched on my long-term interests in the relationships between teachers, learners and computers.

I went to Nigeria for Peter's funeral. There I met some of his Nigerian collaborators who previously had only been names and photographs to me. They asked me to continue in my role. They had lost Peter's detailed vision. I had lost his knowledge of Nigeria and of Yoruba culture.

When I came home I used the Internet to learn from, about, with and for the people I was collaborating with. This involved these elements:

- Learning from Peter's collaborators – I needed to know the project from their side. This was a considerable challenge given the lack of telecommunications infrastructure in rural Nigeria at the time.
- Learning about the geography, economics, politics, history, culture and so forth of Nigeria – so that I could understand my collaborators better, about "development" politics, research and so on. The goal was to see how our work fit into the wider picture and about the related ICT (information and communication technology) projects already in existence.
- Learning with my collaborators – we were doing something none of us had tried before, setting up a Community Digital Information Centre (CDIC) and collaborating at a distance.
- Learning for my collaborators – I had good Internet access and they didn't, so I could seek out what might be useful for them and the CDIC.

Over the years my online learning focus has changed, and my networks have grown both online and offline. My work has included using the Internet for collaborative course design and delivery. I also guide and support various Dadamac projects (www.dadamac.co.uk) where people are collaborating and/or learning together. My current online learning interest is in discovering how we can use the Internet so more people (including people in underserved communities) can benefit from online learning opportunities.

My Online Learning Journey

When I started learning online I just saw the Internet as somewhere to go and read published information. Then I discovered discussion groups. My experience expanded as I learned how to make the most of these groups and the information shared there. Some of the people I met online became my friends, collaborators, teachers, or mentors.

When I think of my own learning using the Internet I don't think of any set courses. I think of ranging freely online, checking links, joining discussion groups and being part of supportive online communities, some short-term, some long-term. Some of the deepest lessons I've learned about the dynamics of online communities, beyond our own Dadamac community, came through work within Minciu Sodas (dadamac.net/network/minciu-sodas) and Coalition of the Willing (dadamac.net/network/coalition-willing).

In addition to joining online groups run by others I have set up and managed groups of my own. I have been able to experiment, and to observe what does (and doesn't) seem to work in online groups. My experiences of online learning are unlike those in mainstream established academia, and the rewards, motivations and rules are also different. I call the space where I do my learning "virtual academia": "virtual" because it is online and "academia" because my studies there are of a postgraduate nature and deeply rooted in the compelling needs of the professional communities within which I work.

Virtual Academia

I will not attempt to define "virtual academia," but I will describe parts of it.

Virtual academia exists only on the Internet. It is a world that is less hierarchical (and more chaotic and spontaneous) than established academia. There is no top-down control. Virtual academia does not have any formal structure because it does not even exist as a formal entity. There are no established boundaries defining what is inside or outside. It exists in a fluid, emergent way and is coming about simply because the Internet exists and enables people to learn.

Learners in virtual academia have the Internet itself as their "home institution." They range freely there without the constraints of established academia. Their studies are completely learner directed and are tied into real-world problems and practical initiatives. The learners are motivated to develop knowledge rather than gain accreditation.

Virtual academia provides many opportunities for fresh insights and knowledge creation through collaborative learning. It is particularly relevant in areas that are newly emerging, where people are responding to needs, finding their own way, facing uncertainty and appreciating opportunities to learn from each other. The Learning Change project (gfbertini.wordpress.com) is a good example of shared knowledge creation. As George Por says in the tagline of his group,

Collective Intelligence & Wisdom (plus.google.com/u/0/communities/100666540255152085162?cfem = 1), "None of us is as smart as all of us."

Virtual academia is suited to people who are trying things out and adapting approaches in the light of experience (elsewhere known as "making mistakes" and "failure").

I go to virtual academia to support and develop my practical work, and also because I'm interested in the ideas and theories behind what I am doing. In doing so I am seeking the following:

- Background knowledge so I am well informed
- Examples of challenges and good practice from other practitioners
- Opportunities to think things through, develop my ideas and put my work in a wider context
- Teachers and mentors who can help me develop further
- Opportunities to benefit Dadamac projects or the people involved in my online communities

In some online groups, I'm extracting my own learning insights as a side benefit of contributing to the main purpose of the group. In others I'm part of a group where collaborative learning is not just incidental, but purposeful. There are certain elements in such groups:

- Group members are learning together and teaching each other.
- Specialists have an appreciation of the types of background knowledge that may be needed by others in the group.
- People confess ignorance or confusion and are comfortable asking questions.
- Links are given and advice is offered to help make up any knowledge gaps.

In virtual academia people often help each other on a one-to-one basis. My teachers have given me tuition in more subjects than I can name, including pattern language, Moodle, using wikis and simple spoken Yoruba: all online, unpaid, informal and individual.

In virtual academia there is peer-to-peer help, but no formal support systems, funding streams, or suchlike. There are no fees for teaching or learning. People put in what time they choose and cover their own costs of going online. They decide for themselves what they need to learn and when their needs have been met. It is easy to dip in and out because virtual academia is demand led, not supply led. There are no set courses and therefore no examinations or accreditation; there is simply self-directed, free-range learning and all the information, knowledge and people networks of the Internet to call on. But, like established academia, virtual academia has a mixture of benefits and disadvantages.

Resources and a Culture of Collaboration

I'm not including any online courses in my discussion of resources, as I'm concerned with more fluid, learner-defined approaches to study. Online learners with high bandwidth often point each other to multimedia resources, such as RSA animates (www.thersa.org/events/rsaanimate), TED talks (www.ted.com) and other video clips. Webinars, for example the GlobalNet21 Community (www.globalnet21.org), are also a useful learning resource.

Physical meetings that previously would have been "for attendees only" now generate resources for outsiders. Some key speakers also contribute from outside the physical walls. The content is available to all learners thanks to opportunities for participation at a distance, live streaming, video recordings, slideshares, podcasts, tweets and so on. I think of this as "the fluid walled classroom" and first recognised it as such through attending Overseas Development Institute (ODI) events (www.odi.org.uk) and the second meeting of the School of Commoning (www.schoolofcommoning.com).

Within virtual academia the culture tends to be a practical and pragmatic one, emphasising cooperation and mutual benefits, rather than competition. Information tends to be shared freely, rather than being locked into books and journals, and is frequently multimedia. Online publication means that information can be shared rapidly, without the costs of paper publishing, and without the delays of editorial control or formal peer reviewing. Informal peer recommendation increases the visibility of good content.

Thanks to software, hardware and infrastructure developments (such as the rise of social media, hardware with increasing portability and functionality, and increasing public Wi-Fi access points), information is flowing increasingly rapidly in peer-to-peer (P2P) ways. The P2P Foundation (p2pfoundation.net) has good examples. Where Creative Commons copyright licences and tools are used it is easy to copy, distribute, edit, remix and build upon published work.

Overcoming Isolation

There is no "freshers" week in virtual academia, no students union, no pastoral care. A free-ranging learning journey on the Internet can be a lonely experience. It helps if you have some kind of guide, mentor, or master. Fred Garnett recognises this need for support in WikiQuals (www.slideshare.net/fredgarnett/wikiquals-show-tell) and suggests the role of "affinity partner."

When I started online learning, discussion groups only functioned through e-mail. Now more choices are available. Increasing bandwidth has led groups to use more real-time online meetings, many including audio and video. These are more social and help to reduce the isolation factor. There may even be fellow students living nearby; online learners in highly populated areas can discover relevant face-to-face meetings through Twitter, Facebook, MeetUp and other online sources.

Experiences in virtual academia reflect the cultures and tools of the various communities the e-learner joins. Entry to Minciu Sodas tended to be through personal invitation, often from the director, Andrius Kulikauskas. Newcomers were welcomed into one of the many interconnected groups, which were further interconnected through a wiki and chat room. Teachers Talking, which is described later, provided course participants with a friendly entry point to a mini-version of virtual academia. In Coalition of the Willing participants typically had high bandwidth, and there were many techies involved. The group used a wide variety of digital tools, and people flowed freely between the different online spaces using whatever was most appropriate to the learning, or collaboration, currently underway. Moving between appropriate online spaces in a fluid way is very natural behaviour in virtual academia, just as people in established academia move between physical spaces.

Assignments and Assessment

In established academia students complete assignments and get feedback and assessment. In virtual academia, contributing to online discussions can have similar benefits to preparing assignments, but the kind of feedback is different.

In formal assessment situations, test questions are posed by teachers, and the learner's task is to provide the right answers. A good question challenges the student to reflect on what is known and then apply that knowledge appropriately.

In online groups people ask and answer questions and enter into deep, well-argued discussions. Someone asking a question can be seen as a "temporary teacher" challenging the other members of the group and stretching their thinking in the best traditions of the Socratic method (en.wikipedia.org/wiki/Socratic_method). Unlike "test questions" these are genuine questions that are unlikely to have any established "right answers." Comment threads on blogs can serve a similar purpose. New ideas and insights can emerge through considering how to reply. Answers that take the discussion forward are acknowledged and discussed further, providing valuable feedback to the person who offered the answer.

This type of questioning and answering can be richer than the questions and answers of formal assignments. When people in a discussion group come from different disciplines and are experts in their own fields, the questions they ask, and the ways they express them, can bring new knowledge and insights to the discussion.

Questions and answers in established academia can be seen as a mixture of learning, teaching and testing. The learning aspect can happen in virtual academia. However, there is no moderator assigned to monitor the learner's progress and make suggestions about future directions. It is up to the learner to find people who will take on such teaching or mentoring roles.

Final Accreditation

In established academia final accreditation provides a permanent reference point and is a key to a place in the job market. Learners in alternative academia are not following set courses so if accreditation is desired, retrospective accreditation is the appropriate approach. WikiQuals is an experiment in retrospective accreditation for people who are outside established academia but doing work that could be seen as academic.

Accreditation provides evidence of knowledge and work done. There are various ways to provide such evidence. Anyone who works online leaves a trail of digital footprints. It's not just a matter of blogs written, comments posted, contributions made to discussions and profiles completed. We continually scatter evidence of our interests through what we do as we find information and "like" it, tweet and re-tweet, make bookings for events, send feedback, contribute photos and so on. Tools to keep track of our footprints, to pull them together and re-present them, are increasingly in evidence.

Working openly online provides the opportunity to build reputation and networks. Collaborations emerge comparatively easily. Finding new paid work, in some areas, may be done as effectively through digital footprints and reputation networks in virtual academia as through formal accreditation and references from established academia. LinkedIn is one example of how our ongoing stories are being told. As LinkedIn says:

> In the future, how will we be judged? Will companies still check our resumes for our alma mater or will they look for other credentials? Using LinkedIn, we not only capitalize on our network, we can also keep an updated resume of the projects we are working on. As resumes like this become more mainstream, prospects improve for those who forgo degrees in favour of practical experience. (From "LinkedIn's Core Mission: Making Its Profiles the Next Generation Resume," via *Techcrunch*, techcrunch.com/2012/11/14/linkedins-core-mission-making-its-profiles-the-next-generation-resume)

Field Work

Students in virtual academia are typically looking at theory related to their practical projects, which can be thought of as their field work.

In my own case, field work has been at locations in Nigeria, Kenya and the UK. The Internet itself is also home to my field work as it is there that I do much of my collaborative work. My field work began with OOCD2000+. The next major project was Teachers Talking, which led to the founding of Dadamac, and its various projects on the ground and online, including the self-defined group of Dadamac learners, and the idea of the Dadamacademy. The ideas that I'm sharing about virtual academia, online learning and online teaching have their roots in my field work and are best understood through reference to it.

Teachers Talking

Teachers Talking (TT) (www.dadamac.co.uk/teachers-talking.html) was an introduction to ICT for some teachers in rural Nigeria who needed to teach the subject. They asked John Dada, of Fantsuam Foundation and the Fantsuam Cisco Academy, to provide computer training. John asked me to design and present an appropriate, practical course. We called it Teachers Talking (About Computers) because the participants came from poorly resourced schools, with no computers, so they would have to explain to their pupils afterwards, not demonstrate. Like most of my projects the shape of Teachers Talking emerged gradually.

Before the course started I set up a TT Yahoo group (dadamac.net/start-of-tt-online-sig). I invited people from my online networks to join me in preparing the best possible experience for the TT participants to have in their short time online. As I was unpaid I had no qualms about inviting other people to help me without payment. An idea emerged of preparing an "online resource cupboard" for the participants to browse through. We wanted them to experience the potential of the Internet during their online sessions by discovering relevant teaching resources and ideas (things that would be useful to them back in their classrooms).

Preparing for the 2004 course provided me with my first experience of running a Yahoo group and of collecting information on a wiki. Subsequent courses included connections through Skype, chat rooms and Web conferencing.

People joined TT to offer their expertise but soon discovered that it was a two-way learning experience. We needed to know details of the course timetable, the availability of resources, access to computers online and offline, and other practicalities. People in the Yahoo group were intrigued to discover details of life in rural Nigeria as the planning progressed. Questions were diverse: Why did we have to invite all the local dignitaries and devote the entire first morning of TT to a formal opening ceremony? What was a mid-morning kunu break? Did John really mean it about participants never having seen a computer before the course? I had unwittingly set up my first cross-cultural online learning group and begun my studies into the related dynamics of such groups.

TT was to be my first visit to Fantsuam, but I knew rural schools elsewhere in Nigeria through working holidays with OOCD2000+. This meant I had connections with "both cultures" in my learning group – I belonged with the course designers with their 24/7 broadband connections, but I was also familiar with the realities being described by John Dada and others helping with the planning in Nigeria.

When I finally presented the TT course some members of the Yahoo group chose to be available for e-mailing. They wanted to get to know the participants personally and support them at a distance. Feedback after the course highlighted how much the participants valued this experience of online learning through being part of an Internet-based, supportive, cross-cultural group.

Through TT, I worked with serving teachers, and also with schoolchildren. I often think about how they, and people in similar communities, can be included in the benefits of online learning.

The TT Yahoo group was the first e-learning community I set up. Since then I have set up and enabled other e-learning and/or collaboration groups, all with slightly different purposes, arrangements and dynamics.

Folabi Sunday – TT Alumnus and Online Learner

I met Folabi (Fola) Sunday through OOCD2000+. He kept in touch via his smartphone. I have helped him online and introduced him to people (potential fellow learners, teachers and mentors) in the Dadamac Community and in Minciu Sodas. Through online contact with them he has developed his practical ICT skills (hardware and software) as well as increased his theoretical knowledge. I also arranged for him to attend a short TT-style course in 2008.

Fola's involvement with a supportive online community has helped him fulfil aspects of Peter's vision back in Ago-Are, Oke-Ogun. Fola is an ICT evangelist, teaching in several schools, and running his own independent, self-funded ICT centre in Ago-Are. He describes himself as a Dadamac learner and calls me his teacher. I say that I learn from him. We are in contact mainly through Google Chat. He also joins Dadamac's monthly online drop-ins (First Thursdays) when possible. He contributes to Dadamac's wealth of information through words, photos and video clips (see Figure 13.1).

The way he gives knowledge as well as gaining it is typical of virtual academia. People are both teachers and learners, contributing to the pool of shared knowledge.

Online Learning in Cross-Cultural Groups

In the TT group I had my first opportunity to observe people from different cultures collaborating online and learning from each other. I was interested in the different kinds of information various people had contributed and the fact that the final beneficiaries of TT would not be just the participants, but also their colleagues, pupils and communities.

When I got home after presenting TT 2004 I thought about everyone involved and the ways information flowed. It began with John and me. We had both brought in other people (for course content expertise and local knowledge), and then the course had been delivered to the rural teachers; afterwards they had gone back to their schools and wider communities. I drew a diagram that I (wrongly) thought covered everything (see Figure 13.2).

216 • Pamela McLean

Figure 13.1 Students at Folabi (Fola) Sunday's independent ICT centre in Ago-Are

As I helped with additional collaborations I discovered that my initial diagram for TT had missed a vital element that influences two-way communication. I had underestimated cultural differences. This oversight happened because, although John and I are from different countries, we had a large measure of cultural overlap. We were therefore able to collaborate effectively from the start in TT and easily include all our contacts, although they had large cultural differences. However, as I discovered later in an appropriate technology training group, if that cultural overlap is missing, all kinds of problems can occur, so someone is needed to bridge the gap. I call this person a cultural mediator. Even in a simple online learning group someone needs to be aware of possible cross-cultural differences and ensure they are mediated. In a complex collaboration, mediation may be needed at several points and for a variety of reasons.

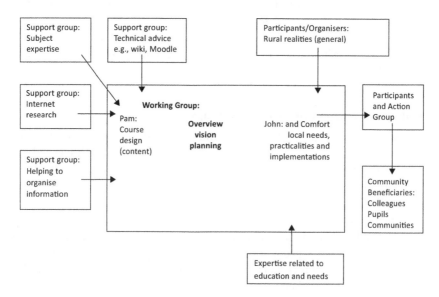

Figure 13.2 Teachers Talking

Online Learning in Virtual Academia • 217

I adapted my TT diagram to include the cultural mediator role. It illustrated the fact that some of the difficulties are to do with communications technology, and some are to do with human communications. Every time there is a relevant difference between people in the group, mediation may be needed to ensure a two-way flow of information. I checked the diagram's validity with other ICT4Ed and ICT4D (ICT for Education and ICT for Development) practitioners. When I checked with Dr (now Professor) Andrew Dearden during PRADSA (Practical Design for Social Action) workshops (www.bgdd.org) he found complete overlap between my diagram of the UK-Nigeria TT project and his UK-India project with a farmer's cooperative in Madhya Pradesh.

We produced a joint poster for the end of PRADSA, entitled "Human-Digital Information Bridge: A pattern for cross-country learning and problem solving networks" (see Figure 13.3). The poster had photos mirroring the various roles in the two locations (not reproduced here due to lack of written permission from the people photographed). It included a diagram covering the complete

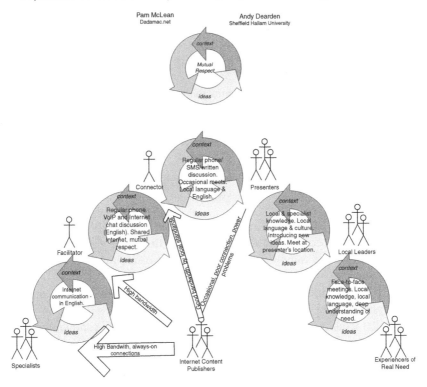

Figure 13.3 Digital Bridge Diagram extracted from poster

chain of two-way communications and cultural mediation. It covered all communication stages and cultural barriers between publishers of information on the Internet at one extreme and extremely hard-to-reach potential beneficiaries (illiterate people, speaking other languages and living beyond the reach of the Internet) at the other extreme.

The extremes of the communication chain in the diagram were illustrated in practice when a TT alumna, with no Internet access, sent a message to the Fantsuam Foundation asking someone there to go online, to contact the TT group, so that the members might search the Internet on her behalf. She was experimenting with a new cash crop (ginger) and wanted extra information before harvest time. She was sharing her knowledge verbally in the local language with people in her, mainly illiterate, local community.

In considering the full potential of online learning there are various possible approaches. We can look at existing educational provision and how it can be extended through online mechanisms. We can also look at the hardest to reach, as in the previous example, to see what online learning barriers exist and how they can be overcome.

The ICT Three-Legged Stool

As I continued my studies I developed a better understanding of the cross-cultural issues in online groups. I saw three main areas where communication breakdown happens:

- Differing relationships to the information content (regarding previous knowledge and present interest)
- Differences in people's usual offline lives that are reflected in online behaviour (community culture, language, concepts, behaviour expected of self and others)
- Different relationships to the communication technology being used (cost, availability, familiarity, etc.)

I summarised the three areas using the mnemonic of an ICT three-legged stool (see Figure 13.4), because all three "legs" need to be firm or the project will fall over.

Information and communication technology projects involve the following:

- I = Information: i.e., content – facts and figures, words, pictures, diagrams, video, messages, etc.
- C = Communication: i.e., people needing/wanting to communicate, needing access to information, needing to provide information, etc.
- T = Technology: i.e., hardware, software, issues of effective use, power supply, maintenance, training, running costs, infrastructure, telecommunications policies, etc.

ICT4Ed&D

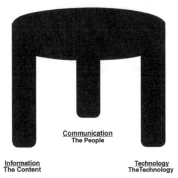

Figure 13.4 ICT Three-legged Stool

Later I refined my definition as follows:

- I = Information/Initiatives/Interests
- C = Communication/Community/Culture
- T = Technology/Tools/Training

Online Teaching, Online Learning and the Three-Legged Stool

I'm cautious about using the word "teacher" as its meaning varies with the cultural context. I prefer the description of "helping people to learn or discover." My understanding of words like "teacher" and "learner" reflects the fact that I trained as a primary school teacher when there was an emphasis on "the child as the agent of his own learning," and I was influenced by the work of John Holt (en.wikipedia.org/wiki/John_Holt_(educator)) and Ivan Illich (en.wikipedia.org/wiki/Ivan_Illich).

I help people to e-learn in three ways related to the "three-legged stool" idea:

- I = "Information/Initiatives/Interests": I help people access information and create new knowledge through various initiatives. I do this by recognising people with overlapping interests and introducing them to each other online, enabling collaborations and information exchange, and pointing to relevant resources.
- C = "Communication/Community/Culture": I build the community side of things by enabling effective communication. I help people feel at ease about contributing online. I help with cross-cultural issues. I often ask additional "who, what, where, when, why, how" questions, at key points in online discussions, where I know the answers will demonstrate areas of cultural difference. This helps reduce misunderstandings and the kind of confusion that can happen when people lack

shared cultural experience, use mismatching generalisations and have inaccurate assumptions.
- T = "Technology/Tools/Training": I give people basic technical tips and training online, usually in spontaneous e-learning sessions. Sometimes it's a matter of demonstrating an additional feature while we are using something in an online meeting. Other times I will use one communication channel in parallel with another to help people develop new skills, supporting someone to move from something familiar online to something unfamiliar.

Examples include these:

- Helping people to start using Skype by having a Yahoo chat beforehand and coming back to Yahoo whenever help was needed.
- Getting people started with Twitter during (typed) Skype group meetings and repeatedly coming back to Skype to compare progress and suggest next steps to take.
- Taking opportunities of individual chats on Facebook, Google Chat, or Skype to support someone moving over to the First Thursday meeting etherpad space to try it out beforehand and gain confidence.

I also respond to individual needs in a mentoring kind of way, often "being available to online callers" who turn up via typed chat channels while I'm working at my laptop.

A Simple Diagnostic Tool

The ICT three-legged stool mnemonic proved useful, so I used the idea to create a simple circle diagram, relevant for all Dadamac projects. It's similar to a Venn diagram, but not exactly so.

We start with the empty circles and our knowledge of two groups (or two people) who need to communicate effectively. In the non-overlapping parts we put all the relevant information we have (or need) about the two groups. In the central area we put the essential elements that need to be established and maintained. This helps us see areas of overlap and difference and the essential core that may need attention from a mediator/facilitator.

"ICT circles" is a diagnostic tool to be used as often as needed to understand key interconnections and blockages. It can have multiple versions, featuring any two groups (or stakeholders) involved in the initiative. Figure 13.5, the Teachers Talking example, illustrates the kind of information that starts going into the different sections, normally in a rough handwritten way, with lots of arrows and icons. We use the ICT circles as a kind of agenda tool to focus discussion and create a shared image of a situation. It's part of a process. The product is a new insight or a mediation action taken, not a tidy diagram.

Online Learning and Online Teaching

My role as an online learner has given me insights about the benefits and disadvantages of virtual academia and has fed into my understanding of how to help others to learn and collaborate online. I appreciate how much of my own state of readiness was thanks to my (distance learning) BA with the UK Open University. I can learn effectively online because I have easy Internet access, motivation, learning skills and, perhaps most importantly, the confidence to ask my own questions and pursue the answers. I am lucky to work in my mother tongue and come from a culture which is written rather than oral. I also have the bandwidth to escape from text and venture into a multimedia world, so my learning resources are rich and varied. Living in a large city I am able to find people with overlapping interests, so I can supplement my online learning experience with face-to-face meetings.

People without the benefits I enjoy may need more help and mentoring to benefit from the opportunities of virtual academia. This suggests the development of more enabling structures, with easy-to-find entry points and available mentors. A new hybrid online learning system might emerge that provides features and benefits of both virtual and established academia.

Teachers and mentors can help free-range learners by accelerating their searches for starting points and strategies. We can point to role models, peers, innovators, useful content, necessary skill development, existing lines of enquiry and appropriate groups. We can make introductions to people who could become fellow learners or collaborators. We can provide opportunities for the learners to explore their questions, interests and ideas in an online environment that is supportive and enriching. We can also look out for potential communication problems, especially in cross-cultural groups, and mitigate

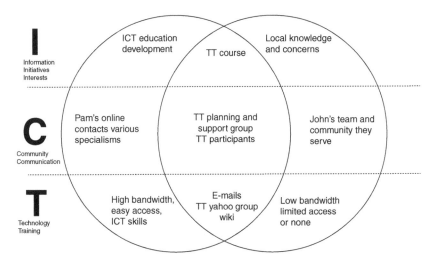

Figure 13.5 ICT Circles (Teachers Talking Example)

them. Ideally we will also be able to provide some one-to-one interaction and mentoring, helping students get a full overview of their studies and consider different perspectives.

Final Thoughts

This chapter is a description of virtual academia and also an example of how it works.

In introducing the idea of virtual academia I mentioned the following:

- It is particularly relevant for studying areas that are newly emerging.
- Theory and practice are closely aligned.
- New ideas and insights are developed by contributing to groups.

When I started work on this chapter, I struggled to find ways to connect my experiences of learning online with the experiences of potential readers who, I imagined, would be working or studying in formal educational establishments and whose assumptions and experiences would be very different to my own. I wanted them (you) to understand my learner-driven experiences in a way that might seem relevant to the mainstream debate about online learning.

I tried to find points of similarity and difference between the culture of mainstream education and the "learning culture" that is my reality. Thus I came up with the concept of my personal online learning experience taking place in "virtual academia" and explored its features. That, in turn, has given me new insights into aspects of my practical work. Writing this was like writing to a discussion group for the way it triggered new insights and understanding. The concept of virtual academia, emerging through the drafting and redrafting of this chapter and accelerated by e-mails and Skype chats, is in itself typical of how things happen in virtual academia.

References

Coalition of the Willing. Retrieved from http://dadamac.net/network/coalition-willing
Collective Intelligence & Wisdom. Retrieved from https://plus.google.com/u/0/communities/1006 66540255152085162?cfem = 1
Dadamac. Retrieved from http://www.dadamac.co.uk
GlobalNet21 Community Network. Retrieved from http://www.globalnet21.org
The Learning Change Project. Retrieved from https://gfbertini.wordpress.com
Minciu Sodas. Retrieved from http://dadamac.net/network/minciu-sodas
Oke-Ogun Community Development Agenda 2000 Plus (OOCD2000+, 2013). Retrieved from http://dadamac.net/initiative/oke-ogun-community-development-network-ocdn
Olanoff, D. (2012, November 14). LinkedIn's core mission: making its profiles the next generation resume. *Techcrunch*. Retrieved from http://techcrunch.com/2012/11/14/linkedins-core-mission-making-its-profiles-the-next-generation-resume
Overseas Development Institute (ODI). Retrieved from http://www.odi.org.uk
The P2P Foundation. Retrieved from http://p2pfoundation.net
Peter Adetunji Oyawale. Retrieved from http://dadamac.net/network/peter-adetunji-oyawale
PRADSA (Practical Design for Social Action) workshops. Retrieved from http://www.bgdd.org

RSA Animates. Retrieved from http://www.thersa.org/events/rsaanimate
School of Commoning. Retrieved from http://www.schoolofcommoning.com
Teachers Talking. Retrieved from http://www.dadamac.co.uk/teachers-talking.html
Teachers Talking Yahoo group. Retrieved from http://dadamac.net/start-of-tt-online-sig
TED Talks. Retrieved from http://www.ted.com
Wikipedia. *Holt, J*. Retrieved from http://en.wikipedia.org/wiki/John_Holt_(educator)
Wikipedia. *Illich, I*. Retrieved from http://en.wikipedia.org/wiki/Ivan_Illich
Wikipedia. *Socratic method*. Retrieved from http://en.wikipedia.org/wiki/Socratic_method
WikiQuals. *First annual report*. Retrieved from http://www.slideshare.net/fredgarnett/wikiquals-show-tell

Part 6
Designers and Producers

Part 6 looks at the commercial provider of online learning, but the efforts described here are a world away from the "tell and test" page turning that characterised the e-learning curriculum which gained such a foothold in the business world; that was focused on cost per head of delivery rather than efficacy of learning impact. The three chapters in this section represent a new era of online learning, one that builds upon social connectedness and knowledge creation through collaboration and sees gaming and simulation as a mechanism to build meaningful learning experiences. Clark Quinn is a thought leader in the use of gaming in education. In his chapter he looks at how to produce online learning that is educationally effective whilst also highly engaging as an experience, and he provides detailed guidance on how to link game design to learning objectives. David Clark and Doug Beckwith show how rich digital media simulations are being used by leading universities to provide a "day in the life of . . ." experience for learners. They provide a 21st-century spin on the approach of "learning by doing." Betts brings yet another focus; he seeks to produce a massively scalable, massively collaborative learning environment that utilises to as great an extent as possible existing content. Collectively these authors are agreed that learning is most effective when it takes place within a socially relevant and engaging context. One that allows the learner to explore his or her world and where content is not a static repository to be tackled in a preset linear fashion but rather a dynamic canvas to be explored, modified and reconstructed. Each, in their own way, point to the power of technology to connect people to each other and to realistic life experience.

14
Gaming Learning

CLARK QUINN

Quinnovation, USA

Editors' Introduction

In this chapter Quinn makes a strong case for the power of games to provide engaging learning while simultaneously building confidence and motivation. This, he claims, is because learning games provide meaningful contextualised practice. He sets out a series of design criteria that must be met in order to produce effective learning experiences. This chapter is a rich repository of practical advice and guidance for the budding game designer, and there are a number of useful flow charts and schematics to help clarify the design process.

Why are we, or why should we be, interested in games for instruction? The answer lies in the gaps we often see in formal education. Most formal learning struggles to provide sufficient and meaningful practice, despite the evidence from research that demonstrates the necessity. Our goals for learning are (or should be) twofold: retention over time until the learning is needed and transfer to all appropriate (and no inappropriate) contexts. Games, properly designed, provide the opportunity for contextualized practice in ways that approximate the benefits of mentored live practice, with few of the downsides.

An oft-ignored dimension to the argument is emotion (or, more technically, the conative elements of cognition: motivation, anxiety, confidence). We need to go beyond just the cognitive and involve learners' hearts as well as their minds. When we focus on learning, we need to tune the experience to reduce their anxiety to a manageable level, increase their motivation and gradually build their confidence, and games do this.

If our goals are retention and training, what are the barriers we're seeing? There are two major barriers to the success of learning (online or not): sufficient practice and contextual relevance. Each of these unpacks, but at the surface they're quite clear: we practice until we get it right, not until we can't get it wrong; and the problems we give learners bear little resemblance to the problems they'll face in the real world. Those two factors are exactly the opportunities that games present.

This chapter will briefly review a framework for meaningful practice that explains why we should design games for learning, and then defines a tested approach to systematically and reliably build learning games that will engage our learners and achieve our learning outcomes.

About Games

Van Merriënboer (1997) distinguishes between the complex problems to be solved and the knowledge needed to solve those problems. The premise here is that if you provide challenges, learners will be motivated to learn the relevant knowledge. The reverse, trying to get them to learn knowledge, will be difficult without an appropriate motivating context. So the focus for meaningful learning, and consequently serious games, is on cognitive skills. The ability to make better decisions in complex environments is what we increasingly need our learners to do.

We need to be clear that this is more than just gamification: adding game mechanics to other activities. Gamification can involve deeply leveraging game mechanics to wrap around practice environments, as Karl Kapp (2012) would have it, but it can also be about adding extrinsic motivation, à la Malone (1981), to make activities palatable, using scores and badges, that otherwise are uninteresting. Here we are advocating intrinsic motivation, not the more trivial exercise of gamification.

Even with meaningful-decision games, there are distinctions. Often, people will term such environments "simulations." However, simulations, technically, are just models of a world. They can be in any legal state, and the learner can take them to any other legal state. A self-effective and self-motivated learner can learn from such an environment, exploring to understand the relationships that matter.

To address the average learner, however, we put the simulation in an initial state and ask the learner to take the simulation to a different goal state that learners can't achieve until they understand the underlying relationships. And, typically, we wrap a story around it. Here we term that a "scenario." Scenarios can be effective learning solutions, but we can make scenarios more effective by tuning them into games. We turn them into games by tuning them, adjusting the parameters until we achieve a state of engagement.

Engaging Learning: Designing e-Learning Simulation Games (Quinn, 2005) laid out how the elements of effective learning practice align with the elements of engaging experiences (see Figure 14.1). The elements of effective practice appear across major learning theories; while not all the elements occur in every theory, they recur repeatedly. Similarly, the elements of engagement emerge across approaches to understanding engagement, not all appearing everywhere but reliably appearing again and again.

This alignment indicates a set of core elements that, when met, ensure that the experience will be both effective educationally and engaging as an experience. These elements should define learning practice, now with an additional

Education	Engagement
Clear goals	Clear or emergent goals
Appropriate challenge	Balanced challenge
Contextualized	Thematic coherence
Anchored	Relevance: action to domain
Relavent	Relevance: problem to learner
Exploratory	Choice of action
Active manipulation	Direct manipulation
Appropriate feedback	Coupling
Attention getting	Novel information/events

Figure 14.1 Alignment of Effective Practice and Engaging Experiences

goal to systematically align them with the elements of engagement, elaborating what is needed to tune a meaningful scenario into a game. The elements need to be elaborated in a unified version:

- Clear goals: The goals the learner needs to accomplish should be or should become clear through play.
- Appropriate challenge: The tasks to accomplish the learner's goals have to be within the learner's reach, but not within his or her existing competencies.
- A story "world": The tasks need to be set in a concrete environment, a world where the actions make sense.
- Meaningfulness: The tasks need to be a real application of the knowledge, accomplishing outcomes in the story world.
- Relevance: The tasks, and the world, have to be of interest to the audience.
- Exploratory: The learner has to have alternative choices of action and commit to a choice.
- Directness: The learner has to act on the world in the ways that make sense in the world.
- Coupled: The world needs to respond in ways appropriate to the learner's action and the world's logic.
- Novel: The world cannot be completely predictable, thus maintaining the learner's attention.

If these elements are appropriately included in our solution, we know our learning experiences will achieve the goals of meaningful practice. The next issue is whether we can systematically design solutions that include these elements aligned for success. If we can't reliably execute against these elements, this is all just wishful thinking. To put it another way, we now know learning should be hard fun, but can we make it so?

Designing Games

How do we systematically go from a learning objective to a game design? We need to be able to use the framework to develop a game that achieves a particular learning outcome reliably and repeatedly. We need a design process.

Newer approaches, such as Michael Allen's Successive Approximation Model (2012), suggest the process should be a waterfall model, but iterative and formative. To go from a scenario to a game, you have to tune, and that entails cycles of evaluation and revisions.

You need expertise for each of the elements of the game: graphics, audio, dialogue writing, interaction, video and any other elements you'll use, as well as the software engineering for development. While sometimes a person will be good at more than one, the ideal is to have the appropriate expertise. In the real world, of course, you have to use who you can get, but try to get diversity ideally (and valuably) as early in the process as possible.

For reference, a four-step process of analysis, specification, implementation and evaluation is used to talk about design. Analysis is gathering requirements, constraints and needed outcomes. Specification details the solution. Implementation builds the solution, and evaluation measures the solution against the needed criteria. We go through each of these stages, looking at what we need to add to the usual approaches we take. We will dig in a little deeper in the specification phase, covering modelling and pragmatics of the design process.

Analysis

Unlike pure game design, learning games have to start with the learning objectives, and, as our design criteria tell us, a learning game needs to have learners doing something meaningful. A problem is that expert performance is compiled away, inaccessible to conscious inspection. We need a way to talk about meaningful goals that subject matter experts (SMEs) can comprehend.

Sid Maier, one of the game designers' game designers (alluded to in the same reverent tones as Will Wright, Raph Koster and few others), once famously said "a good game is a series of interesting decisions" (Carless, 2003). The extension for our purposes is that a serious game is a series of important decisions. If we believe that, then our learning goals largely need to be about learners being able to make better decisions than they could beforehand; this gives us a way to think and talk about game design for ourselves and our SMEs.

It is, consequently, useful to structure games as a decision, precipitated by a situation, set in a story world (see Figure 14.2). There are alternative choices and consequences of those choices. This, alone, would make a better multiple choice question, what Quinn (2005) called a mini-scenario. However, the consequences of those decisions often lead to other situations requiring subsequent decisions (they travel in packs). This constitutes the basic structure of a game. The goal is to create a digital environment that can support the delivery of this structure as an experience.

The term "decisions" can work with SMEs to get the discussion turned to fruitful objectives. If we can isolate the core decisions learners need to be able to make after the learning experience, we have the necessary core around which to

Gaming Learning • 231

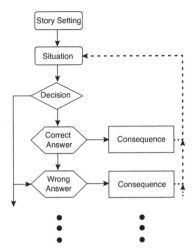

Figure 14.2 Game Structure

build learning games. Getting the decisions, whether from SMEs or otherwise, is the key element, and also the first step in analysis. Ideally, we get these in the form of behavioural objectives (Mager, 1975) – with performance, context and measurable outcome – that we can map into decisions, but it may be the reverse; we get the decisions and map them to behavioural objectives. Regardless, we want the specificity of outcome that comes from such rigor in definition.

Decisions don't exist in a vacuum, but instead play out in a context, and learning in context is more effective than in the abstract. So we need to discover the context in which these decisions occur. Ideally, we find all such contexts, to provide greater freedom in creating a setting that will align engagement with effective education. We need to understand the constraints that make those settings differ and also the things that distinguish those settings from ones in which the decisions aren't relevant.

In the real world, the consequences of decisions may be complex. From the point of view of learning games, however, we have to choose whether and how to explore those nuances. For specific training, you may choose to have right answers and wrong answers, and in the cases of more educational goals you may prefer to have ambiguity and create opportunities for discussion. Note that we will have to build in all the complexity we think important and provide feedback about the relative value of each decision. This is doable, but it is not trivial.

Importantly, people make decisions based upon clues that trigger particular models, and mistakes often come from bringing in the wrong models, which we term "misconceptions." These are useful in learning game design, as they give us alternatives to the "right" answer that can be made sufficiently challenging. When we want to ensure that learners aren't carrying on misconceptions beyond the learning experience, we need to make these compelling alternatives to more appropriate choices. When we do, we have a chance to remediate those misconceptions before it counts, after the learning experience.

Along with these decisions are consequences of the decisions, good and bad. We need to know what happens, and with what likelihood. Is a choice terminal, in that it means you've failed (or won), or does it lead to a more desperate attempt? We need to document those consequences to build into the potential outcomes of choices in the game.

We also have to be quite clear about the causes of the situation and the factors that change the basis of decisions and alter the consequences. When does the situation change? Are some things probabilistic? If so, what are the factors that affect those likelihoods? How much of this is just due to chance? Document those factors and the estimates of their likelihood.

There are constraints or factors that we'll consider, and some that we'll ignore, as they're not crucial. We're not going to model the whole world, and practically, we have to keep our scope reined in to what we can actually develop and deliver. Do be explicit about what you are and are not modelling, as there may be ways to increase scope or reasons to have some extra factors.

Finally, and arguably most importantly, we need to understand our audience. Traditionally in learning design we establish what must be learned and where learners currently are in their development. In this case, we also need to understand learners' "likes": what motivates them, what they think is important and what they care about. We will leverage this in building in the engagement.

Pragmatic Considerations

At this stage, we should document what we have discovered and circulate it. You will want SMEs and stakeholders to know what has been determined as important and get their amendments and approval to proceed. You should produce an analysis summary that documents the decisions you intend to embed, the settings in which they occur, the alternatives to the right answer (that capture the ways learners reliably go wrong) and the consequences of choices right or wrong.

Typically, you'll want to get sign off here from stakeholders and SMEs that they agree with what you have documented. There will likely be feedback that results in some changes. If you are doing this on a contract basis or under some constraints on schedule and resources, it is strongly recommend that you insist in the agreement that they circulate it to all parties and consolidate the feedback, and that you'll only do one round of updates, so your response to the consolidated feedback is final and otherwise it constitutes a scope change.

Specification

At this point we are ready to start considering potential design solutions. The goal is to have a fully realised storyboard that documents the design ready for sign off before implementation. There are intermediate stages including documenting our evaluation metrics and potentially several intermediate levels of specification.

Previously we indicated that design should be iterative; but how do you know when to stop iterating? All too often, the answer can be "when we run out of time and/or money," which is not the right answer. The answer should be "when we've achieved our design goals." To do that, you need to specify your design goals in ways the game can be assessed against. If you are running out of resources at a faster rate than you are achieving your design goals, you may reset your scope, or consider lower levels of success, but at least you are doing so consciously.

We need to be specific about what will determine a successful outcome. This may have been part of the brief or potentially emerged from the learning goals we documented in the analysis phase. As in other learning technology interventions we need to specify usability goals (to eliminate usability as a factor if we're not succeeding on our other goals) and learning outcomes with an independent validation. For a game, however, we need to go further to stipulate engagement goals to a level that can be tested against. You can't say it's a game, only your learners can tell you. As this suggests, engagement goals are subjective; learner opinion is key, and we can use metrics like ratings, preference over other ways of learning or a willingness to pay for the experience. Whatever we choose, we need to be concrete.

With these criteria specified, you are ready to move to the challenge, and fun, of specifying a game design. The ultimate goal is a realised world or story setting, an initial state of affairs, a clear (or emergent) goal, embedded decisions and an appropriate level of challenge and appropriate interactions.

This is the point to get creative. You need to find the intersection between the contexts in which these decisions occur and settings that interest the learner. And you will need to use well-known creative techniques such as diverging, deliberately populating the space of possible solutions, before converging. Exaggeration is your friend. You don't have to tie it to the real world; for example, you can consider fantastic settings – medieval times (potentially with magic), science fiction (also known as "the future"), etc. Even if you're tied to the real world, ramp up the stress – e.g., you are not just saving the life of a patient, you are saving the ambassador's daughter! In the real world, there will be real motivations, and you want to approximate that here, but you have to use story tools to do it. Realise that you are not writing a story; rather, you are creating a background story within which the players will tell their own story by their actions.

What we're talking about here is experience design. That is, consider the learner's trajectory of anxiety, motivation and confidence explicitly as your proceed. We're moving from learning being about content to being about the experience. Give learners the opportunity to make important decisions.

The principles of media usage apply here (Clark & Mayer, 2003). It's easy to jump into overemphasising media as opposed to the quality of the experience.

Too much of what is developed in trying to create engaging learning is overproduced and underdesigned. Minimalism is a good principle here (Carroll, 1990). As Antoine de Saint-Exupery (1939) said: "Perfection is attained not when there is nothing more to add, but when there is nothing more to remove."

The characters are one element to consider. What role would players naturally be in when making these decisions, and which of those would be appealing (or how can you make it appealing)? And what are the other characters they'll have to interact with? While you want to make the role relevant, you likely want to minimize descriptive details of the character the player plays so he or she can more easily identify with the role. The one exception is in the case of a deep game, when you might want to let the player customize the character to build allegiance. In the case of other characters, it helps to flesh out their motivations and perhaps have a signature flaw. Try to avoid stereotypes, however. Commercial game designers will flesh out characters more than actually shows in the game, just to have that depth to draw upon.

Another element to consider is how to make the alternatives to the correct answer at each decision point sufficiently compelling. You want to make the challenge sufficient and simultaneously discriminate between learners who understand the relationships and those who do not.

Practically speaking, once your team has converged on a rough idea of a story world, characters and important variables, you probably should get approval before you go too far. Getting sign off on the rough concept is highly recommended. In fact, it has been my personal experience that the concept is typically finalized by the time of the end of the analysis. If so, minimize the handoffs and waiting time, and put your initial concept into the document that also summarizes the outcome of the analysis.

At this stage, when you've got an approved concept, it's time to flesh it out. This is hard to discuss conceptually rather than tacitly, as it's an iterative process where you "sweat the details." You'll be writing dialogue, creating the look and feel and rending graphics, working out the interface design, scripting any animations, locking down any audio and accomplishing any other necessary tasks.

One of the ways to keep the experience from feeling too deterministic is to have some pools of alternatives to pull from, randomly. For example, after every successful decision in a game that includes a series of them, there might be feedback from a boss; if it's the same phrase every time, it can be less than desirable. You could have just a handful of different ways to say it and pull from them randomly. Similarly, if you're giving players a different set of things to work on, you can pull the names and statuses randomly from a pool. In a project management game, we had a pool of roughly 20 different projects, each with four different levels of scope (low, medium, high and ridiculous) that we chose randomly. Both schedule and budget were generated randomly within a range, as well. This combinatorial approach provided an essentially unlimited replay possibility.

You should be running interim representations in front of representatives of the audience and getting feedback. Again, it's an iterative process. If this is a situation where you need much and varied practice, going beyond a fixed scenario, there's another element involved as well: modelling.

Modelling

One of the important decisions is how the interactions are controlled. This might seem to be an implementation detail, but it turns out that the nature of the interaction determines many other aspects. In general, practice should be "until you can't get it wrong," which typically means considerable practice. If you don't need much practice, and minimal exposure is sufficient, you can consider hard-wired solutions – e.g., branching scenarios. There are also human-driven solutions (e.g., Wills, Leigh, & Ip, 2011), but here we are talking about technology-implemented solutions. In general, you'll want to build a model-driven experience that adapts on the fly, getting harder until the learner is successfully practicing the full decision. This requires building a model of the world.

Whether we implement via a model interaction or hard-wired responses of a branching simulation, the research and design we do is largely similar, short of modelling. At the point of determining to do a model-driven game, with variability, chance, adaptivity and more, there's an extra level of work that has to happen. In most cases, when you're practicing to really get the skill down, you want to take this step.

Modelling the world can be qualitative or quantitative, but it needs to happen. You'll set parameters that will stipulate how much one action affects a particular variable and under what conditions. Ultimately, you create a model of the world and the relationships in it. The model is set in an initial state, and the learner takes actions that affect the state of the model, until the state reaches a terminal state (win or lose; see Figure 14.3).

In short, you need to determine how to represent the world in terms of variables that change based upon the learner's actions and the rules that determine what those changes are. The model needs to support the initial state and map learner choices into effects on the model that allow the learner to, if they fully understand the relationships embodied in the model, navigate successfully to the goal state. This implies, necessarily, that you have to model the relationships involved in the decisions. The engine processing learner actions runs rules that process the changes to the model based upon the relationships in the model and then calculates what next action should be presented to the learner, assembling the choices from a decision template populated with elements representing the current state (see Figure 14.4).

This actual modelling is a challenging but important task. Not everyone can do it; a quick check is that anyone who can write his or her own macros or

236 • Clark Quinn

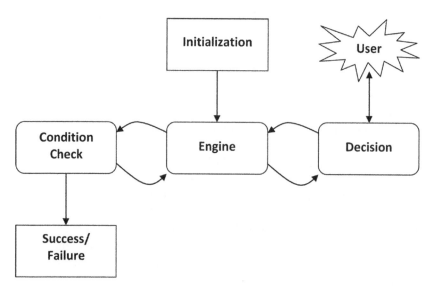

Figure 14.3 Game Model

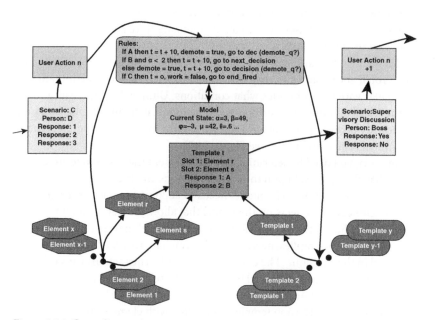

Figure 14.4 Game Processing

mail-processing rules is probably capable. Certainly a game designer or software engineer should be able to capture the world in terms of such a model, but a designer has to be the one to stipulate the world. A colleague once opined that it takes a team of at least two: one to brainstorm what needs to be in the world, and another to capture it. The reason it takes two is that there is an inherent tension between the tasks: one must diverge in coming up with ways to enrich the world in meaningful ways, and the other must converge on a finite representation. Her point was that very few people can do both things at the same time.

Once we've chosen the implementation, an important element is the way in which you keep the game from being too deterministic. In a game that's driven by a real simulation, a model of the world, this is done through probability, having some events occur unpredictably. These events should have some effect on the game, affecting underlying metrics. The contingency factors collected at the analysis stage now come into play. You may adjust those probabilities for pedagogical reasons. For instance, if something doesn't occur very often in real life, but is really important when it occurs, you might increase the frequency with which that event occurs. If it's a fixed implementation, you don't have the freedom to have randomness; however, you should consider throwing unexpected bits of humour or cultural references into different paths to reward exploration, with the caution that such can be done well or poorly. Testing is a useful filter on these experiments.

Pragmatic Considerations

The end result of the specification process should be a complete storyboard, documenting the design before you start implementing. This document needs to include the story world, characters, core variables, initialization settings (which can include some randomness as well, supporting replay) and terminal conditions (win/lose). Then, for each decision type, you need to capture the screen template, elements that will be displayed and the consequences of learner actions as rules that change the values of the model, including what template you go to next (see Figure 14.5). For every screen, or screen type, the look and logic should be represented.

This document again needs to go through the sign-off process before beginning implementation. In the waterfall model this would be firm, but in iterative development, you will be prototyping elements of your design. You should be iteratively prototyping every time you have a question to be answered. We'll pick this up again in evaluation.

And a caveat: some proportion of your stakeholders (perhaps as much as 90%) will not fully understand how the storyboard relates to the actual learner experience, particularly if elements of the screens will be populated by rule so placeholders are present. Consequently, consider finding a way to represent a sample learner experience as part of the submission for approval. It can be a prose recitation, a set of annotated slides, or an animation. For real games and big projects, they'll go as far

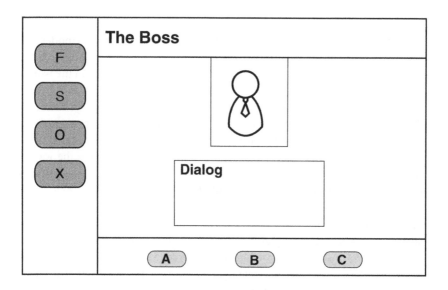

Dialog: *"What's this I hear?"*

Response: A. *"Nothing"*
B. *"Nothing, sir"*
C. *"I resign"*

Rules:
If A then t = t + 10, demote = true, go to dec (demote_q?)
If B and α < 2 then t = t + 10, go to next_decision
else demote = true, t = t + 10, go to decision (demote_q?)
If C then t = 0, work = false, go to end_fired

Figure 14.5 Storyboard Sample

as programming a sample (e.g., in Flash) that doesn't have all the underlying logic, but has a hardwired experience of play. What you want to avoid, having developed against an approved storyboard, is stakeholders seeing the resulting experience and saying "that's not what I expected." You want to minimize possibilities for miscommunication to derail your project. Again, stipulate contractually that there be one round of consolidated feedback and revision.

The processes of analysis and design, together, involve gathering the needed information and consolidating that into the necessary form for sign off. Then the storyboard is developed using any breakdown of team that makes sense, for example an instructional designer handling the text and rules and a graphic design person doing the look and feel and user interface (UI) design for a storyboard. The result is signed off before development (see Figure 14.6).

Gaming Learning • 239

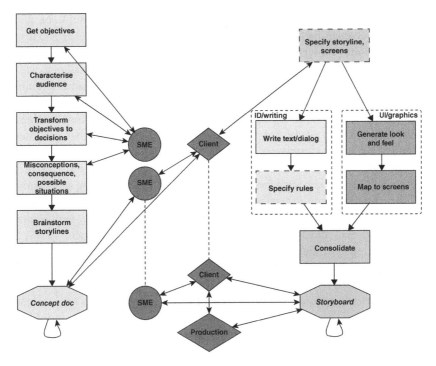

Figure 14.6 Analysis and Specification

With a signed-off storyboard in hand, you're ready to transition from the iterations of evaluation for specification process to the iterations around a real implementation.

Implementation and Evaluation

Implementation consists of two stages. The first is the low-tech prototyping that precedes the finalization of a storyboard, and the second is the development of a fully programmed game for testing and refinement. Each has its own issues. This chapter is largely about design, so the main discussion here will be on the impact of implementation and evaluation on the design process.

For the prototyping stage, you should ideally stay with the lowest-fidelity technology you can use. One of my students fully developed a game design using pieces of paper showing the possible screens with a cycle of asking "what would you do here" and then showing the resulting screen. Much can be done with sticky notes, paper and simple screen mock-ups (whether presentation software or diagramming tools).

We typically don't use paper and nowadays use many digital technologies to do even low-tech prototyping, but we want to postpone levels of investment as late as possible. The reason is simple: once you invest in implementation, it becomes increasingly hard to justify significant revisions. You want to be able to throw out anything you do before the storyboard is finalized.

For a branching scenario, the implementation is easy. You can do it in raw HTML, in PowerPoint, with essentially all commercial e-learning tools and with special purpose branching scenario software. Fully modelled games require more complex implementation.

When you move to the coding phase, you want to design for revision. You don't turn a scenario into a game, you tune it into a game. Which means that even after you've specified the storyboard, some of the values you chose for the model will not be quite right. Once you start playing you realise this is taking too long, that is too fast, this isn't changing fast enough, or that value isn't adapting sufficiently. The way you will know is that the user experience doesn't achieve the "flow" zone (Czikszentmihalyi & Czikszentmihalyi, 1988). Expect that you'll have to play with the parameters of the game and that you'll need to refine and test again.

A warning here: there are experienced developers using software tools who have largely done simple tasks such as animations. In such situations, their ad hoc coding skills have been adequate. When it comes to games, however, you need a software engineer. The difference is that software engineers know to not hardcode values into the software but use constants to refer to those values. Then, if you want to tune an interaction, you change the constant's value and the references throughout the code will change. The alternative is that the coder hunts through the program for every instance of the value and ends up missing some. There are other benefits as well, like proper task breakdown of the structures so the code is malleable in other ways.

A question that always arises is what tool to use for games. Everyone wants a tool that's easy to use yet powerful, but it is likely that such a tool is fundamentally impossible. The nuances of the models are such that there's no simple way to capture them; the tool will inherently have to have the power of a full programming environment, with the same overhead. You can't get away with anything that really isn't at least a programming language, or else you will need to have such a specialised interface that learning to use it is as complex as learning to program.

On the other hand, any programming environment you can use that meets the delivery environment should be sufficient. As long as you can embed the media elements and control the interactions, it should suffice. For example, great games have been created in HyperCard, about as simple a programming language as you could possibly have.

The question more importantly is about delivery platform. Games have been delivered in everything from Web pages to gaming consoles, with computer-based games in between. These days, handheld platforms, specifically tablets and smartphones, are increasingly desirable as target environments.

The choice of delivery tool is dynamic enough that identifying solutions is still an open question. At the time of writing, HTML5 seems positioned to own the Web and mobile delivery space, but tools for HTML5 are still early. There are currently hybrid solutions as well, at least for mobile, where mobile Web can be embedded in a platform-specific environment for greater access to hardware options, but at a trade-off of capability versus custom development for the specific platform. The best solution will be the intersection of what's available at your time of development and the environment familiar to your development resources.

Testing early and often is a mantra for software engineers and game designers, and the same should be true for you. If you have a question or an idea, test it. Think you've nailed an interaction? Test it. Do iterative testing: first simulated in your mind, then tested within the team, then with the next most proximal victim (e.g., subject) – for example, a pliable individual in the organisation not involved in the project. You want to do as much testing with the real audience as possible, but get as many of the problems out of the way before you use them. The usability field found that iterating between expert review and user testing was a valuable approach (e.g., Nielsen, 1994), as well as that only a handful of experts was sufficient to find most of the major flaws. A parsimonious approach focusing on the most valuable feedback is to be lauded.

Real game designers test many things. Your developer should be testing against software bugs, platform compatibility and other technical issues. You will want to be testing against usability issues (verifying that the design you verified is good), then educational impact and finally game experience. The latter is totally subjective, but you can't decree it's a game, only your players can tell you. It doesn't have to be compelling, but for the fastest learning curve and most effective outcomes, it should be.

There continues to be a concern over cost. Games are liable to be more expensive than designing a knowledge test, but if that doesn't have any real outcome, it's throwing money away. Instead, look at the cost of not doing meaningful practice and consider that consequence. The short answer is that if you get the design right, there are lots of ways to implement it. Games can be done on a very frugal basis, even if it's just creating a series of branching scenarios to provide sufficient practice. At some point, however, the ability to provide essentially unlimited replay on a fixed-cost basis has to overcome the cost barriers, and when they do, there's little better.

Go Games

Learning games are powerful practice environments, but they require rigor to develop. We need to systematically incorporate the following elements:

- Clear goals
- Appropriate challenge
- A story "world"
- Meaningfulness
- Relevance

- Exploration
- Directness
- Coupled
- Novel

Initially, you need to gather information about the needed decisions, identify the consequences and probabilities as well as the settings in which they occur, and understand audience interests. This information will allow you to choose an appropriate model world, build in choices, balance the challenge and flesh out the details. You'll want to use exaggeration to ramp up motivation and use the right media for the task. And you'll need to model the world if you're going beyond hardwired or human-driven solutions.

You will want to do this in a systematic and pragmatic way. You'll want to use the right resources, constrain scope and risk, and manage stakeholder expectations. You'll also want to match implementation level to learning need throughout the process, including final delivery. And you'll need to iteratively test and tune.

If you do so, however, you'll have realised the opportunity to offer engaging practice and achieve meaningful outcomes. We have to get out of the habit of focusing on knowledge-based objectives and recognise that the ability to apply knowledge is the real goal. We can't expect knowledge tests to have any meaningful impact, and we need to shift. Once we recognise that, learning games become our most viable solution. Learning can, and should, be hard fun.

References

Allen, M. (2012). *Leaving ADDIE for SAM*. Alexandria, VA: ASTD Press.
Carless, S. (2003). Interview: Bruce Shelley – The Mythology of Empires. *Gamasutra*. Retrieved from http://www.gamasutra.com/view/feature/2779/interview_bruce_shelley__the_.php
Carroll, J. M. (1990). *The Nurnberg funnel: designing minimalist instruction for practical computer skill*. Cambridge, MA: MIT Press.
Clark, R. C., & Mayer, R. E. (2003). *e-Learning and the science of instruction*. San Francisco: Pfeiffer.
Csikszentmihalyi, M., & Csikszentmihalyi, I. S. (1988). *Optimal experience: psychological studies of flow in consciousness*. New York: Cambridge University Press.
de Saint Exupéry, A. (1939). *Wind, sand, and stars*. New York: Reynal & Hitchcock.
Kapp, M. K. (2012). *The gamification of learning and instruction: game-based methods and strategies for training and education*. Alexandria, VA: ASTD Press.
Mager, R. (1975). *Preparing instructional objectives* (2nd ed.). Belmont, CA: Lake Publishing Co.
Malone, T. W. (1981). Towards a theory of intrinsically motivating instruction. *Cognitive Science, 5*, 333–370.
Nielsen, J. (1994). Heuristic evaluation. In J. Nielsen & R. L. Mack (eds.), *Usability inspection methods*. New York: John Wiley & Sons.
Quinn, C. (2005). *Engaging learning: designing e-learning simulation games*. San Francisco: Pfeiffer.
Van Merriënboer, J. J. G. (1997). *Training complex cognitive skills: a four-component instructional design model for technical training*. Englewood Cliffs, NJ: Educational Technology Publications.
Wills, S., Leigh, E., & Ip, A. (2011). *The power of role-based e-learning*. New York: Routledge.

15
Lights, Camera, Action: Experiential Learning with Digital Media Simulations

DAVID JAMES CLARKE IV AND DOUGLAS BECKWITH

Toolwire, Inc., USA

Editors' Introduction

The authors draw upon years of experience in the design of online learning environments to argue that a new age of learning by experience can be enabled by the availability of low-cost, photorealistic, immersive digital simulations. They trace the development of the art and show how early deficiencies can now be countered. Two example case studies provide a detailed insight into the power of this style of experiential learning to transform the way we think about higher education provision on both sides of the Atlantic; the results make for compelling reading. The chapter closes with a review of a range of exciting developments that are just around the corner and which have the ability to take this initiative to yet another level.

Introduction

Lecture ◊ homework ◊ exam ◊ repeat; that, in essence, is the model of higher education today. Experiential learning is largely absent from this model.

Over 100 years ago, the time-tested "apprenticeship model" gave way to the teacher-centred classroom as a result of the Industrial Revolution. When a craft-based economy transformed into a service-based economy, hands-on learning declined in prominence. Instead of providing skills, teachers increasingly assumed the responsibility for drilling facts.

In recent years, our society has undergone another radical transformation sparked by the growth of the Internet and widespread access to information. In this day and age, there is no shortage of content at one's fingertips. As our abilities to acquire knowledge quickly increase, the utility of knowledge storage decreases. As a result, the focus of educators must extend beyond mere knowledge transfer to place a greater emphasis on teaching fundamental 21st-century skills, including the abilities to think critically, solve problems and communicate effectively. Yet for all of the emphasis on these cognitive skills, opportunities to

243

apply and practice these skills – the very essence of the apprenticeship model – have not been incorporated in the learning model. Contemporary education has been almost exclusively one-way, teacher to student, with far-removed and delayed graded assignments, often with little to no feedback, as the only form of "interaction."

Today's global economy requires an agile workforce – one that can skill and re-skill at an accelerated rate. The emergence of the Information Age has created a massive demand for a new breed of workforce-ready graduates prepared to contribute in a digital economy. Today's instructors face the daunting challenge of preparing students with the right skills to achieve success in this ever-changing 21st–century workplace. This task is compounded by tight budgets and ever-increasing class sizes.

In order to adjust to these changes, our educational systems require more authentic forms of information delivery and assessment that are based on two-way interactions and can be delivered in ways that are scalable, sustainable and support learning institutions' long-term goals.

Immersive Experiential Learning – Bringing Learning to Life

Through dozens of published books and our work for several online education providers, the authors have spent the past two and a half decades wrestling with the basic incongruence between modern education and modern life. Solving this problem is the driving force behind our work at Toolwire, Inc., where David James Clarke IV and Douglas Beckwith serve as the vice-president of learning solutions and senior fellow, respectively.

At Toolwire, working to develop online experiential learning solutions for higher education and corporate training, we begin by asking a basic question: Why can't today's classroom be as engaging as a video game, as hands-on as an internship and as addictive as Facebook newsfeeds?

Among several innovations, we developed a learning solution called Toolwire Learnscapes™. These are digital media simulations that immerse students in photorealistic settings with interactive video characters. These learning platforms facilitate self-paced, day-in-the-life "virtual apprenticeships" that expose students to realistic work environments. Using green screen technology, our virtual scenarios, which unfold in boardrooms, hospital wards and courtrooms, break the fourth wall of the classroom and place students inside their education. At the heart of the Learnscape is real-time interaction in meaningful and relevant settings that bring learning alive, not through contrivance, but because they call for application, practice and extension of knowledge acquired.

Within each Learnscape episode, "virtual mentors" impart valuable information and provide encouragement to build the students' confidence as they engage with course material. Through Learnscapes, law students have the opportunity to visit a jail to conduct pretrial interviews with clients, and aspiring nurses can stand bedside taking patient histories and checking medications. These simulations allow students to learn by doing and make mistakes within a low-stake environment. Learning occurs through successes and mistakes because students discover in real time what works and what does not. Students are required to make decisions, and the "virtual mentors" give feedback during the play of the Learnscape, when the feedback is most relevant, not at some later more formalised time.

There are some aspects of education that even the most sophisticated learning platform cannot replace. We recognise that relating to virtual avatars is no replacement for building student-teacher relationships and that online forums cannot replace an on-the-ground community of learning. This statement assumes, though, that there are student-teacher relationships and learning communities as part of the traditional classroom setting. Sadly, this is not always the case. At Toolwire we believe online learning can work in tandem with traditional classrooms to expand educational opportunities materially. While classrooms provide a foundation for the learning process, online experiential learning offers customized learning solutions tailored to fit a student's individual needs. One way we like to visualize the complementary nature of class-based and online learning is through the cognitive learning map seen in Figure 15.1. This diagram illustrates how experiential learning can supplement brick-and-mortar schoolrooms to catalyze the learning process and convert short-term knowledge into deeper understanding through a process we call cognitive encoding.

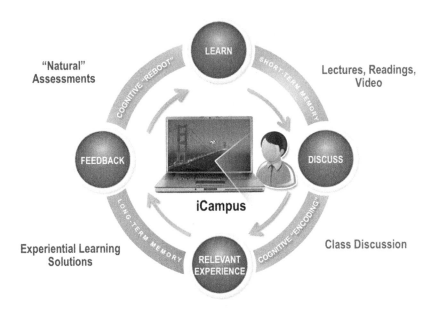

Figure 15.1 The Cognitive Learning Map

This chapter provides an overview of Toolwire's interactive learning platforms, which are built around pedagogical methods proven to increase student engagement and promote deeper learning through real-time interactive educational transactions that are both relevant and meaningful to students (Bacow, Bowen, et al., 2012). Reflecting on first-generation digital learning solutions and previewing future technologies still early in development, this chapter offers both a macro-view of the evolution of this rapidly changing field and an in-depth look at learning tools already in use in classrooms around the world. Digital media simulations can be developed for virtually any type of course and are especially ideal for topics such as health care, business, education, law, orientation and first-year general education.

Let's take a closer look.

Theoretical Foundation

Toolwire's learning solutions are not only built to match a 21st-century lifestyle and economy but also leverage recent cognitive learning research. From advanced brain imaging to longitudinal cognitive studies, we know more today about how the brain works than ever before.

The underlying pedagogical approach for digital media simulations is inspired by the experiential learning philosophy of "learning by doing" and is grounded in Itiel Dror's (2006) research on the cognitive learning process.

Dror's research demonstrates the extent to which memory and skill acquisition are context reliant. What matters is not just what we learn but also the settings in which we learn. "Specificity of encoding makes retrieval easier when it is in a similar context," Dror writes. "Thus, the learning environment should be as similar as possible to that back at the workplace, where the learners are expected to recall the information and to modify their behaviour" (p. 2). That modification can only take place when timely, specific feedback is given in a relevant, meaningful context so students can learn from successes and mistakes by mapping their learning directly to an experience that has just taken place.

The importance of cultivating students' intrinsic motivation, a fundamental attribute of lifelong learners, draws from aspects of multiple learning theories, including constructivism (Vygotsky, 1978), flow theory (Csíkszentmihályi, 1990), situated cognition (Brown, Collins, & Duguid, 1989), cognitive load theory (Sweller, 1994) and game impact theory (Smith, 2008). The common thread among these schools of thought is the emphasis on the importance of making experiences personally relevant to each student's unique interests and educational goals. At Toolwire, we believe that contextualized learning in real-world situations is inherent in both relevance and learning goals. Digital media simulations include open-ended assessment activities that build on stored knowledge and skills, consequently facilitating greater student expression and more effective knowledge transfer. The forms of new media made possible by contemporary cutting-edge technologies can be used to create context, relevance and interaction in ways never possible before in traditional one-way media.

Keys to Success – Addressing Previous Barriers to Adoption
First-Generation Immersive Learning Environments
Immersive learning platforms are not new in the world of teaching and training. Simulations have been used since the late 1990s in military and medical applications. However, these early simulations were designed for specific tasks and were prohibitively expensive for widespread use across universities and corporations.

The first generation of virtual learning environments capable of widespread adoption appeared in 2003, only two years after the first volume of *Teaching and Learning Online* was published. Though greeted by the learning community with fanfare and excitement, these first-generation virtual learning environments fell short of expectations.

A September 2011 *Campus Technology* article titled "Is There a Second Life for Virtual Worlds" (Ramaswami, 2011) cited a number of barriers that hindered the adoption of first-generation virtual learning environments. These barriers included the following:

- Steep learning curve for teachers
- Lack of technical competencies such as scripting and building
- Lack of technical support
- Lack of interoperability with other technologies
- Bandwidth limitations and firewalls
- Costs of development and maintenance

Drawing from lessons of the past and benefiting from a confluence of new technologies, today's digital media simulations address these barriers in ways that have enabled them to be scalable, personalised and ready for primetime. The following are a few important advancements that are contributing to the widespread adoption of today's digital media simulations.

No Teacher Left Behind – The Importance of Student and Teacher Support
Ramaswami (2011) pointed to lack of technical support as one of the primary concerns expressed by instructors. Eero Palomäki (2009) noted technical problems as being a major issue related to virtual world usage, and Ramaswami (2011) echoed this sentiment when he suggested that "using adequate computers and equipment are only one side to this problem. Another is the availability of IT support for the educators and students."

The need for greater IT support was further underscored by Bacow and colleagues (2012) when they listed the first of their six strategies for overcoming obstacles involved with developing online courses as "Provide generous support for faculty adopting online teaching" (p. 23).

We may therefore conclude that in order for learning institutions to be comfortable entrusting their student with new technologies, every aspect of the user experience, including usability, accessibility, security and customer support, must be considered.

At Toolwire, we have a Learner Advocacy team that is responsible for ongoing support and contributes to ongoing platform improvement and innovation. The team is supported by a customized training portal (library.toolwire.com) that provides access to the following resources:

- An actual digital media simulation orientation
- A two-minute instructional video developed with virtual locations and characters used in these simulations
- A faculty PowerPoint guide
- A quick guide illustrating key features and functions
- An FAQ addressing common questions
- A feedback submission button

User-Friendliness and Accessibility

Steep learning curve was another critical barrier cited by Ramaswami (2011). In terms of user-friendliness and accessibility, Toolwire's digital media simulations offer a vast improvement over first-generation simulations. Toolwire's easy-to-use simulations are essentially plug-and-play.

The online deployment of our digital media simulations provides many advantages.

Delivering these solutions online, in a browser, as opposed to a downloaded piece of software, allows institutions to scale courses easily up or down and, if so desired, make system-wide modifications or adjustments. For students, these simulations are available around the clock, around the globe, which enables them to practice at their own speed and revisit the simulation as many times as necessary.

Higher-Order Instructional Design

Toolwire's simulations introduce an innovative instructional design approach called natural assessment, which assesses students naturally as they progress through the storyline in each simulation episode. This approach moves beyond current methodologies to develop what might best be described as enhanced, authentic assessments. This authenticity is created when students are placed in real-world situations and asked to make decisions and take actions related to the work required in them. Authentic assessments ask the question, "How effectively can you perform in an authentic situation?" not "Can you take a test and recite facts?"

Embedded throughout these experiences, signpost interactions provide multi-branching opportunities. Depending on the quality of students' decisions and actions, students either progress through the storyline or receive additional support through remedial content that can be delivered in multiple modalities within the simulations such as text (an e-mail or text message), audio (a phone voice message), or video (a meeting with colleagues) (see Figure 15.2). As the action in the storyline takes place, students receive feedback, not "answers," that helps shape their course of action, much as performance feedback is given in a performance review or in an on-the-job coaching engagement. This formative feedback allows them to "learn by doing" rather than waiting only for formal feedback at the end of the activity.

At the completion of each episode, information provided by students in the experiential assessment is captured, automatically formatted into an easy-to-read document and delivered to instructors for grading. Thus the built-in assessment capabilities of digital media simulations provide a more effective way of gauging knowledge transfer and the students' ability to select and apply appropriate learning in real-life situations.

Cocreation and Best Practice Design Approaches

From first-generation immersive learning platforms, Toolwire learned that requiring instructors to handle the development, maintenance and administrative responsibilities was simply not sustainable on a large scale. For this reason, Toolwire developed a cocreation methodology (see Figure 15.3) that strategically leverages an institution's instructional design and subject matter experts at critical checkpoints by giving practitioners and subject matter experts a central role in shaping the learning experience. Cocreation is a best practice approach that is extremely conducive to sustained adoption; this cocreation approach guarantees that LearnScapes address the institutions' learning objectives and academic outcomes because the partner institutions have set the academic priorities and goals.

The final product provides increasing value with every use as the upfront effort is amortized over time in order to provide a consistent, instructionally sound way for institutions to introduce the vital missing link of experiential learning into their programs.

The cocreation model enables instructors to focus on what they do best – impart knowledge and mentor students – while Toolwire handles the mechanics of hosting, maintaining, supporting, programming and creating digital media. On average, a series of four to six simulation episodes, each about 20 or 30 minutes in length, can be developed in about 90 days.

Figure 15.2 Screenshot of an Assessment from a Health Care Learnscape™

Lights, Camera, Action: Experiential Learning • 251

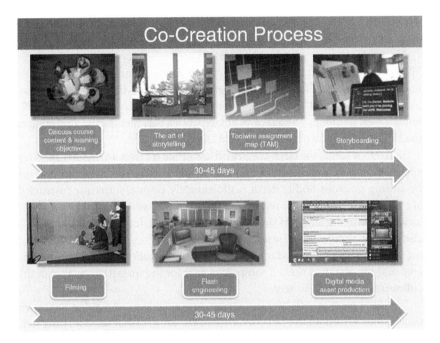

Figure 15.3 The Toolwire Cocreation Process

Case Study: The University of East London – Law Program

A good example of the cocreation process comes from the University of East London (UEL), which worked with Toolwire to develop digital media simulations for its law program.

Working with UEL, we created a simulation situated within the Inns of Court and the surrounding areas. UEL has a diverse student population, so ethnic and gender representation along with age profiles were key considerations within the scripts and storyline. Preproduction started with the curriculum owner and instructional designer, who established the aims and objectives in a flowchart. With the introduction of a scriptwriter and subject matter expert, we created an overarching storyline that converted the course's learning objectives into a narrative format.

Locations required digital photography and raw video footage to provide panoramic views for each of the virtual environment creations. For this simulation, UEL was careful to acquire permission for some virtual location photos on judiciary premises. Production for these simulations used green screen technology.

Court etiquette nuances extended down to a variety of minute details, which required judicial choreography and direction. The subject matter expert ensured that behavioural aspects, accents, voice inflections and delivery were all authentic. As demonstrated in this example, casting expertise is an important competency introduced by the movement towards digital media simulations that are designed to immerse students fully in the most authentic and engaging experiences possible.

Virtual locations in this legal simulation are authentic, adding to the credibility of the experience. Students interact with an experienced colleague outside Fountain Court, a long-established set of commercial barristers' chambers, based in the Temple, London. They also meet at Ede & Ravenscourt – the well-known legal outfitters – and receive advice from a barrister during a meeting at the Wig and Pen Pub close to the Royal Courts of Justice.

In the first scene, the clerk at a British law office receives an urgent call. "Our client Jordan Jones was convicted in the crown court yesterday on two charges of causing grievous bodily harm. Unfortunately counsel currently instructed are unable to attend on the return date in two weeks where the judge will hear pleas before sentencing." As the storyline unfolds, the learner must interview a client in jail as part of the legal research process. In these scenes, the questions the learner decides to ask ultimately influence the quality of information gathered and the ability to build a compelling case for the magistrate as part of the culminating final assessment.

The final piece of reflective learning requires students to develop their own conclusions regarding the final outcome of the judge's findings. The final sentencing scene is set in an actual courtroom; these real-life locations would otherwise be entirely inaccessible to UEL students (see Figure 15.4).

The Result: Higher Satisfaction, Improved Marks

UEL's digital media simulations have proven hugely popular. In a survey of its students, UEL discovered that 97% of respondents found these digital media

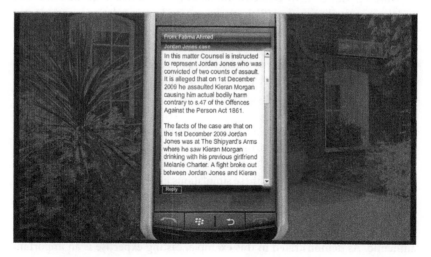

Figure 15.4 Screenshot from University of East London Law Program Learnscape™

simulations either "very useful or extremely useful" in preparing them for their assessment. A total of 94% reported returning to scenes and assessments to reinforce learning, and 92% said the characters within the storyline positively contributed to learning. Equally insightful were some of the individual student comments:

- "It was much better than reading about it in a book. Doing something helps me learn."
- "I was engaged as it was useful to my studies and linked to the assessment."
- "I liked it as I felt part of the action. I think that helped me learn."
- "I could go back to bits that I didn't understand at first."
- "I liked the characters; they were real. I could just imagine meeting them."
- "Don't tell the lecturers, but could we have fewer lectures and more of this type of learning?"

For educators, it doesn't get much better than feedback like this. While researchers have demonstrated the cognitive value of experiential learning, this feedback demonstrates that students also appreciate the ability to take more control of their learning experience. The fact that 94% of the students reported returning to the scenes illustrates the power of having embedded "teachable moments" that are on-demand and can be revisited – a powerful new reality made possible by these digital media simulations.

The inclusion of these learning solutions also appears to have a positive impact on student performance. The mean average student mark and the pass rate for the course's practical role assessment both increased substantially from the previous year. In the coming years, it will be exciting to watch as more evidence such as this emerges from research institutions about the power of digital media simulations to increase student engagement leading to improved learning outcomes.

Case Study: The University of Phoenix – First-Year Sequence Program

One of the leaders in the development of digital media simulations is the University of Phoenix (UOPX). UOPX, one of the largest providers of online education in the world, has made digital media simulations a focal point of its First-Year Sequence program – a series of eight introductory courses addressing foundational skills in subjects such as communications, personal finance, psychology, and health and wellness.

First-year retention is one of the most important and least understood challenges facing higher education today. Half of all student drops occur in the first 20 units. At the University of Phoenix, a large percentage of students are single parents in their late 20s. Many are female, and many are underemployed. These students want better lives for themselves and their families. They want to be good role models, and they want a sense of accomplishment and achievement.

The university's primary challenge was designing courses to address the specific needs of these students. To meet this challenge, the university adopted a more student-centric curricular architecture that was more relevant to student life. In addition, the university's vision, spearheaded by Executive Creative Director Doug Beckwith, PhD, JD, was to create highly immersive and engaging digital media experiences that allowed students to apply course concepts in self-directed authentic workplace environments.

In all, the university has co-created over 20 immersive episodes across many of its First-Year Sequence courses and is currently developing several new digital media simulation series (see Figure 15.5). The breadth of digital media simulation applications at the University of Phoenix is noteworthy. One of the criticisms of first-generation virtual learning environments is that instead of exposing students to new experiences, many virtual learning environments simply replicated classroom-like environments and teacher-centred instructional approaches in virtual learning environments. UPX has focused its development on exposing students to environments and scenarios beyond those that the students would normally have the opportunity to experience.

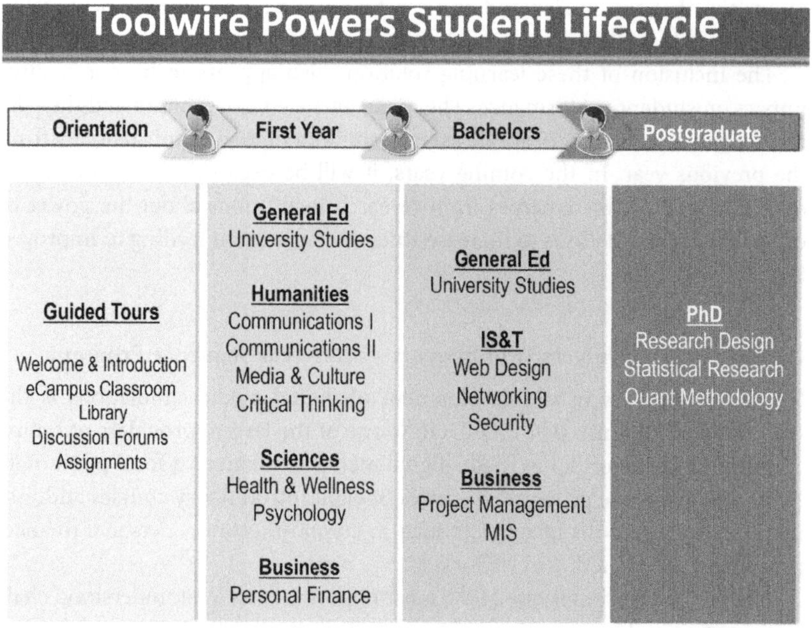

Toolwire Powers Student Lifecycle

Orientation → **First Year** → **Bachelors** → **Postgraduate**

Guided Tours

Welcome & Introduction
eCampus Classroom
Library
Discussion Forums
Assignments

General Ed
University Studies

Humanities
Communications I
Communications II
Media & Culture
Critical Thinking

Sciences
Health & Wellness
Psychology

Business
Personal Finance

General Ed
University Studies

IS&T
Web Design
Networking
Security

Business
Project Management
MIS

PhD
Research Design
Statistical Research
Quant Methodology

Figure 15.5 Toolwire Powers the Student Lifecycle at University of Phoenix

As an example, personal finance is one of the courses in the university's First-Year Sequence. For this 9-week course, the university developed four digital media simulations that typically take about 30 minutes to complete. In each of the four episodes, a "virtual mentor" named Monica provides support and guidance on certain critical, predefined lessons such as money management. During the student's self-guided personal learning journey, other characters act as inquisitors who test the student's knowledge.

The inclusion of "virtual mentors" is extremely valuable. Personal finance is an important core-knowledge topic that surprisingly is absent in the experience of most students and is typically a subject matter taught through the example of parents and family members. Students without these positive role models in their lives, therefore, are at a higher risk of making poor financial decisions. Monica, the "virtual mentor," was created with these students in mind. In one scene, Monica tells the student, "I made a lot of mistakes when I was young, but I was lucky enough to meet this great accountant before I got into too much trouble. He really helped me with some great advice. I'll introduce you to him if you want – Lloyd is his name. He's here in town."

Monica learned the hard way – by making mistakes. Providing students tangible opportunities to practice – and make mistakes – in safe environments is an invaluable service, especially for courses such as personal finance.

As other universities rush to compete in the online education market, UPX now views its investment in digital media simulations as a way to differentiate its courses from other online offerings. What is particularly interesting about UPX's large investment in digital media simulation is this: as many universities and colleges in the US compete to attract the best students by investing in more expensive facilities and student services that will help them top the ranks for expenditures per student in popular publications such as the *US News & World Report*, UPX is investing heavily in technologies which will help it lower the delivery cost per student while at the same time improving the student experience.

The Results: Student, Teacher and Administrator Feedback

Digital media simulations, which have been in use at the University of Phoenix since 2010, have been a huge success. Perhaps the greatest testimony to the effectiveness of these learning solutions is the university's continued investment in the development of digital media simulations in a growing number of courses.

The university does not share quantitative metrics related to the impact of digital media simulations. However, at the 2012 Sloan-C Emerging Technologies Conference and the US Distance Learning Association (USDLA) Annual Conference, the university shared the following qualitative student feedback from a spring 2012 personal finance course:

- "The [simulation] activities are some of the best ideas to be introduced as part of our academic progress. They make a longer-lasting impression in memory because of how they require students to interact."
- "Great. Love the [simulations]. Very effective and clever."
- "I really like [these simulations] and think you should allow more assignments with this technology."
- In addition, the university's executive creative director, Dr. Doug Beckwith, commented: "When it came time to add real-life elements to our First-Year Sequence, it made perfect sense to build the hands-on assessments around immersive experiential simulations. This 'technology apprenticeship' approach has been a big success for students and the college."

The Future of Digital Media Simulations

In the coming years, the incorporation of game-based learning features, elements of social network communication and the focus on increasingly personalised whole-student" adaptive learning engines will be among the most profound advancements driving the continued adoption of digital media simulations. Elemental to that approach is the fact that one of the key insights from game play and social media networking – the desire for and reliance upon relevant, contextualised and immediate feedback – must be taken into account in any improvements in educational design, learning processing and meaningful feedback mechanisms. In addition, online experiences will incorporate universal learning objectives in order to allow for increased reuse and collaboration across multiple organisations.

Game-Based Learning

Building upon today's multi-branching digital media simulations, future simulations will incorporate game design techniques. In a game, while the developer determines the rules and bounds of a given environment, the player drives the course of action. Unpredictable outcomes within a game structure of rules and goals will allow the platform to work as an even more dynamic system. These future interactive digital media simulations will be based upon courses of action made meaningful to students through contextualized relevance of the learning goals and opportunities for students to make educated decision choices and to experience and learn from the consequences of those choices.

Gee (2007) argues that good video games incorporate principles that parallel recent research about how humans best learn. He points to the following key characteristics:

- Create opportunity for identity
- Allow customization
- Foster interaction

- Motivate production
- Encourage risk taking
- Develop cross-functional teams
- Explore/think laterally/rethink goals
- Inspire pleasant frustration
- Design situated meanings
- Deliver "just-in time" and "on-demand" results
- Promote challenge and consolidation
- Develop a sense of ownership

Incorporating more game-like features will further enhance student engagement by allowing students to set personalised goals and experience meaningful achievements. Dynamic scoring mechanisms will track performance in direct correlation with students' increased comprehension. For students, witnessing the cascading consequences of their decisions will draw them into the story and, most importantly, spark their intrinsic motivation to pursue key learning objectives.

Future digital media simulations will increasingly support both individual and team experiences. In "individual mode," students will be able to develop their unique identity and sense of ownership as they defend their analysis and ideas. Students' research experiences will generate adapted prompts in a meta-cognitive activity that will better prepare them to interact with team members in a productive manner. A "team meeting" mode will facilitate group planning, constructive conflict, project-focused resolution and, of course, ranking based on performance and points scored. A "team story" mode will immerse each student in his or her role to think critically and creatively while fostering communication and collaboration. In fact, communication and collaboration will permeate the entire experience throughout all modes. This is the foundation of multiplayer interactions between team members within the game-like digital media simulations of the future.

Whole-Student Adaptive Learning

Another exciting advancement will be the integration of "whole-student" adaptive learning. Within the next few years, student-facing learning platforms will provide richer, more multimodal content in ways that are increasingly customized to individual student needs.

Adaptive learning is already in use in courses that assess concrete answers. This "intelligent tutoring" approach levels and remediates a student's subject comprehension by returning the student to concepts requiring review and delivering simple feedback. This type of adaptation is ideal for one-dimensional subject matter – such as mathematics – because it focuses on problems with clear right and wrong answers. The challenge is providing contextual adaptive learning for problem-solving subject matter.

Future generation learning platforms will extend this adaptive learning approach beyond the "prescriptive" or "intelligent tutoring" systems already in use. The whole-student adaptive learning model of the future will apply to subjects where creativity, analysis and decision making (best answer) – not just problem solving (one right answer) – are required. In other words, adaptive learning will be a powerful tool for preparing students for the complexities of the real world. This approach will introduce a new dynamic to learning previously unavailable to educators. Most importantly, it will be developed and delivered in a way that is scalable and widely accessible to all.

Adaptive learning simulations will provide powerful student-centred learning experiences. Students' learning profiles will be dynamically updated at key, predetermined moments as they create presentations, analyse scenarios, make decisions and solve problems. These systems will also empower instructors to provide more effective remediation. The engine driving these digital media simulations will provide instructors with information to offer individual tailored support to their students.

Benefits to Instructors

A fear expressed by instructors and administrators today is that online learning solutions will weaken the quality of the educational experience by diminishing the human interaction. To the contrary, machine-guided adaptive learning platforms will enable instructors to provide even stronger, more effective mentoring than ever before by more clearly illustrating what makes each individual student unique.

Future simulations will make it even easier for instructors to track student performance and intervene with timely, targeted mentoring and guidance in a way that will improve learning interactions with students. Tapping into students' unique abilities in order to guide them to success is what has always motivated teachers. The challenge has always been that connecting with students at a meaningful level grows increasingly difficult as class sizes expand. While a teacher in a classroom of 35 may have a basic notion of students' strengths and weaknesses, the performance metrics inherent in digital systems will track each individual's learning experiences, showing precisely the kinds of problems and situations that cause them trouble. These innovative tools will allow the teacher to address those weaknesses on an individual basis.

Through adaptive learning technologies, education is rapidly approaching the point where instructors will be empowered to serve a greater number of students more efficiently and effectively than ever before.

Summary

The emergence of online learning couldn't have arrived at a better time. Institutions are struggling to achieve sustainability, and employment prospects for recent graduates are bleak. For many millennials, college diplomas offer little more than the "privilege" of taking an unpaid internship and moving back in with their parents. Not surprisingly, more and more people are beginning to question the value of an education that offers decreasing returns on increasing tuitions.

Classrooms are sacred institutions and should not be tinkered with lightly. So what is most exciting about this next generation of online learning tools is that they offer solutions that are refined and meet the needs of the three crucial stakeholder groups: students, instructors and administrators. We've been stuck with a faltering system in large part because, while there is no shortage of ideas for educational reforms, few solutions have been able to satisfy all three invested parties. As a result, it is a fascinating time to be researching and working in the field of online education.

References

Bacow, L. S., Bowen, W. G., Guthrie, K. M., Lack, K. A., & Long, M. P. (2012). Barriers to adoption of online learning systems in U.S. higher education. *ITHAKA*. Retrieved from http://www.sr.ithaka.org/research-publications/barriers-adoption-online-learning-systems-us-higher-education

Brown, J. S., Collins, A., & Duguid, S. (1989). Situated cognition and the culture of learning. *Educational Researcher, 18*(1), 32–42.

Csíkszentmihályi, M (1990). *Flow: the psychology of optimal experience.* New York: Harper and Row.

Dror, I. (2006). *It is not what you teach, but what they learn that counts!* Retrieved from http://www.immagic.com/eLibrary/ARCHIVES/GENERAL/BLOGS/F070319S.pdf

Gee, J. P. (2007). *What video games have to teach us about learning and literacy.* Palgrave MacMillan.

Palomäki, E. (2009). *Applying 3D virtual worlds to higher education.* Master's thesis, Helsinki University of Technology.

Ramaswami, R. (2011). Is there a second life for virtual worlds? *Campus Technology.com.* Retrieved from http://campustechnology.com/articles/2011/09/01/is-there-a-second-life-for-virtual-worlds.aspx

Smith, A. (2008). *Game impact theory: the five forces that are driving the adoption of game technologies within multiple established industries.* Interservice/Industry Training, Simulation, and Education Conference. Retrieved from http://www.modelbenders.com/papers/Smith_Game_Impact_Theory.pdf

Sweller, J. (1994).Cognitive load theory, learning difficulty, and instructional design. *Learning and Instruction, 4,* 295–312.

Vygotsky, L. S. (1978). *Mind in society.* Cambridge, MA: Harvard University Press.

16
Towards a Method of Improving Participation in Online Collaborative Learning: Curatr

BEN BETTS
University of Warwick, UK

Editors' Introduction

It is easy to be excited by, and carried away with, the idea that social media, social networking and game-based collaboration are the panacea for all learning ills. Indeed, who has not tried to leverage the power of these technologies into their learning programme design? Generally, though, what we see is functionality bolted onto traditional designs with no clear rationale for how they can be used by learners or what behavioural characteristics they are trying to promote. Betts has taken a radically different approach; in this chapter he reports on a learning environment, Curatr, that largely employs pre-existing content to partially populate a space where learners collaboratively make sense and share experience. He presents some fascinating insights into the delicate balancing act of stimulating quality collaborative acts and points to a relationship between participation and final academic outcome. Readers will find many valuable pointers on how to leverage participation in their programmes together with a synthesis of ideas presented in the form of a collaborative learning cycle.

My Big Idea

Four years ago I did something really stupid. My company was engaged with the University of Warwick on a long-term research project when the topic of PhDs came up. Like the naïve youngster I was, I jumped into the programme. At the time I was somewhat disillusioned by the world of online learning. I had come into the field expecting a revolution in education, but what I found was a dull and expensive medium that often fell short of expectations. Fortunately, the rise of social networking and social media technologies was starting to promise an entirely different future. A future where online learning could be truly collaborative on a massive scale. This sounded much better, a real vision for the future of education. There was just one problem. How could you get people to do it?

The backbone of successful collaborative learning is participation. Typical implementations of e-learning, especially in the corporate world, tend to revolve around a model of learning management system (LMS) plus courseware. The LMS serves as a tracking and enrolment database; the courseware serves up content in an instructionally interesting manner. Getting learners to participate in this sort of experience tends to be a challenge. What's more, this model does little to facilitate collaboration – most learners are isolated from each other.

In the academic world, well-facilitated collaborative learning experiences are readily found to be as effective, if not more so, than their classroom counterparts. But good online facilitators and good collaborative courses are somewhat thin on the ground. Unfortunately this model also fails to take advantage of online learning's key asset, its scalability. Where a moderator is always required to nudge participants into action and shape their discussion, massive scaling simply isn't a possibility.

My ambition was to create an innovation in learning technology to fill this void. An innovation that meant an online course could not only scale massively, but also be massively social. I didn't want to rely on the need for expensive courseware; I wanted the richness of the experience to come from the participants themselves. And so it was that I began researching under the title "towards a method of improving participation in online collaborative learning environments."

The Problem With e-Learning

When Benjamin Bloom (1984) conducted his famous 2 sigma study, he stumbled across the evidence that proved what many teachers have suspected for a long time – that students learn much more effectively in a one-to-one environment than in the classroom. He called the finding the 2 sigma problem, in that whilst it improved student outcomes by two standard deviations, it was impractical given the requirement of a teacher for every student. Bloom's study highlighted a number of other methods for significantly improving attainment; student participation and cooperative learning being two good social examples.

Bloom's study does not stand alone. Academic theories as to the impact of social context on learning have been gaining popularity for more than a century. Whilst some have studied the nature of knowledge to suggest the impact of social constructivism, stemming from Vygotsky (Woo & Reeves, 2007), others have studied the role of social context on the learner's behaviour (Bandura, 1977). Finally, there is also a strand of academia focused on the nature of learning within a group or a community (Lave & Wenger, 1991). These approaches might be described as learning with others, learning in the presence of others and learning from others. Computer supported collaborative learning (CSCL) has risen as a field in its own right in the last 10 years. The *Journal of CSCL* readily documents the industries' attempts to apply social context within a distance-learning environment.

Since Bloom's 1984 study we've witnessed the rise of online learning and with it the prospect of infinitely scalable education. "Social" has taken a bit of a back seat as individualised and self-directed e-learning has risen in popularity. But the first forays into online learning have not been entirely successful.

Despite empirical studies suggesting that well-designed online learning can be more effective than its classroom counterpart (Sitzmann, Kraiger, Stewart, & Wisher, 2006), e-learning hasn't won many popularity contests. The cost of developing one hour of bespoke e-learning is quoted as somewhere in the region of $30,000 (Chapman Alliance, 2010). This is a stunning figure when you consider the vast time requirements of most accredited qualifications. Should we be spending millions developing e-learning content?

Fortunately there is an easier answer; the world is full of rich content. With the rise of open educational resources and social media, we have been inundated with quality reference content on most subjects. Tapping into this resource would seem sensible – concentrating less on making the perfect content and more on letting learners curate already existing content for themselves. Such a notion would not only lower costs, but also start to recognise the decades of research highlighting the importance of social context in a learning environment.

Building on our Understanding

Many online learning activities are typified by the presence of the "next" button: virtual slideshows, which users must page through one at a time to arrive at mastery of a subject. This form of presentation is easy to achieve and instructionally sound in principle; but in practice it often fails to engage the learner in the activity. It was the word "engagement" that got to the heart of my research; just how can we better engage people online?

Self-determination theory (SDT) is a macro-theory of intrinsic motivation proposed by Edward Deci and Richard Ryan (2000). They suggested that in order for an individual to be engaged and intrinsically motivated by an activity, that activity must fulfil three key needs: autonomy, competence and relatedness.

Autonomy is the notion of free will – that we choose which activities to participate in and our strategies of participation within them. Generally speaking, e-learning doesn't offer a great deal of autonomy; the pathways the learner must follow tend to be preset. But where experiments in autonomy have been conducted, giving users more control has been correlated to better learning outcomes (Sitzmann et al., 2006). This would seem to indicate that a less linear instructional path might be of some value for improving the engagement of participants.

That isn't to say we shouldn't offer some structure; there exists a degree of tension between the notion of a completely nonlinear approach and standard instructional design practices. From Vygotsky's notion of the zone of proximal development to Jerome Bruner's concept of scaffolding, creating a framework around which learners can build their understanding is seen as a fundamental principle of instructional design (Holzman, 2009). We would hardly be adding value if we gave students random free reign to explore whatever concepts they wanted in whatever order they desired.

Indeed, the notion of one thing after another, of building up understanding one piece at a time, is a link between autonomy and competence.

Deci and Ryan (2000) assert that we all enjoy getting better at something that matters to us. Fundamental to achieving this is the balance between our current level of ability and the difficulty of the task at hand. In order to gain competence, the difficulty of the task must increase in step with our level of ability. Csikszentmihalyi (1990) suggests that a user who experiences this balance can become completely immersed and engaged with an activity, an experience he calls "flow" (see Figure 16.1).

People experiencing a state of flow are said to be completely absorbed in an activity, to the detriment of attention being given to anything else. If the challenge is beyond the participant's current level of ability, that participant is thought to experience stress, and attention is diverted away from the activity. Similarly, if the challenge of the activity is somewhat below the participant's level of ability, the participant is said to experience boredom and lose interest in the activity. The extent to which participants experience flow has been shown to be significant in the level of motivation reported for a learning activity and may lead to higher-quality learning outcomes (Ryu & Parsons, 2012).

Csikszentmihalyi's theory of flow is often quoted in game-design textbooks and as such it was in this direction that I turned for inspiration when implementing measures of competence. By adopting game-like behaviours, we could encourage users to explore the nonlinear paths we set for them, whilst also gaining in competence within the overall instructional process.

Deci and Ryan's final need, relatedness, gets to the heart of our requirement for a more socially orientated learning experience. Like other previously mentioned theories, SDT suggests that relating to others is a requirement for an engaging activity. As such we wanted to orientate our experience to give as much prominence to the participants as to the instructor.

With these needs in mind, I set three objectives that a new innovation would need to fulfil in order to create an engaging, social, learning experience:

- To use any Web-addressable resource as a "learning object," which learners could explore in a nonlinear fashion as a part of a learning experience
- To illustrate competence and advancement within the experience by using a game-like mechanic

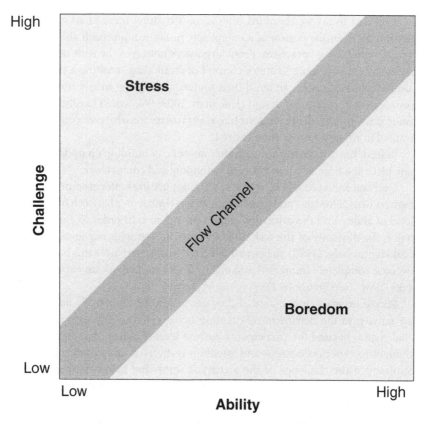

Figure 16.1 Adapted from Csikszentmihalyi's Flow for an Activity (1990)

- To enable learners to interact with each other and the teacher throughout the experience

Teachers would be able to use the approach to rapidly create online learning experiences in which learners could interact with learning content, the teacher and other students. By reflecting, commenting and adding their own content, users would be able to curate a learning experience for themselves. In honour of this notion we called the program Curatr.

Curatr in Action

Following on from the notion that "the world is full of rich content," we wanted to devise a method that would present a seamless navigation experience regardless of where the content was located or what it looked like. This was a challenge as presenting many different types of content in a single interface could easily make for a disjointed user experience. To further complicate matters, we also

Participation in Online Collaborative Learning • 265

needed to devise a user experience that didn't necessarily list out the content in a set order. Rows of links implicitly suggest an order, which was something we were trying to escape.

To best facilitate both requirements we settled on a highly visual approach that would see us represent learning objects as "circles on a canvas," encouraging exploration and forgoing linear navigation systems. Figure 16.2 shows a screenshot of how this interface works; each circle on the screen is representative of a learning object. Clicking on any circle pops up additional information about the linked learning object, including a picture and a description, and a link to "view" the learning object in full.

In Figure 16.2 we are viewing what we came to call the "Curatr's gallery" but in more standard terms would be the course content. The circles themselves do not have labels visible as standard – the user must "roll over" each circle to see its name or click it for more information. This is a design consideration that runs counter to most user experience guides but is specifically chosen to encourage users to explore content instead of judging the content by name alone. In addition to this "gallery," each student has his or her own blank gallery. This is gradually populated by the student bookmarking and adding content as he or she progresses through the course.

Students do not leave the Curatr platform even when viewing an object in full – we use an iFrame to display content within the system so users never leave the portal itself. Figure 16.3 shows a YouTube video being viewed with the ability to comment directly below.

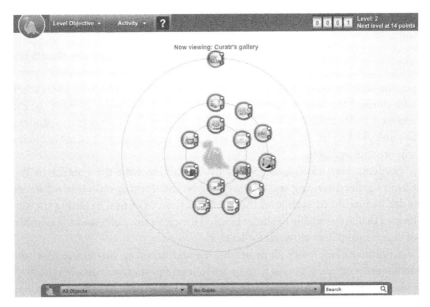

Figure 16.2 Viewing the Curatr's Gallery with the 'Circles on a Canvas' Approach

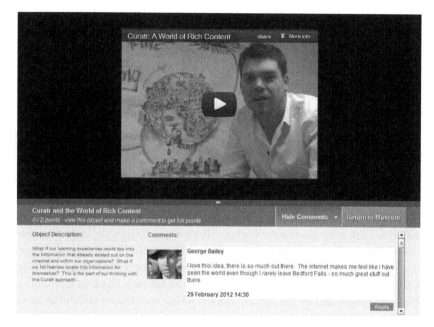

Figure 16.3 Viewing a Learning Object

Playing the Game

To illustrate competence and advancement through this nonlinear course, Curatr uses game-like mechanics. Essentially the whole learning experience is transformed into a game whereby students must earn experience points to unlock new levels of content.

Whilst the Curatr's gallery appears nonlinear at first glance, the objects are actually arranged into a series of levels, which help scaffold the learner's journey through the content. This is the result of conscious input from the teacher who devised the course content and suggested in what order content should appear. Circles closest to the centre are the highest-level objects this student has unlocked so far. As the student earns more experience points, more circles will become available.

Students earn experience points by interacting with the content in the Curatr's gallery, viewing and commenting on the learning objects in whatever order they wish. At each level the teacher sets an objective, outlining the key lessons that are available to students using the circles available and the number of experience points required to "level up."

Comments and views alone are not enough to prove the nature of a student's understanding. As such, in order to level up, students will often have to pass through an "end-of-level gate," or a test of their understanding, as well as achieve the necessary experience points.

Participation in Online Collaborative Learning • 267

End-of-level gates are questions set by the teacher and come in a number of forms, including multiple choice questions (MCQs) and peer-marked questions (see Figure 16.4).

Peer-marked questions challenge students to write short essay responses to discussion questions for the class to then vote for their favourite response.

In addition to free text responses, participants can also be asked to make a contribution in other ways: finding a Web site or uploading a document, for example.

Following successful completion of an end-of-level gate, a "level up" message is displayed, new content becomes available and the next level objective is made clear.

Interacting With Other Users

If the circles allow for autonomy, and the game allows for competence, then the ability to talk, share and mark others work focuses on stimulating relatedness – students' need for engagement – in Curatr.

Students can interact with each other in a variety of ways – joining in the discussion of a learning object or marking each other's work, for example. Students

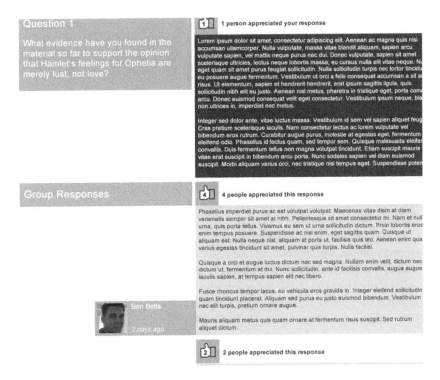

Figure 16.4 Responses to a Peer-marked Question

using Curatr also have their own blank gallery of objects that can be filled and shared with others, a kind of learning portfolio.

By default, a student's gallery of objects will include objects they have bookmarked from the course content, answers they have given to end-of-level gates and learning objects they have added back themselves. Adding and sharing learning objects can earn a student bonus points, if allowed by the teacher. Students can curate the content they collect into guides and collections for others to browse. Particularly exceptional contributions might be bookmarked by the teacher, automatically sharing a student's learning object with the rest of the class.

Recognising Quality With Badges

A fair challenge to our method thus far is that we've very much focused on rewarding the action of contributing, more so than the quality of that contribution. In recognition of this we instituted the concept of badges, awards that can be given out to recognise particularly useful contributions. Typically, the teacher makes the awards, but some are triggered by student actions, such as sharing an object with other students.

Badges form a part of each student's playercard, their record of achievement. Playercards are public to the group and show the badges, points and contributions a student has made on the platform.

The Effect of Game Play on Participation

Traditionally, the level of participation in an online social learning experience has been somewhat dictated by the role of the teacher, cajoling and directing conversation. The Curatr approach of first scaffolding out an experience and then letting peers support each other in the learning experience has been effective in minimizing this role. Game-like behaviours have revolutionised the way we look at gaining participation. We've found that the effective intrinsic use of mechanics like points and levels can shape students' behaviours towards those we want them to exhibit.

However, there is a balance to be had. Where we push students to comment on every object, we see creativity and morale drop. When we free students to level up without making contributions, we see a slackening off in participation.

Typically, rules like the 90-9-1 approach (Nielson, 2006) to online social communities have defined the level of participation one expects from a community; 90% of users will not contribute (lurkers), 9% will make some comment or reaction (contributors) and 1% will create original content (creators). Curatr's game play attempts to shape behaviour in such a way that statistics like these are overcome. Such is the effectiveness of this approach that it is entirely normal for 100% of users in a Curatr environment to participate as both contributors and creators (see Table 16.1). But the balance has to be right. Ask too much and students lose the will. Demand too little and Nielson's rule can come back into effect.

In cohort 1, we offered three points for adding an object, a big boost. We offered a point for a comment, but we didn't make it obvious. The comments area was closed until students opened it, and we never explicitly said participants would get a point for commenting. On further inspection, many of the objects added by students added little value; we had lost hold of quality as they spammed in links to spurious Web sites to get their amount of "added objects" up and gain points.

In cohort 2 we took away points for adding an object. We then made it very obvious that points would be awarded for commenting and defaulted the comment box to be open. The swing was profound – twice as many comments and a much more even spread of participation. Moreover, the objects that were added were generally of a much better quality.

Getting the balance right is a key factor to how you shape participation. But one thing you can take from those numbers either way is that Neilson's theory

Table 16.1 A comparison of two classes running the same course, but with slightly tweaked Curatr game mechanics

	Cohort 1			Cohort 2	
Student	Objects Added	Comments Made	Student	Objects Added	Comments Made
1	63	119	1	6	160
2	67	68	2	6	75
3	11	24	3	8	106
4	12	65	4	3	90
5	16	5	5	3	96
6	19	12	6	6	70
7	11	8	7	3	68
8	11	1	8	12	85
9	39	12	9	4	57
10	19	17	10	2	80
11	5	9	11	1	27
12	5	5	—	—	—
13	19	7	—	—	—
14	4	47	—	—	—
15	21	7	—	—	—
16	8	24	—	—	—
Sum	330	430		54	914
Mean	19.41	25.29		4.91	83.09
Median	12	4		12	82.5
Teacher	—	9		—	63

is toast. It is a rule of thumb, but happily it's one we can overcome. Previously this had been done by the teacher poking, prodding and threatening students into action. This isn't to say that the role of the teacher is undermined in Curatr; even in the aforementioned example, where the teacher contributes more, so do the students. But the intensity with which one must prowl the halls given the scale at which classes can take place is entirely more manageable – students contribute more than the teacher.

A Case Study of Curatr in Practice

The Service Operations Management Certificate run by Warwick Business School in the UK is an entirely distance learning accredited course, aimed at team leaders and managers who work in service processing environments: banks, call centres and the like. The 24-week course is designed to familiarise participants with the basics of operations and process management whilst creating tangible improvement projects to be deployed back in the work environment.

The course is split into four modules of 6 weeks and was designed from the ground up to run using the Curatr platform. Each module follows the same design template; an introductory level followed by six further levels which build on a participants' understanding and push them to do more as the weeks progress. Whilst early levels merely required the viewing of learning objects, later levels were made harder such that participants had to earn additional experience points by commenting, adding new material and organising content in order to earn enough points to "level up." At the end of each module the participants were asked to complete a 1,500-word assignment applying the principles to their own workplace.

All four modules were created within a week, using a combination of freely available material, resources previously created and some specially prepared content. The end result was a learning experience that would occupy students for in excess of 10 hours per week for 24 weeks – 240 hours of learning. No course credit is offered for participating online, it is entirely optional as the only element that attracts credit is the final assignment for each module.

In the latest cohort to participate, 35 students undertook the course, with 33 going on to complete the course. Each module comprised of between 45 and 80 learning objects, along with instructions to make comments agreeing or disagreeing or building on elements of the material whilst connecting it back to each participant's own workplace.

On average each student made 109 comments over the 24-week period. The comments tended to be detailed, thoughtful and considered; the average student wrote over 4,000 words in comments and contributions. These ideas and contributions were then funnelled into students' end-of-module assignments, which yielded phenomenal real-world outcomes, with instances of organisational savings of up to £1m being found through the ideas students created.

As a result of these outcomes, course enrolment is up significantly; cohort 2 had 35 students, cohort 3 carried 57 enrolments.

Participant Views

- "The website is fantastic. I was concerned about how I would learn, but the format of a game-like site is excellent and helps to motivate. So far the content has been great ... now trying to put it into practice within my work environment. My creative juices are flowing and I find myself rather excited and enthusiastic to do as much as I can and look forward to see some results." – *M. M., Office Depot*
- "I'm learning loads and feeling so much more confident when discussing strategy and process improvements as a result of doing this course. Found myself using terms like 'standardisation' and 'variability' in a meeting this week!" – *E. C., NFU Mutual*
- "Our staff like the Curatr style of learning. I've been impressed with what they are sharing with me." – *J. M., Wealth Learning, Coutts, UK*

Participation and Performance

After the Warwick course had finished, a detailed analysis considering the impact of participation on performance was undertaken. The results were fascinating. Amongst the bottom five contributors in terms of participation in online discussion, the average final mark was 64.05. Amongst the top five the average final mark was 71.75 – a difference of 7.70 and a shift of 1.5 standard deviations in outcome; the difference between an upper second and first class honours pass.

When we compared the number of experience points a student had earned with the average final assignment mark he or she obtained, a similar picture emerged; those who earned the most experience points generally got better marks. The correlation was shown at the 99% confidence level.

We can surmise from this data that the level of participation a student exhibits in an online collaborative learning environment is a good indicator of his or her likely academic performance. This isn't to say that we know participation is the cause of good performance; we just know it is a potentially strong indicator. In Curatr, we think we've found a vehicle for promoting participation, but it's more about the method than it is about the software itself.

Applying the Method

As a result of our research we now propose the Collaborative Learning Cycle (CLC) as a framework around which to build successful online collaborative learning experiences. Built on the work of Lave and Wenger (1991), Nonaka

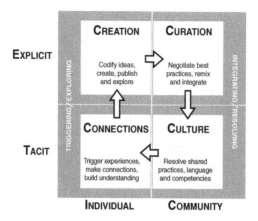

Figure 16.5 The Collaborative Learning Cycle

and Takeuchi (1995) and Garrison, Anderson, and Archer (2001), the CLC indicates the sorts of behaviours one should look to leverage to create meaningful online learning experiences.

Whilst nudges and the "gamification" of an experience do not guarantee you meaningful insights in and of themselves, such techniques can be used to shape behaviour in ways that make users more likely to participate in meaningful ways. For Curatr, we use our nonlinear interface and points for viewing to trigger initial connections. We then build on this by asking people to make comments, source their own content and explore ideas in conjunction with their peers. This brings about a natural curation process, as the group weeds out ideas of little use and concentrates on integrating the best ideas into their own thinking. This can result in a shared culture emerging; one in which everyone starts talking the same language and shares the same practices.

The CLC offers a lens with which to view the collaborative learning process, allowing instructors to scaffold an approach that facilitates each step. Curatr is just one application of the underlying methodology we advocate. We hope to have demonstrated that the overreliance on courseware specialists to produce learning content is unnecessary, as is the bottleneck produced by the requirement for a moderator to motivate and direct conversation in a collaborative learning environment. Free your learners to work together in achieving their goals and you might just be surprised at the results.

References

Bandura, A. (1977). *Social learning theory.* Englewood Cliffs, NJ: Prentice Hall.
Bloom, B. S. (1984). The 2 sigma problem: the search for methods of group instruction as effective as one-to-one tutoring. *Educational Researcher, 13*(6), 4–16.
Chapman Alliance (2010). *How long does it take to create learning?* Retrieved from http://www.chapmanalliance.com/howlong

Csikszentmihalyi, M. (1990). *Flow: the psychology of optimal experience.* New York: Harper Perennial.
Deci, E. L., & Ryan, R. M. (2000). The "what" and "why" of goal pursuits: human needs and the self-determination of behavior. *Psychological Inquiry, 11*(4), 227–268.
Garrison, D. R., Anderson, T., & Archer, W. (2001). Critical thinking, cognitive presence and computer conferencing in distance education. *American Journal of Distance Education, 15,* 7–23.
Holzman, L. (2009). *Vygotsky at work and play.* East Sussex: Routledge.
Lave, J., & Wenger, E. (1991). *Situated learning: legitimate peripheral participation.* Cambridge: Cambridge University Press.
Nielson, J. (2006). *Participation inequality; encouraging more users to contribute.* Retrieved from http://www.useit.com/alertbox/participation_inequality.html
Nonaka, I., & Takeuchi, H. (1995). *The knowledge-creating company: how Japanese companies create the dynamics of innovation.* Oxford: Oxford University Press.
Ryu, H., & Parsons, D. (2012). Risky business or sharing the load? – Social flow in collaborative mobile learning. *Computers & Education, 58*(2), 707–720.
Sitzmann, T., Kraiger, K., Stewart, D., & Wisher, R. (2006). The comparative effectiveness of Web-based and classroom instruction: a meta-analysis. *Personnel Psychology, 59,* 623–664.
Woo, Y., & Reeves, T. (2007). Meaningful interaction in Web-based learning: a social constructivist interpretation. *The Internet and Higher Education, 10*(1), 15–25.

Endpiece

Putting the Learner in Charge – A Pedagogy for Online Learning Comes of Age

BRIAN SUTTON AND ANTHONY "SKIP" BASIEL

Learning4Leaders, UK, and Adobe Education Leader, UK

As we look back over the chapters presented in this edition we may well ask – What does all this tell us? Is a new pedagogy for online learning any more apparent now than it was 12 years ago when we reviewed the first volume?

There certainly appears to be a tangible difference in the way both teachers and learners view and interact with online learning materials. To fully appreciate just how significant this mind-set change has been it is perhaps worth revisiting some elements of the endpiece from the first volume and performing an audit of our progress.

Features of Online Learning Identified in the First Volume

In 2001 we closed by saying the following – "Online learning, however, has much more to offer than easier text exchange between student and teacher. On the basis of the material in this book the following features of online learning should be of interest to teachers and learners." The following list was offered:

- Easy access to and interrogation of high volumes of diverse learning resources, including texts, pictures, library materials, learning tools and other aids to learning assembled by teachers and institutions
- Ease of access to other materials from other sources, including non-educational sources
- Ease of access to communicate electronically with experts, inside and external to the institution
- Dialogue: teacher-student, student-student, specialist closed groups, open groups, in real time (synchronous) or over a period (asynchronous), one-to-one, one-to-many, one-to-many ones (e.g., one teacher to many individual webcams) and many-to-many
- Routine recording of all transactions in an accessible form capable of adaptation and access as lessons from other students' experience and concerns, threads of discussions and development of arguments,

frequently asked questions and for quality assurance and accessible archives
- Access to a range of personal support by e-mail with tutor and mentors, or through specialist or peer discussion groups
- Ease of navigation to sources and persons – within and outside the packaged materials – according to the interests and needs of the learner
- Logging or tracking of activities for personal records or sharing
- Multiple levels of engagement via navigation buttons – to different depths of understanding, different volumes of data, difficulty of learning activities – according to the interest or the capability of the learner
- Feedback loops, either from the teachers, peers and others or from within the materials themselves through progress checking, quizzes and online assessments
- Linkages to other media, such as sound, video and TV
- Ease of access to simulation of dangerous or complex activities for learning purposes
- Choice of learning styles within the same package according to the needs of the learner
- Opportunities for working "live" in collaboration with others from anywhere in the world

So how do we measure up against this wish list?

Has the Reality Met the Expectation?

After a cursory glance at this list we might be tempted to congratulate ourselves on a job well done. It is certainly true that many of our current online experiences exhibit most, if not all, of these features, and in some areas we have gone beyond the possible expectations. However, a deeper review of the features reveals an underlying assumption that may well have been true 10 years ago but is no longer valid as a working hypothesis. There is an assumption that whilst learner choice and control may be a desirable outcome any such choice would likely be exercised within a learning environment specified and constructed by expert educators using materials that by and large would be created by those same experts specifically for the purpose of learning. It would appear that it was okay to exercise choice but only within predetermined boundaries. Learners after all need to learn what is good for them, and they are not in a position to exercise too much discretion in choosing what is and is not a valuable source of knowledge.

In 2001 the idea that technology would launch a revolution in learner-generated content and that in a "hyper-connected" world the wisdom of the crowd would come to dominate opinion about what is and is not good or valuable was far from the minds of the contributing authors. Discussion about how to get students to engage with materials provided by the teacher (such discussions are still at the forefront for many educators) now appear to be rather naïve and quaintly old-fashioned. If an online resource is deemed by the community to be relevant, engaging and useful you will not be able to stop people from engaging with it; further more, if they don't like the current format they will repurpose it, augment it and tell everyone how great it is.

Educational artefacts are now created by anyone, anywhere in the world, and they represent the terrain any would-be lifelong learner has at his or her fingertips. In a world where job prospects may rest more on a dynamically updated history of personal experience backed up by personal recommendations and digital footprints we see that the unique selling point of higher education, namely accreditation, may be in danger of being devalued.

Hyper-connectivity not only has the potential to increase the pace of social change, but may also make it more volatile. As such the internet has not produced a new kind of identity. Rather, it has been instrumental in raising awareness that identities are more multiple, culturally contingent and contextual than had previously been understood.

It would appear then that when we talk about online learning we are dealing with something with much greater reach than just a system that allows learners to study at their own pace in order to prepare themselves to gain a formal accreditation based largely on other peoples' conception of problems stated in terms that in all probability have little contextual relevance to the learner.

So How Are We Doing Against Our 2001 View of How It Might Be?

In the first volume we closed by suggesting that any new pedagogy that fully embraces online learning was likely to be based upon some or all of the following:

- Learning will be learner managed. Learner responsibility will extend to the relevance of the learning to the learner's longer-term development and applicable to his or her current interests and activities.
    - We see real signs that this is indeed taking place. In chapter 8 we saw how young people excluded from formal education negotiate their own learning agenda and create their own learning experience. Chapter 13 introduced the concept of "free-range" learning and "alternative academia" as we glimpsed a world where learning is driven by contextual needs.
- There will be a major switch in emphasis from the selection, processing and packaging of content by the teacher to the selection, processing and adaptation of materials by the learner.
    - Chapter 16 introduced a commercial system that allows learners to curate their own content and employed game theory to encourage

learners to explore different levels of material, whilst chapter 5 provided insight into the reasons why learners choose open educational resources.
- Interactions between learners and learners, learners and experts, and learners and nonexperts will be a major source of advice, reassurance and monitoring of progress.
  – We saw in chapter 4 how students co-created self-regulation strategies within a "community of survival," and chapter 3 showed how scaffolding cognitive processes is as important as providing engaging content.
- Networking and collaboration between individuals or groups of learners will be a key learning activity and will extend globally.
  – We see some persuasive examples of this taking place in chapters 8, 9 and 11.
- A new role of educational producer will appear, linking the educational aspirations of teachers and learners with the expertise of material designers.
  – This presaged the emergence of the open educational resource movement discussed in detail in chapter 5 and chapter 6.
- Assessment will accommodate a wide range of learning outcomes, judged as comparable to, though different from, those specified.
  – Chapter 7 provides principles to guide the design of a more dynamic style of online learning; chapter 14 introduces game theory and shows how to design gaming into learning. Chapter 15 shows how rich digital media simulations can be used in a wide range of situations to provide previously unimaginable levels of experiential learning and assessment, and, finally, chapter 16 includes references to collective assessment of co-created learning objects.

Overall, then, we see that online learning has indeed moved on and is producing educational environments and experiences that are capable of living up to the long-hoped-for promise of online learning.

What More Might We Expect in the Future

It is now an accepted trend that technology is getting smaller and less expensive every 18 months (or less). This trend is emerging with the use of mobile learning (m-learning). Technology will continue to converge with the growth of tablets, e-book readers, small handheld devices and new wearable information and communication technology. Computer interfaces will also continue to evolve from keyboards to touch screens and voice interactions.

A shift to immersive e-learning events will no longer have the learner sitting outside the screen looking in, but rather will shift perspective to have the online student at the centre looking out. Engaging new media content will continue to develop with next-generation augmented reality, alternative reality game design and telecommunication that blends the resources of GPS technologies.

The next volume of this book will not be on (dead tree format) paper, but rather provided to us in blended new media delivery of the future to involve all our senses and perceptions. You, the readers, will be the authors, and learning will never be the same again.

Notes on Contributors

Khalid Alshahrani holds a lecturer position at King Fahad Naval Academy in Saudi Arabia. Since 2003 he has been teaching English in face-to-face and blended learning classes. His research interests include computer assisted language learning (CALL) and investigating e-learning in the sociocultural settings of higher education.
Contact – alshahranik@kfna.gov.sa

Yun-Jo An is an assistant professor of instructional technology in the Department of Educational Technology and Foundations at the University of West Georgia. Her research focuses on online learning and teaching, scaffolding ill-structured problem solving, learner-centred technology integration and teacher professional development.
Contact – yunjoan912@gmail.com

Paul Bacsich works at Sero Consulting and also owns the consultancy company Matic Media Ltd, which specialises in benchmarking e-learning and on virtual universities. Before becoming a consultant he was director of special projects at the UK e-University (UKeU), was a professor at Sheffield Hallam University with long-standing interests in e-learning and worked at the Open University.
Contact – paul.bacsich@sero.co.uk

Narend Baijnath is the pro vice chancellor of the University of South Africa, with responsibilities for Information and Communications Technology, open distance and e-learning, community engagement, academic planning, organisational architecture and open education resources. He was recently appointed to the board of governors of the Commonwealth of Learning.
Contact – baijnan@unisa.ac.za

Anthony "Skip" Basiel has been a thought leader in e-learning for almost two decades. He has won national recognition for e-learning research and development projects from the UK Higher Education Academy, the (UK) e-Learning Network and the National Peer Awards. He has worked the full range of the e-learning design and development spectrum with a focus on evaluation strategies.
Contact – abasiel@gmail.com and abasiel.wordpress.com

Douglas Beckwith Douglas Beckwith, a senior fellow at Toolwire, is a pioneer in online learning. Dr. Beckwith formerly served as a college dean and the executive

creative director of curriculum innovation at the University of Phoenix, where he championed the use of rich media throughout the university's curriculum.
Contact – dbeckwith@toolwire.com

Ben Betts is an industry thought leader working at the intersection of business, learning and technology. He is CEO of HT2, a learning technology company, and a research engineer at the University of Warwick's International Digital Laboratory. Ben specialises in social and game-based learning principles, with a focus on engaging learners in online collaborative learning.
Contact – ben@ht2.co.uk

Curtis J. Bonk is professor of instructional systems technology (IST) at Indiana University and adjunct in the School of Informatics. Previous to IST, he was a professor of educational psychology and an accountant/CPA. Curt's interests are global education, emerging technologies for learning, open education and extreme learning. His books include *The World Is Open, Empowering Online Learning, The Handbook of Blended Learning* and *Electronic Collaborators*.
Contact – mypage.iu.edu/~cjbonk/ and cjbonk@indiana.edu

Len Cairns – Len is associate dean (engagement and international) in the Faculty of Education, Monash University, Australia. He has been a visiting scholar at a number of European and US universities and currently teaches in leadership (school and organisational).
Contact – Len.Cairns@monash.edu

David James Clarke IV with 25 years of industry experience and an entrepreneurial spirit, David James Clarke IV is an industry expert in the education and e-learning industries. Prior to his work with Toolwire, Clarke was the founder of Logilent, an online learning provider, where he developed live, hands-on learning platforms. Clarke has served as a technology professor at the University of California, Berkeley, and has authored over 34 books in publication.
Contact – dclarke@toolwire.com

Ian Cunningham chairs the educational charity the Centre for Self Managed Learning. He is visiting professor at Kodolányi János University of Applied Science, Székesfehérvár, Hungary, and he chairs the social enterprise Strategic Developments International Ltd.
Contact – ian@stratdevint.com

Richard F. Heller retired in 2006 from the post of professor of public health in the University of Manchester, UK, having previously been professor of clinical epidemiology in the University of Newcastle, Australia. He is the founder and coordinator of the Peoples-uni (peoples-uni.org).
Contact – rfheller@peoples-uni.org

Phil Ice is the vice president of research and development at American Public University System. He is the recipient of three Sloan-C Effective Practice of the Year Awards (2007, 2009 and 2010), Sloan-C's Gomory Award for Data Driven Quality Improvement and the AliveTek/DLA Innovation on Online Distance Learning Administration Award. In 2010 he received the Adobe Higher Education Leaders Impact Award.
Contact – pice@apus.edu

Mike Howarth Mike currently works at University College, London, where his fusion of academic lecturer and education media experience assists the staff training team refine video e-learning. His expeditions to Peru, Iran and Tanzania started a career as a senior BBC education producer of geography, science and nature programmes.
Contact – michael.howarth@mhmvr.co.uk

Jackie Hee-Young Kim is an assistant professor at Armstrong Atlantic State University in Savannah, Georgia, where she has taught online classes and childhood education courses for the past six years. She has authored many articles related to Web-based learning and teaching in professional journals and has given many presentations at professional meetings.
Contact – Jackie.kim@armstrong.edu

Melissa Layne is the director of research methodology at American Public University System. Her research spans the practical, theoretical and policy-related areas of distance education. Recent research and subsequent publications include topics on retention in online environments, adaptive and personalised learning, self-paced instructional design, informal learning and quality assurance in online learning at the institutional, program and course levels.
Contact – mburgess@apus.edu

Pamela McLean is an Internet and learning explorer. She is cofounder of Dadamac Ltd (www.dadamac.co.uk). She is driven by a mixture of curiosity and relationships with people. Her explorations have been richly rewarded by what she has learned and what others say she has taught them.
Contact – pamela.mclean@dadamac.net and Twitter @Pamela_McLean

Giles Pepler works at Sero Consulting, where he has managed studies of e-maturity in Scotland's colleges and in adult/community education in England and annual surveys of ICT in education at further education colleges in England. Before joining Sero he was an FE college principal and a secondary school headteacher.
Contact – giles.pepler@sero.co.uk

Clark Quinn integrates creativity, cognitive science and technology to develop learning and performance strategies for business, education and government

organisations. After an academic career, Dr. Quinn has served as an executive in online and e-learning initiatives and has an international reputation as a speaker and scholar, with three books and numerous articles and chapters.
Contact – clark@quinnovation.com

Gabriel Reedy is a lecturer in higher education at King's College London, where he leads a postgraduate programme in education for health care professionals. His research includes work in educational technologies, OER, online learning and practice-based learning.
Contact – gabriel.reedy@kcl.ac.uk

Pamela Ryan although now semi-retired, has had affiliations with the University of South Africa for 40 years and continues to work at that university as an independent consultant. Originally a professor of English studies, she migrated into management to become executive director to the pro vice chancellor.
Contact – pamflintstone@gmail.com or on Twitter @foregone

Brian Sutton is owner and managing director of Learning4Leaders and a visiting professor at Middlesex University. He has been involved with e-learning since the mid-1980s and is currently in demand as a speaker and as a learning consultant; he works with global clients to specify, design, build and deliver integrated learning programmes for managers and leaders in all disciplines.
Contact – Brian@Learning4Leaders.com

Ian Terrell works as a consultant for TerrellTA, engaged in several educational and evaluation projects. He retired as director of professional development in education at Middlesex University in 2012 after building an open access online community for about 500 educators using practitioner research for school improvement.
Contact – ianterrell25@gmail.com

Mark Weyers is the founder and director of the independent academic development centre, the International Institute of Academic Development (IIAD). Previously, Mark worked at the UCL Centre for the Advancement of Learning and Teaching (CALT) at University College London.
Contact – dr.m.weyers@gmail.com

Tarek Zoubir is a learning technologist at Middlesex University, UK. He is currently using a variety of technologies across department directorates and boundaries to enhance existing blended teaching and learning designs.
Contact – t.zoubir@mdx.ac.uk

Index

NB: numbers in italics indicate drawings, figures or tables

A

Adamson, V. 89
adaptive self-regulation, elements of 56; social interaction paths 67
Alexander, S. 11
Allen, M. 230
An, Y. J. 38, 44, 45, 48
Anagnostopoulos, D. 5
Anderson, T. 4, 5, 6, 272
Angeli, C. 10
Arbaugh, J. B. 6, 7
Archer, W. 4, 5, 6, 272
Argyris, C. 137
Atkins, D. E. 96, 148
augmented reality 279
Awofeso, N. 156
Ayres, P. 119, 120
Azevedo, R. 38, 39, 44, 53

B

Bacow, L. S. 246, 248
Bacsich, P. 80, 89
Bain, J. D. 115
Bandura, A. 55, 61, 261
Barnett, R. 112
Basiel, A. 8
Basmadjian, K. G. 5
Bassok, M. 41
Baylor, A. L. 47
Beaudin, B. 11
Beetham, H. 20
Bell, P. 45
Bell, S. J. 84
Bennett, B. 132
Bertalanffy, L. 120

Biggs, J. B. 115, 116, 117
Black, P. 28
Blaschke, L. M. 195
Bloom, B. S. 261, 272
Bollen, K. A. 70
Bonk, C. J. 10, 11, 20, 27
Bonner, S. 61
Boud, D. 8
Bowen, W. G. 246
Bransford, J. D. 41
bring your own device (BOYD) 145
Brophy, P. 88
Brown, A. L. 38, 41
Brown, C. 204
Brown, J. S. 246
Brownell, G. 79
Bruner, J. 38, 263
Brush, T. 39, 44
Bulu, S. T. 41, 42
Buzzetto-More, N. 85

C

Cairns, L.G. 8
Callan, S. 201
Campbell, J. 187
Campbell, P. 7
Campione, J. C. 41
Canning, N. 201
Carless, S. 230
Carr-Chellman, A. 118
Carroll, J. M. 234
Carson, S. 77, 82, 83, 86, 87
Celani, M. A. A. 8
Certified Membership of the Association of Learning Technology (CMALT) 97

Chad, K. 89
Chan, T. 11
Chandler, C. J. 79
Chandler, P. 119
Chang, C-F. 5
Chapman, L. J. 177
Chase, W. G. 114
Chen, C. 42
Chi, M. 35, 37, 41
Chiarelli, S. 58, 61, 62
Christensen, C. M. 197
Clark, M. 54
Clark, N. 79
Clark, R. C. 233
Cleveland-Innes, M. 5, 7, 8
Clink, K. 81
cognitive load theory (CLT) 114
cognitive presence 7
CoI-TLP merging: graph 16; model 17
CoI-TLP model, merging the best of both worlds 3–17
Coleman, E. B. 41
collective self-regulation, coping together 53; why 54; sample discussion topics 55
Collins, A. 246
Collins, H. 8
Collins, P. 182, 187
Combs, A. 121
Community of Inquiry (CoI) 4, *9*, *10*; North West Quadrant 13; North East Quadrant 13; South West Quadrant 14; South East Quadrant 15
Conceptions of Teaching *24*
Connaway, L. S. 84, 89
Conole G. 118
continuous professional development: post graduate 157
Coomey, M. 8, 10, 12, 22, 131, 142, 170
Coppola, N. W. 6
Critten, P. 8, 187
Cromley, J. G. 38, 39, 44, 53
Crook, C. 20
Csikszentmihalyi, I. S. 240

Csíkszentmihályi, M. 11, 240, 246, 263
Cunningham, I. 132, 137, 138
Curatr, increasing participation in online collaborative learning 260
Cuskelly, E. F. 10
Czerniewicz, L. 204

D

D'Antoni, S. 96
dadamac 208
Daniel, J. 80
Davis, E. A. 42
Davis, K. A. 42
Dawes, G. 132
Deci, E. L. 262, 263
Dede, C. 26
Dee, C. 81
Dee-Lucas, D. 11
Denzin, N. K. 167
de Saint Exupéry, A. 234
Devlin, M. 24
Dewey, J. 7, 164
dialogue, involvement, support, control (DISC) 4, 22
Digital Education Brighton 145
Digital Media Simulations 243–59; Immersive Experiential Learning 244; cognitive learning map *245*; theoretical foundation 246; Toolwire co-creation process *251*; future of 256
Doherty, P. 11
Dooley, K. 122
Driscoll, M. 20, 21
Dror, I. 246
Duchastel, P. 118
Duffy, T. 119
Duguid, S. 246
Dunlosky, J. 37
Dunnett, R. 145
Dynamical Systems Theory 120
dynamic and static modes, online 134
Dynamic Architecture for Learning Design *124*

E

Ehlers, U. D. 25
Eisenberg, M. B. 84, 88
Elobaid, M. 85
Engle, R. A. 37
Entwistle, D. 24
Entwistle, N. J. 24, 115
Eraut, M. 164
Esslemont, C. 83
Ewing, J. M. 11
expert versus novice learners 119

F

Ferrara, R. A. 41
Field, K. A. 79
Fill, K. 118
Flavell, J. H. 37
four roles for development professionals 138; a model *139*; theory 138; design 139; manage 140; interact 140
Fredericksen, E. E. 6
Frederiksen, J. 49
free range learners 211, 221
Fridkin, S. 40
Funaro, G. M. 10, 11

G

Gagné R. M. 114, 118
game based learning 256
gaming learning 227–42; analysis 230; analysis and specification *239*; designing 229; game model *236*; game processing *236*; implementation and evaluation 239–40; modeling 235; specification 232–4; storyboard *238*; structure *231*
Garrison, D. R. 4, 5, 6, 7, 8, 21, 272
Garton, S. 7
Ge, X. 35, 36, 37, 42, 44, 45
Gee, J. P. 256
Gelder, T. 121
Gemmell, I. 148
Geng, F. 79, 80, 82

Gibbs, P. 187
Giddens, A. 201
Glaser, R. 35, 37, 41
Gleick, J. 122
Godwin, S. 78, 80, 83
Gonzalez, C. 112
Google and OER's 88–9
Graesser, A. C. 37
Graham, C. R. 27
Greene, J. A. 44
Greenhow, C. 26
Gregor, S. D. 10
Gregory, A. S. 79
Griffiths, J. R. 88
Gunawardena, C. 6
Gurrell, S. 96
Gurtler, T. 54
Guthrie, J. T. 38

H

Hacker, D. J. 37
Häkkinen, P. 28
Hall, E. T. 177
Hämäläinen, R. 28
Hammond, A. L. 96
Hampden-Turner, C. 136
Hampton-Reeves, S. 78, 84, 85, 88
Hannafin, M. 39, 45
Hara, N. 10
Hargittai, E. 79, 85
Hase, S. 195
Haygood, D. 79
Head, A. J. 78, 84, 88
Healey, M. 112
Heindel, A. J. 53
Heller R. F. 148, 149, 154
heteragogy 195
heutagogy 195; *see also* peeragogy, heteragogy
Hiltz, S. R. 6
Hmelo, C. 47
Hofstede, G. 136
Holzman, L. 263
Horton, J. 80
Hotseats 162, 167

Hounsell, J. 115
Howarth, M. S. 176, 187
Hoyle, R. H. 70
Hughes, J. E. 26
Human-Digital Information Bridge 217
Hwang, A. 6

I

ICT three-legged stool 218–19; diagnostic tool 220
instructional design versus learning design 118
Ip, A. 235

J

Jackson, P. W. 135
Jamali, H. R. 81
Jarrett, C. 177
Jenkins, A. 112
Jiao, Q. G. 62
Johnson, L. 79
Johnson, M. 177, 187
Jonassen, D. H. 35, 36, 37, 42, 45, 149
Jones, A. 80
Jones, J. 28

K

Kagitcibasi, C. 54
Kahn Academy 79, 142
Kalyuga, S. 119, 120
Kanuka, H. 5
Kapp, M. K. 228
Kay, D. 89
Keats, D. 157
Kember, D. 24, 25
Kenyon, C. 195
King, A. 41, 42, 48
Kinzer, C. 47
Kirschner, A. 28
Koestler, A. 133
Kolb, D. A. 164
Kop, R. 28
Koper, R. 118
Kovach, R. 61
Kraiger, K. 262

Krajcik, J. 47
Kramarski, B. 39
Kuntz, A. M. 177

L

Lakoff, G. 177, 187
Land, S. M. 35, 36, 37, 39, 42, 44, 45
Lane, A. 79, 80
Laurillard, D. 28, 187
Lave, J. 163, 164, 261, 271
Lawrence, J. A. 37
Learnscapes 244–56
Lee, A. 156
Lee, K. J. 115
Lee, M. 47
Leigh, E. 235
Levine, A. 79
Levine, K. 79
Lewis, M. 41
Lewis, R. 11
Lim, S. 79, 84
Lin, X. D. 41, 47, 48
Lincoln, Y. S. 167
Linn, M. C. 42, 45
Littlejohn, A. 81
Locke, C. 187
Lorenzen, M. 85
Lovett, M. 82, 87
Luckin, R. 134, 143

M

Mager, R. 231
Malone, T. W. 228
Margaryan, A. 81
Marra, R. M. 8
Marshall, C. 79
Martinez-Pons, M. 59, 70
Marton, F. 115
Mason, R. 10, 11
Matusiak, K. K. 84, 88
Mayer, R. E. 82, 114, 233
McAndrew, P. 78, 80, 82
McClure, R. 81
McConnell, D. 12
McCormick, C. B. 37

McCrory, R. S. 5
McCune, V. 115
McDowell, E. A. 79
McGrath, W. 11
McMichael, C. 149
Medeiros, N. 89
Meichenbaum, D. 69
Menchen-Trevino, E. 79, 85
metacognition 37; components of *38*; question prompts *43*
metacognitive maps, process visualization 46–7
metacognitive processes in ill-structured problem solving: strategies for 35; seven strategies for improving *40*
metacognitive training 39; IMPROVE method 39–41
metaphor: and video 180; activity within live online conversation 187
Mevarech, Z. 39, 41
Meyer J. H. F. 118
Meyer, K. 5
Miller, G. A. 114
Miller, P. 89
Mills, J. 54
Mitra, S. 194, 199
MOOCs 21, 28, 80, 81
Moore, J. L. 8
Moos, D. C. 44
Mulder, F. 80
Muller, D. A. 115

N

Naidu, S. 7
Nicholas, D. 81, 84, 88
Nielson, J. 241, 268
Nonaka, I. 271

O

O'Connell, D. 134
OER: barriers to adoption and use 96–109
OER practice: implications for 90; use in academic settings 97

Oliver, K. 39
Oliver, M. 7
Oliver, R. 11, 12
Online Educational Resources (OER): common ways of finding *86*; educational level sought 81; how used 80; impact on student attainment 87; location found 81; reasons for accessing 78; searching for 77; type of resources being sought 79
online learning: interactive role 141; P mode and S mode 141
online paradigm grid *23, 36, 132*; dimensions and tensions 170–3
Onwuegbuzie, A. J. 62
Orr, S. 24

P

Paas, F. 114, 120
Palloff, R. M. 20, 28
Palomäki, E. 247
Pan, B. 88
Papert, S. 24
Paris, S. G. 54
Parsons, D. 263
pathways to improved productivity 28
Paulus, T. M. 5
Pawan, F. 5
Pedersen, S. 41, 42
peeragogy 195
Pelz, W. 6
Peoples Uni 147–59; conceptual diagram *151*; problem and solution *152*
Perels, F. 54
Peterson Bishop, A. 88
Philip, K. E. J. 156
Pickett, A. M. 6
Plenderleith, J. 89
Post, T. A. 35, 37
Powell, S. G. 37
Pratt, K. 20, 28

Q

Quinn, C. 119, 228, 230
Quintana, C. 46, 47

R

Rada, R. 11
Ramachandran, V. R. 177
Ramaswami, R. 247, 248
Reed, K. 148
Reeves, T. 261
Reigeluth, C. M. 36, 48
Reimann, P. 41
Repman, J. 11
Reynolds, F. 154
Richardson, J. C. 6
Rimmershaw, R. 11
Rivkin, I. D. 41
Robelia, B. 26
Ross, G. 38
Rothblum, E. D. 54, 62
Rotter, N. G. 6
Rourke, L. 5, 6
Rovai, A. P. 5
Rudestam, K. E. 21
Russell, A. 168, 169
Ryan, R. M. 262, 263
Ryu, H. 263

S

Säljö, R. 115
Salmon, G. 154, 155, 168, 169
Sandars, J. 148
Santos, A. 80
Savery, J. 119
Saye, J. W. 39, 44
scaffolding 6, 12, 36, 38, 39, 41, 83, 101, 201, 263, 268, 278; soft 44–7, 49–50
Schmidt, J. 157
Schmitz, B. 54
Schnotz, W. 120
Schoenholz-Read, J. 21
Schon, A. D. 164
Schunk, D. H. 54, 55
Schuwer, R. 77, 83
Schwartz, C. W. 55

Scofield, M. R. 153
Searls, D. 187
Secules, T. 47
Seely Brown, J. H. A. 96, 148
Seibert, D. 38
self-determination theory 262
self-regulated learning (SLR): comparison of traditional and adaptive self-regulation 64–6; environmental influences 62; general guiding principles 68; role of the instructor 63; specific strategies 69
Selwyn, N. 20
Sharma, M. D. 115
Sharpe, R. 20
Shea, P. J. 6
Simon, H. A. 114
Sinnott, J. D. 35, 37
Sitzmann, T. 262
Skinner, D. 24
Smith, A. 246
Smith, G. G. 53
Smith, R. 79
Smolensky, P. 121
Snyder, B. R. 135
social enterprise model 153
social networking 26, 78, 80, 89, 109, 157, 256, 260
social presence 6
SOLO taxonomy *116*; practical application of model 123–4
Solomon, L. J. 54, 62
Solomon, N. 8
Stanley, E. E. 81
Stannard, R. 87
Stapleton, S. 80, 86
Stein, B. S. 41
Stenhouse, L. 164
Stephenson, J. 8, 10, 12, 22, 131, 142, 170, 187
Stewart, D. 262
Stone, S. 79
Swan, K. P. 6
Sweat-Guy, R. 85
Sweller, J. 114, 119, 246

T

Tabbers, H. 114
Tait, A. 204
Takeuchi, H. 271
task analysis, mental representation 57
Taylor, S. 148
Teachers Talking 214–15, *216*; ICT circles *221*
teaching learning paradigm (TLP) 8
teaching presence 5
Thille, C. 82
Thomas, P. R. 115
Thompson, M. 11
Torres-Ayala, A. T. 53
traditional learning theories, impact on instructional design 113
Treloar, C. J. 148
Trompenaars, F. 136
Tuovinen, J. E. 114

U

Unisa 195–6; signature courses 197–8; two-fold benefits *202*

V

Vallance, E. 135
van Gerven, P. 114
Van Merriënboer, J. J. G. 114, 228
virtual academia 209; see also free range learners
virtual mentors 244
Vizcarro, C. 11
Vojt, G. 81
Volmink, J. 149
Voss, J. F. 35, 37, 45
Vygotsky, L. S. 38, 54, 246

W

Waite, T. 201
Wallace, P. 20, 21
Walther, J. 6
Warren, K. J. 11
Waters, E. 149
Web 1.0 and Web 2.0 25, 26, 157, 171–3
Web 3.0 and beyond 26–7, 157
Webb, M. 28
Webcam 182
Weiler, A. 84
Weinberger, D. 187
Wenger, E. 163, 164, 261, 271
Whipp, J. L. 58, 61, 62
White, B. 49
Whitelock, D. 11
WikiQuals 211–13
Wild, M. 119
Wiley, D. 96
Wiliam, D. 28
Willemain, T. R. 37
Williams, R. 8
Wills, S. 235
Wilson, R. 79
Wilson, T. 11, 80
Wineburg, S. 38
Winkler, M. 121
Winn, J. 79
Winograd, P. 54
Winters, F. I. 44
Wisher, R. 262
Wolfe, C. R. 37
Wong, W. 79, 84, 85, 88
Woo, Y. 261
Wood, D. 38

Y

Yalcin, S. 5

Z

Zetter, R. 112
Zhang, M. 47
Zimmerman, B. J. 41, 54, 55, 58
Zittle, F. 6

Lightning Source UK Ltd.
Milton Keynes UK
UKOW06n0608230316

270725UK00013B/343/P